Online
INTERVIEWS
in Real Time

Online
INTERVIEWS
in Real Time

Janet Salmons

Vision2Lead, Inc., and Capella University School of Business and Technology

SAGE

Los Angeles | London | New Delhi
Singapore | Washington DC

For information:

SAGE Publications, Inc.
2455 Teller Road
Thousand Oaks,
    California 91320
E-mail: order@sagepub.com

SAGE Publications India Pvt. Ltd.
B 1/I 1 Mohan Cooperative
    Industrial Area
Mathura Road, New Delhi 110 044
India

SAGE Publications Ltd.
1 Oliver's Yard
55 City Road
London EC1Y 1SP
United Kingdom

SAGE Publications Asia-Pacific Pte. Ltd.
33 Pekin Street #02-01
Far East Square
Singapore 048763

Printed in the United States of America

Library of Congress Cataloging-in-Publication Data

Salmons, Janet, 1952-
Online interviews in real time/Janet Salmons.
    p. cm.
Includes bibliographical references.
ISBN 978-1-4129-6895-9 (pbk.)
    1. Interviewing. 2. Telematics. 3. Online chat groups. 4. Research—Methodology. 5. Real-time data processing. 6. Telecommunication. I. Title.

H61.28.S25 2010
001.4'33—dc22   2009037020

This book is printed on acid-free paper.

09   10   11   12   13   10 9 8 7 6 5 4 3 2 1

Acquisitions Editor:	Vicki Knight
Associate Editor:	Lauren Habib
Editorial Assistant:	Ashley Dodd
Production Editor:	Karen Wiley
Copy Editor:	Amy Rosenstein
Typesetter:	C&M Digitals (P) Ltd.
Proofreader:	Andrea Martin
Indexer:	Holly Day
Cover Designer:	Arup Giri
Marketing Manager:	Stephanie Adams

Contents

Detailed Contents

List of Figures

List of Tables

Visual Map of Book Topics in Context of Knowledge Creation

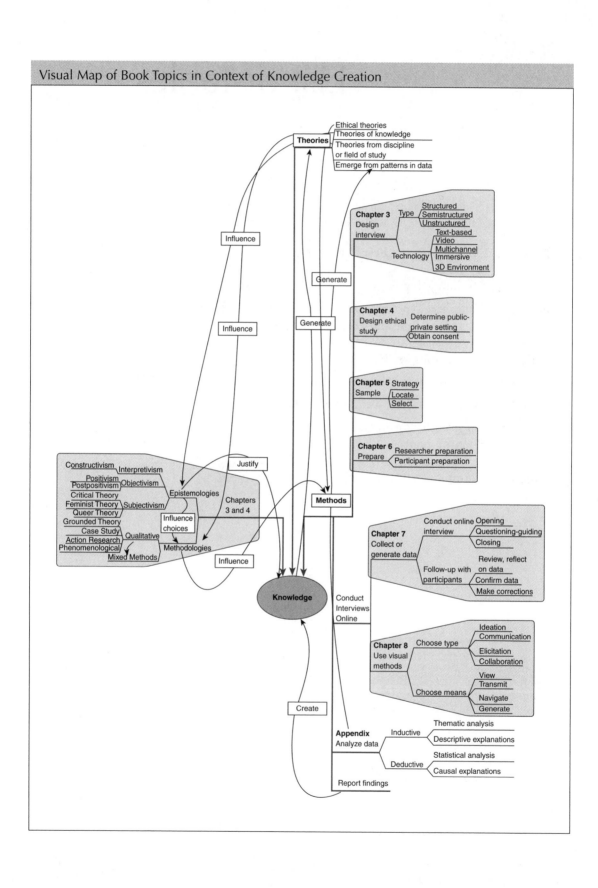

Preface

The saying goes, "If a farmer fills his barn with grain, he gets mice. If he leaves it empty, he gets actors." Like actors, researchers are always looking for an opening. If a means for communication opens, intrepid researchers will find a way to adopt it to their own objectives, shaking up the academic status quo along the way.

In parallel to the evolution of Information and Communications Technologies (ICTs), data collection research methodologies are evolving. When online methods of communication opened up, researchers used them to share information. When information became available to download, scholars used it for secondary and background research. As interaction on the World Wide Web became popular, researchers observed from the sidelines or as participants and action-researchers. As it became possible to protect private data, researchers found ways to conduct surveys online. Now that people can use ICTs to experience meaningful person-to-person interaction, researchers are taking notice. With many free or inexpensive options for communicating in real time, it is not surprising that researchers are looking for ways to collect data through online interviews.

For the purpose of this book, the term *online interviews* refers to interviews conducted with ICT. The primary focus is on interviews conducted with synchronous technologies, including text messaging, videoconferencing or video calls, multichannel meetings, or 3-D immersive environments. Asynchronous technologies are discussed as well because activities to prepare for or follow up on the interview may be carried out using e-mail, blogs, social networking sites, or websites.

Interview research is the most personal form of data collection. The interviewer cannot simply stand back to observe subjects or analyze their survey responses. Whether the subject of inquiry is personal or not, the interviewer must actively engage the interviewee, gaining personal trust and professional respect to elicit information-rich responses. Some level of relationship is inherent in the exchange, if only for the time period of the interview. When interviews occur online, researchers must devise and learn new ways to build trust and motivate individuals to contribute. Researchers also must devise and learn new ways to design studies, recruit participants, and meet ethical research guidelines.

When options expand, typically the complexity of decision making increases as well. Why would a researcher choose to conduct an interview online rather than in person? What special considerations are needed for the design, the sample, and the analysis? What skills will the interviewer need? What online approach is most suitable for the study? The terms *Internet studies* and *Internet research* have been used primarily to describe research that uses online methods to study behaviors that occur online (Markham, 2005). This book takes a broader view, suggesting that online methods are appropriate ways to study behaviors that occur online *or* offline.

My own online interview research on collaborative e-learning is described throughout the book. It provides one example of online interview research using a groupware meeting platform that allowed me to interview participants in five countries from my office in Boulder, Colorado. This dynamic experience provided the impetus for the book. The online interview approach to data collection was convenient and low cost, but those practical reasons are not what have ignited my curiosity. Even for someone familiar with online communication, the online research process, from initial recruitment to final follow-up, far exceeded my expectations. The data I collected were categorically richer and deeper than I had anticipated. Relationships built with research participants—who I recruited online and have never met in person—have endured. Several of them contributed chapters to a book I edited: *Handbook of Research on Electronic Collaboration and Organizational Synergy* (Salmons & Wilson, 2009).

I was—and am—intrigued by the potential for using verbal, visual, and textual elements to extend the usual question-and-answer verbal exchange that characterizes what we call an *interview*. That potential expands with the availability of each new communications technology. As more people use these technologies to build online social and professional networks and communities, new cultures are emerging. This trend has led me to explore methodologies from field study and visual methods from disciplines such as anthropology and sociology. In this book I have tried to bring some key ideas that are transferable from varied research traditions into online research.

Along the way I discovered other researchers who use synchronous technologies, including Second Life, shared applications, and videoconferencing in research interviews. The Researchers' Notebook, a feature in each chapter, and related links on the companion website offer examples drawn from their studies. Profiled researchers' work illustrates a few of the many ways online interview research can be conducted to serve a variety of research purposes.

Organization of the Book

The book is organized to encompass both scholarly and practical issues involved in designing and carrying out online interview research. The body of each chapter presents material on interview research that provides both foundation and context for discussion of *online* interview research. The primary focus is on the use of in-depth interviews in qualitative research; where relevant, mixed methods designs are discussed.

Chapters 1–3 offer the foundation for the second part of the book. These chapters introduce the scholarly purpose of interview research and describe ways researchers can align technology selection to the purpose of the study at hand. Chapters 4–8 offer background, guidance, and models to assist researchers to design, plan, and conduct online interviews. The book closes in Chapter 9 with a discussion of evolving trends in online communication and areas for future exploration and study.

Some consistent features are offered in each chapter; they are indicated with icons to allow for ease of navigation through the book:

- This icon 🔭 points you to the Researchers' Notebook.
- 📖 Research Tips and ⚖️ Ethics Tips in the margins point readers to important practical reminders.
- Key Concepts 🔦 summarize main ideas from each chapter.
- Assignments ✎ may be used as the basis for formal or informal learning about online interview research.
- New key terms are bolded, and definitions can be found at the end of the chapter under this icon: 📖. All the terms also are included in the Glossary of Terms.
- Other ancillary materials related to the topics of the book are available on the book's companion website (www.sagepub.com/salmons study) 🖥. This site is important to instructors and learners who want access to up-to-date resources. When technologies change and new resources emerge, new material will be posted.

Chapter 1. Real Interviews in an Online World

In Chapter 1 you will discover reasons why researchers choose to collect data through online interviews. You will look at distinctions between different kinds of synchronous and asynchronous communications that can be used for scholarly interviews.

Chapter 2. Online Research With Technology

In Chapter 2 you will explore online communications tools and ways verbal and visual features can be used for scholarly interview purposes. You also will consider options and issues for selection of the appropriate technologies for carrying out the research.

Chapter 3. Interviews for Scholarly Research

In Chapter 3 you will examine interrelationships between epistemologies, theories, methodologies, and methods in research design. You will focus specifically on the variations of the in-depth interview for data collection.

Chapter 4. Design for Credible and Ethical Online Research

In Chapter 4 you will delve into research design considerations for online interview research. You will survey ethical issues in online research and determine what ethical issues might need to be addressed depending on interview approach and public or private setting.

Chapter 5. Sampling: Selecting Participants for Online Interviews

In Chapter 5 you will explore types of sampling and selection of research participants for online interviews. Building on prior chapters, it will explore the implications of design for sampling and participant selection.

Chapter 6. Preparing for a Live Online Interview

In Chapter 6 you will look at the preparation of interview questions or prompts, planning for use of communication tools in the interview, and the interviewer's preparation to listen to the research participant.

Chapter 7. Conducting the Synchronous Online Interview

In Chapter 7 you will look at practical steps for carrying out an online interview. Four kinds of interviews are described using text-based, video-conferencing, online meeting spaces, or immersive virtual environments. You also will look at steps for following-up with interviewees to verify and complete the data collection.

Chapter 8. Visual Research and the Synchronous Online Interview

In Chapter 8 you will look at technologies that offer researchers and participants the opportunity to communicate using visual modes in online interviews. A Typology of Online Visual Interview Methods is introduced, with alternatives to use in text-based, videoconferencing, online meeting spaces, or immersive virtual environments.

Chapter 9. Online Communications and Online Interviews: Trends and Influences

In Chapter 9 you will look at trends in online communication and ways they may influence online interview research. You will reflect on emerging issues for researchers, theorists, and thinkers about the future for qualitative and mixed research methods in an online world.

Back Matter

The Appendix contains a literature survey about qualitative data analysis. A Glossary of Terms and References conclude the book.

Research is conducted to create new knowledge. We need new knowledge—theoretical and practical—that reflects the new realities of our digital age and connected, interdependent world. Online researchers have the opportunity to model the process of global connection and make unique contributions. I hope this book will inspire you to be one of them!

Janet Salmons, Ph.D.
Boulder, Colorado

Acknowledgments

This book would not have been possible without the A-Team of e-teams: Panaena Bina and Cole Keirsey. You have my gratitude for your patience, thoughtful insights, and excellent feedback!

A heartfelt thank-you goes to Vicki Knight, Acquisitions Editor at SAGE Publications, for unflagging support and enthusiasm for this book.

The book benefited greatly from the constructive comments and suggestions provided at various stages of the manuscript by the following: Jane M. Agee, The University at Albany, State University of New York; Penny L. Burge, Virginia Tech University; Kim H. Knight, Roger Williams University; Suzanne Havala Hobbs, University of North Carolina at Chapel Hill; Kathryn J. Roulston, The University of Georgia; Joe Bishop, Eastern Michigan University; Jill Sperandio, Lehigh University; Karen L. Tonso, Wayne State University; and Marcus B. Weaver-Hightower, University of North Dakota.

I appreciate and recognize the trailblazing work of researchers who shared their thoughts and questions about online interview research and contributed worthwhile examples for the Researchers' Notebook:

- **Jon Cabiria, Ph.D.** Professor of psychology at Baker College and the Pennsylvania Institute of Technology. Research interests: intersection of online social networks and human behavior.

- **Wendy L. Kraglund-Gauthier, Ph.D. candidate.** Editor/instructional designer, Continuing and Distance Education at Saint Francis Xavier University in Nova Scotia, Canada. Research interests: distance and online learning.

- **Susan O'Donnell, Ph.D.** Senior research officer, People-Centred Technologies National Research Council Institute for Information Technology, and adjunct professor, Sociology University of New Brunswick Fredericton, New Brunswick, Canada. Research interests: role that videoconferencing is playing in support of local economic and social development in remote aboriginal/First Nations communities in Northern Ontario.

- **Monique Sedgwick, Ph.D.** Assistant professor at the School of Health Sciences, University of Lethbridge in Alberta, Canada. Research interests: nursing and rural health.

- **Stephen Thorpe, Ph.D.** Consultant, Zenergy in Auckland, New Zealand. Research interests: facilitation in online communities.
- **Lynn Wilson, Ph.D.** Executive director, SeaTrust Institute. Research interests: environmental and ocean policy, collaboration in science and policy.

Real Interviews in an Online World

1

Explore, and explore. Be neither chided nor flattered out of your position of perpetual inquiry.

—Ralph Waldo Emerson, 1838

After you study Chapter 1, you will be able to do the following:

- Describe how interviews contribute to scholarly studies;
- Identify reasons why researchers choose to conduct interviews over the Internet;
- Compare and contrast evolving characteristics of synchronous and asynchronous online communication; and
- Discuss ways to think about "richness" of online communication.

Interview Research: A Window Into the Lived Experience

Each individual experiences the world in a uniquely different way. Each finds significance in life events by interpreting and reinterpreting meaning through lenses of memory, culture, and prior occurrences. Researchers who want to understand the complex human drama often choose interviews as an entrée into another's observations, thoughts, and feelings.

When individuals respond and share their stories, researchers can observe nonverbal signals and listen to verbal expressions. The potential fullness of this active exchange has traditionally motivated researchers to choose face-to-face conversations when collecting data for qualitative and mixed-methods research. Implications of physical setting and the demeanor of the interviewer are carefully considered to develop the rapport and trust necessary to collect robust data.

Must individuals sit in the same room to have a meaningful dialogue? In many areas of life and work, activities that people previously assumed would need physical proximity are now conducted via electronic communications. Scholarly activities are included in this trend. Contemporary researchers expect to use computers when writing about research design, analyzing data, and creating reports of their findings. Researchers routinely use the Internet to study the existing literature in their fields through online journals and databases. Scholars expect to discuss their work along the way with far-flung colleagues through e-mail lists, blogs, social media, and interactive websites. Increasingly, researchers are using the Internet to collect data as well.

Emerging **Information and Communications Technologies (ICTs)** offer new ways to conduct research interviews. Access to the Internet and the wide availability of sophisticated software mean that researchers can easily talk directly with subjects in their homes or offices. **Online interviews** are a viable alternative because researchers can choose from varied communication options to best fulfill the purpose and design of the study.

Synchronous and Asynchronous Communication

Online interaction is typically categorized according to the ability to send, receive, and respond to messages at the same time, **synchronous communication**, or at different times, **asynchronous communication.** The medium may be new, but none of the many modes of electronic communication is wholly unique to the online environment. Whether face-to-face or online, communication typically mixes verbal and nonverbal, written and symbolic visual modes. In person, synchronous real-time communication occurs when people meet or talk on the telephone. Online, synchronous communications can include written, verbal, and/or visual exchange. By attaching a headset and logging onto a free online service, people can use **voice over Internet protocol VoIP** instead of the telephone, making it possible to have free conversations with anyone in the world with similar access to a computer. By adding a Web camera, researchers and participants can use desktop videoconferencing and see each other while they converse. Researchers can adopt platforms designed for online meetings for interview purposes, using shared whiteboards and other tools that allow them to see materials and artifacts in addition to talking with and seeing each other. Or, they can interact in immersive 3-D virtual environments such as **Second Life,** where they are represented by the avatars they design.

Asynchronous communications, which do not constrain people to participate at the same time, occur when people correspond by letter or read and write print publications. Online asynchronous communications occur when people correspond by e-mail or through short text messages sent back and forth using cell phones or computers. People communicate asynchronously when they make posts and respond to others in discussion **forums**, on social media sites, **wikis**, or blogs.

Each ICT has its own set of opportunities and limitations. Online, asynchronous communication entails two types of displacement—time and space—while synchronous communication entails one type of displacement—space (Bampton & Cowton, 2002). Synchronous modes bring people one step closer together, yet many people find the reflective pause between message and response leads to deeper consideration of the matter at hand.

The choice between synchronous and asynchronous modes—or the choice to blend them—is significant. Because the online environment offers many modes of communication, researchers can match the characteristics of the media to specific design requirements of their inquiry. These requirements depend on the characteristics of interviewer and interviewee and constraints inherent in the study context. Depending on the purpose and design of the study, interviewers may choose a verbal communication mode that allows them to ask questions and interpret immediate responses or choose a written mode that allows interviewees to take time to think about the question and respond. Factors for selection of technology tools are explored in depth in Chapter 2.

The Internet: The Medium Warms

The word *Internet* simply does not mean the same thing today as it did even a decade ago. As a result, many criticisms of electronic tools as inadequate for the nuanced, sometimes emotion-filled communication intrinsic to research interviews need to be re-examined. Early comparisons of behavior and communication focused on what was lost in the migration from in-person to online interactions. Some critics expressed concern that text-based e-mail messages and static websites disallowed development of intimacy, **immediacy**, or a sense of presence. In 1998 one participant described an asynchronous, text-based online discussion:

> It is a cold medium. Unlike face-to-face communication you get no instant feedback. You don't know how people responded to your comments; they just go out into silence. This feels isolating and unnerving. It is not warm and supportive. (Wegerif, 1998, p. 38)

Like the globe, the Internet is "warming." The Internet now allows for instant feedback so contrasts between online and face-to-face communications are less stark. Indeed, direct comparisons become harder to make as the online reality becomes more distinctive, and ways of experiencing it encompass more dimensions.

In contrast to the earlier linear forms of information search and retrieval of information, contemporary online behavior is more communicative and reciprocal. Internet users follow links from site to site with ever-branching discoveries leading to new questions to explore. The ever-evolving cyberspace "does not imitate the real world, but rather creates a rapid, new, immediate, multi-layered world" (Sade-Beck, 2004, p. 3). In this multilayered online world, the concept of "presence" is itself evolving.

> Presence is not simply the opposite of absence. Technologies of communication are not just substitutes for face-to-face interaction, but constitute a new resource for constructing a kind of connected presence even when people are physically distant. In the regime of "connected" presence, participants multiply encounters and contacts using every kind of mediation and artifacts available to them: relationships thus become seamless webs of quasi-continuous exchanges. The boundaries between absence and presence get blurred and subtle experiences of togetherness may develop. (Licoppea & Smoredab, 2005, p. 321)

In the physical environment, "presence" is an either-or situation—you are either present or not. Online, people feel present in different ways, including the following:

- *Environmental presence:* the extent to which the environment itself recognizes and reacts to the person;
- *Personal presence:* the extent to which the person feels physically present in the environment;
- *Social presence:* the extent to which the person has the feeling of being together and communicating with others to achieve meaningful interactions, establish and maintain relations, and create productive social systems in online environments; and
- *Cognitive presence:* the extent to which the person feels the potential to participate in critical thinking and community of inquiry (Baños et al., 2008; Garrison, Anderson, & Archer, 2004; Heeter, 2003; Kehrwald, 2008; Suler, 2003).

Recent evidence shows that people feel deeply present with others online. Familiarity with Internet-based interactions using varied communications technologies in daily professional, social, and family life enhances their comfort in the medium and strengthens the connections they make online.

COMMUNICATION RICHNESS

Media Richness Theory (MRT) provides one way to classify different kinds of Internet communication by distinguishing between "lean" and "rich" media based on "the capacity for immediate feedback, the number of cues and channels utilized, personalization, and language variety" (Daft & Lengel, 1986, p. 580). Daft and Lengel argued that "rich media" allow people to provide and receive immediate feedback, check interpretations, and understand multiple cues via body language, tone of voice, and message content. Others believe it is important to assess richness in terms of the potential for creating immediacy and, as noted above, a sense of presence. "Rich" media results in greater socio-emotional communication, reduces the physical or psychological distance between individuals, and fosters affiliation (Erickson & Herring, 2005; Kahai & Cooper, 2003; Mehrabian, 1971; O'Sullivan, Hunt, & Lippert, 2004).

Researchers have demonstrated that while text-based communication is "lean," as a medium according to MRT it can be used effectively as a way to conduct interviews. O'Sullivan and colleagues found that some people use cues in online text that consist of "novel ways of expressing immediacy that have no parallel with conventional immediacy behaviors" when trying to shape a receiver's sense of closeness (O'Sullivan et al., 2004, p. 472). For example, to enrich text-based dialogue and make up for lost social cues, online communicators use textual and graphic images and symbols such as emoticons (Erickson & Herring, 2005). Ross (2001) suggests that in the fast or immediate back-and-forth of electronic communication that parties are actively engaged in interpreting each other's messages and questioning meanings in a way that may enhance understanding. A thoughtful assessment of online communication "emphasizes understanding between parties rather than a simple notion of channel capacity" and questions the assumption that decreasing richness as Daft and Lengel defined it means less ability to process information and build understanding (Ross, 2001, p. 76).

Simeon Yates coined the term *say-writing* to describe the ways that **Computer Mediated Communication (CMC)** encourages and supports a new type of genre that combines features of written mode with features of spoken mode (Yates, 1996). Other researchers make similar observations:

We concluded that the virtual [text chat] interview went some way towards bridging the oral/written divide. Although clearly in written format, the type of comment was very oral in nature. The researchers and participants paid little attention to spelling and grammar, as the nature and meaning of the conversation took precedence over the correctly written word. As such, the transcript very much resembles a "written conversation." (Connor & Madge, 2001, para. 10.18)

Computer networks are often considered a *medium* of communication distinct from writing and speaking. CMC exchanges are typically faster than written exchanges (e.g., of letters, or published essays which respond to one another), yet still significantly slower than spoken exchanges, since even in so-called "real-time" modes, typing is slower than speaking. (Herring, 2003, p. 2)

Just as online written dialogue has characteristics of verbal communication, it also allows for some of the subtleties associated with **nonverbal communication.**

NONVERBAL COMMUNICATIONS AND ONLINE INTERVIEWS

Researchers making use of diverse combinations of communications technologies to carry out interviews grasp meaning from varied verbal and nonverbal cues. To do so they must re-examine the ways such cues are defined and interpreted.

Nonverbal cues affect any interview process. Ong (1990) observes that "'words, words, words' mean nothing unless built into a nonverbal context, which always controls meanings of words" (p. 1). Interviewees reveal depth of expression and display cultural and social norms that often guide nonverbal behavior (Fontana & Frey, 2003; Kalman, Ravid, Raban, & Rafaeli, 2006).

Four modes of nonverbal communication are as follows:

1. *Chronemics* refers to the use of pacing and timing of speech, and the length of silence before a response in conversation.

2. *Paralinguistic* communication or paralanguage describes variations in volume, pitch, and quality of voice.

3. *Kinesic* communication includes facial expressions, eye contact or gaze, body movements, or postures.

4. *Proxemic* communication describes the use of interpersonal space to communicate attitudes (Gordon, 1980; Guerrero, DeVito, & Hecht, 1999; Kalman et al., 2006).

The Social Information Processing (SIP) theory argues that "when most nonverbal cues are unavailable, as is the case in text-based CMC, users adapt their language, style, and other cues to such purposes" (Walther, Loh, & Granka, 2005, p. 37). When participants communicate with text-only e-mail, the timing of response, silence, or nonresponse provides researchers with chronemic nonverbal data. When people chat or text message in real time the length of time between post and response provides pacing and turn-taking in the conversation. Conversations can overlap, with many participants effectively "speaking" at once, as often happens in online chats. As Jacobsen (1999) describes it, "cyberdiscursivity" is a dynamic rhetoric allowing for mutual, reciprocal "textual creation/recreation" (p. 9). Network latency and multitasking by participants introduce effects that are different from face-to-face contexts, and which can lead to misinterpretation of temporal cues. The interviewer may believe the participant is struggling with a slow response, when in fact he or she has been distracted by an incoming e-mail.

In synchronous chat or asynchronous e-mail, interviewees control when they choose to respond (Mann & Stewart, 2000). There can be pauses in face-to-face interviews, of course, but in an e-mail interview the delay in interaction between researcher and subject can range from seconds (virtually real time) to hours or days. In planning the interview with participants, the researcher usually wants to accommodate the participant by allowing some degree of freedom to determine pace of response. The way participants exercise such freedoms may or may not offer further insight. Slower responses may indicate more powerful reflection on the deeper meanings of the inquiry (Bampton & Cowton, 2002; James & Busher, 2006). On the other hand, quick replies may indicate lack of adequate consideration by the interviewee.

If the gap between questions and answers is too long, responses and follow-up probes can lead to discontinuous responses, and the thread of interview is lost (James & Busher, 2006; Kitto & Barnett, 2007; Mann & Stewart, 2000). The researcher may be left to wonder why the interviewee has not responded. The interviewee may simply be busy or need more time to devise an answer. However, it also is possible that there may be a problem with some aspect of the question, and the respondent is reluctant to ask for clarification (Bampton & Cowton, 2002; Kitto & Barnett, 2007). When an interview takes too long and loses focus, enthusiasm can wane for the interviewee. Similarly, if the researcher is too slow to respond, participants may doubt the researcher's commitment and engagement in the research (James & Busher, 2006).

Uncertainty of meaning for chronemic cues in the e-mail interview may be addressed by creating some protocols for timing and follow-up, and for the anticipated length of the interview. The researcher must strike an appropriate balance between allowing interviewees time to respond as they wish and maintaining the momentum of the dialogue (Bampton & Cowton, 2002).

While text-based exchanges can foster the trust and rapport necessary to collect data, verbal interchange in real time provides additional nonverbal as well as verbal data. The rich media interview brings researcher and participants together in real time and in a virtual space, allowing for increased immediacy and presence. In interviews conducted with Web-based applications together with audio through VoIP or telephone, researchers listen to interviewees and collect data on chronemic and paralanguage aspects of their responses. Researchers using videoconferencing or video calls can use some level of kinesic communication, such as facial expressions and gestures, although eye contact may be more difficult to attain. When a shared whiteboard or shared immersive space is used, haptic movements become part of the kinesic communication process. Proxemic communication, interpreted as physical distance between communicators, is not applicable or must be reinterpreted for online contexts.

A further issue of nonverbal cues and online interviews involves determining when an interview is nearing its end. If the interview participant fails to respond, it may be a signal that he or she wants to withdraw from study but does not want to tell the interviewer (Hunt & McHale, 2007).

In a face-to-face interview, the interviewer can usually sense when time is running out and adjust his or her approach to the discussion accordingly, ensuring that certain issues are tackled as a matter of priority. It is less easy to sense when an online interviewee is ready to conclude the interview unless he or she states so explicitly (Bampton & Cowton, 2002). In addition, the interviewer has less control over the interviewee deciding to terminate the interview. An online interviewee can end the interview at the press of a button, whereas an interviewee in a face-to-face interview has to physically leave or request the interviewer to leave (Chen & Hinton, 1999; James & Busher, 2006). The online interviewer has fewer options for recovering a difficult interaction (such as apologizing for an inappropriate question, requesting that the interviewee remain, or retracting a line of questioning) before the interviewee simply logs out (James & Busher, 2006).

Scholarly research guidelines require that an interview be complete for the data from the interview to be used without conditions. When the interviewee fails to complete the interview, the researcher must decide whether to use partial information that was collected or to discard the data (Hunt & McHale, 2007). Careful design (see Chapters 3 and 4), participant selection (see Chapter 5), preparation (see Chapter 6), and alignment of ICT with interview approach (see Chapters 2 and 7) can optimize the potential for successfully engaging the participant through all stages of data collection.

Why Conduct Interviews Online?

Researchers opt to conduct interviews online for a variety of reasons. One obvious reason common to almost all online researchers is cost, since online interviews can be planned and conducted without the time and expense of travel. However, cost is one among many considerations for this important decision. Online researchers report significant reduction or elimination of constraints that would make in-person interviews impractical. An increased pool of study participants is possible, including geographically dispersed, international, disabled, or socially isolated individuals (Ahern, 2005; Bowker & Tuffin, 2007; Connor, 2006; Mann & Stewart, 2003). When research participants are in locations that limit access to outsiders, such as hospitals or closed workplaces, it might be possible for a researcher to have a virtual presence where a physical presence would not be allowed.

Online participants may be more relaxed because they are communicating with the researcher in the comfort of a familiar environment. As a result, they may be willing to discuss sensitive or personal matters, such as emotions or disorders that are hard to reveal in person (Cabiria, 2008a; Hunt & McHale, 2007; Mann & Stewart, 2003). People who have difficulties with spoken language or people who speak in different languages can participate more easily.

Researchers may choose online interviews to honor the principle that "research questions that explore an online phenomenon are strengthened through the use of a method of research that closely mirrors the natural setting under investigation" (Geiser, 2002, p. 3). As one researcher described the choice, "Online rather than face-to-face interviews were adopted because the researcher decided to query our target population directly within the context of their (and our) interest in Internet use" (Chou, 2001, p. 574). People who are actively involved in virtual communities, social media, or immersive environments have online identities, friends, and colleagues. Online interviews allow researchers to better understand the participant's cyber experience.

Some researchers choose to conduct interviews online because they intend to create a more egalitarian research medium. In such a medium, participants may feel better able to influence the direction of the research. Greater disclosure, mutuality, and reciprocity between the researcher and the participants may emerge in a more egalitarian setting (James & Busher, 2006; Seymour, 2001). Others opt to interview online as a way of overcoming interviewer effects. The following quotations illustrate such choices.

> Many researchers have been motivated precisely by the apparent abilities of the Internet to sidestep, transform, highlight or reinvent some traditional formations, identities and inequalities. Researchers concerned with issues of marginalized identities and fragmented communities may have been drawn to the Internet precisely as a domain of political opportunity. (Hine, 2005, p. 242)

> In cases where face-to-face interviews might be influenced by personal visual characteristics associated with age, gender, class, prestige, ethnicity and standards of ability researchers may choose the online environment where such distinctions are less overt. (Seymour, 2001, p. 148)

Not all researchers will choose to conduct their interviews online. Some researchers simply believe that establishing an interviewer-interviewee relationship online is "difficult if not impossible" (Fontana & Frey, 2003, p. 6). Common reasons for researchers to eschew online interviews include the following:

- Researchers need to be able to observe the interviewee and/or the research setting.

- They need a full range of verbal and nonverbal communications that are only available when people are physically present.

- The subject matter is highly sensitive and physical proximity is needed in case the researcher needs to comfort the research participant.

- The target research demographic lacks access to information and communications technologies.

Certainly, some types of research do require interviews with close or on-site observation, control of the surroundings, and communication options available when people are face-to-face in the same room. However, even when researchers choose to conduct interviews in person, they may find that online communication is useful for other kinds of interaction with interviewees. Researchers might use online chat for interview preparation or e-mail to follow up on the initial interview. It is unlikely that all interview research could transition into the online environment, nor would that be desirable. Some researchers will stick to established interview modes while others will find that new media options allow for meaningful interaction at various stages of the process. By understanding how all available alternatives work, researchers can make an informed choice based on the nature of their study and the strengths and constraints of available online tools.

Relevant Trends

Communications over the Internet continue to increase. Other significant developments are contributing to the twenty-first-century experience—and pervasiveness—of the Internet. A few trends are particularly relevant to online researchers. The **digital divide** is shrinking. This means there is a greater likelihood that target populations have the needed tools and skills for online research participation. Although there is still a divide between those with regular access to the Internet and those without it, more people now access the Internet at home, work, school, public spaces such as libraries, or anywhere on mobile devices. Indeed, increased **mobile access** is moving the Internet off the desktop. People can get access anywhere on phones and handheld devices.

When people go online they find greater capacity for user-generated content and **interactivity**. The Internet is ever more user-driven, with more social activity occurring online. (See the book's website for updated technology tool usage and access trend data.)

Changes in technologies allow for richer communications—by any definition—and for more opportunities to develop a sense of presence. Digital natives born to a wired world and digital immigrants who migrated from analog to digital both use ICTs for social, cultural, and professional exchanges. More people use the Internet in their daily work and social lives (Lebo, 2004; Rainie & Horrigan, 2005). More people use the Internet to access information and to conduct their own research on health and consumer issues (Fox & Fallows, 2003; Madden, 2005). In personal and social life, people find that the Internet helps preserve ties when distance makes contact in person impossible. More people interact with others online for informal, school, or work purposes. They are familiar with weblogs (Rainie, 2005), e-mail, and messaging (Shiu & Lenhart, 2004). More people are experienced with access to online media by using Internet radio, watching webcast concerts, and downloading music and digital pictures on their home computers (Rainie & Horrigan, 2005).

These shifts make new approaches for online research possible. Changing usage patterns for casual users enlarge communication options for researchers. When people become acquainted with a technology through personal use, they will be less intimidated when expected to apply it in an academic or professional setting. Broader access and increased comfort levels mean a larger pool of potential participants who are capable of participating in online research.

Closing Thoughts

An unanswered question for online researchers relates to the potential impact of a "cyberspace effect." Does cyberspace as the interview medium or location make people more open and willing to communicate, or does it make them more secretive? Does cyberspace encourage or enable them to provide different kinds of information than they might provide in face-to-face interviews (Hunt & McHale, 2007)? As more researchers study online interview methodologies, they will lay the groundwork for future researchers who will be prepared to make informed choices about the ideal online setting and medium that correspond to the needs of their research designs.

Communications technologies that offer rich and persistent communications benefit the online researcher. Undoubtedly, functionality and access will continue to evolve—and may have changed significantly between the time I write this and the time you read it in print. That is why updates to this book are available on the book's website.

Researchers' Notebook: Stories of Online Inquiry

How do researchers put into practice ideas and principles presented in *Online Interviews in Real Time?* The Researchers' Notebook offers practical examples drawn from my own research and from studies conducted by other innovative online researchers who generously shared their experiences with me. This Chapter 1 Notebook introduces each researcher; I weave experiences and suggestions as relevant in Researchers' Notebooks to complement each chapter of the book. On the book's website you will find links to websites and articles if you would like to learn more about their work.

RESEARCHERS IN THE RESEARCHERS' NOTEBOOK

- **Jon Cabiria, Ph.D.** Professor of psychology at Baker College and the Pennsylvania Institute of Technology. Research interests: intersection of online social networks and human behavior.

- **Wendy L. Kraglund-Gauthier, Ph.D. candidate.** Editor/instructional designer, Continuing and Distance Education at Saint Francis Xavier University in Nova Scotia, Canada. Research interests: distance and online learning.

- **Susan O'Donnell, Ph.D.** Senior research officer, People-Centred Technologies National Research Council Institute for Information Technology, and adjunct professor, Sociology University of New Brunswick Fredericton, New Brunswick, Canada. Research interests: role that videoconferencing is playing in support of local economic and social development in remote aboriginal/First Nations communities in Northern Ontario.

- **Monique Sedgwick, Ph.D.** Assistant professor at the School of Health Sciences, University of Lethbridge in Alberta, Canada. Research interests: nursing and rural health.

- **Stephen Thorpe, Ph.D.** Consultant, Zenergy in Auckland, New Zealand. Research interests: facilitation in online communities.

- **Lynn Wilson, Ph.D.** Executive director, SeaTrust Institute. Research interests: environmental and ocean policy, collaboration in science and policy.

Why Do Researchers Choose to Conduct Interviews Online?

When I originally decided to conduct research on e-learning, it was clear that a global sample would be important to understand a global phenomenon. The need to reach an increased pool of participants without costly travel motivated me to look at online research options. My research had a global scope but, alas, my budget was strictly local. Although cost was an important reason to choose online interviews, it was not the only or most important reason.

The study involved expert interviews with online instructors who teach with collaborative methods; the purpose of the study was to refine the Taxonomy of Online Collaboration (Salmons, 2009). This taxonomy is a model that provides a graphic notation system for mapping collaborative projects. To gain meaningful input from interviewees I needed an interactive, visual way to communicate. Because my target sample—online college and university instructors—was comfortable with using the Internet, technology did not present an obstacle to participation.

As an experienced presenter of webinars, I was familiar with the audio and visual features of Elluminate, an online meeting platform. Elluminate includes a shared whiteboard where I could present the model and invite interviewees to illustrate their examples with it. VoIP made verbal exchange with participants in five countries possible—without long-distance phone charges. The archiving feature of Elluminate enabled me to save a record of all aspects of such an exchange for future viewing and transcription. Together, these features made online interviews preferable to a face-to-face discussion—even if cost had not been a factor.

Finally, this study illustrated the principle that research questions that explore an online phenomenon are strengthened when the study context closely mirrors the environment under investigation (Geiser, 2002). I felt that the online interviews allowed me to "walk the talk" by collaborating online with research participants in ways that reflected the subject of the study—online collaboration.

Other researchers have their own reasons for choosing to interview online. Like me, Dr. Lynn Wilson had a limited travel budget and research participants from all over the world. Her research involved expert interviews with ocean scientists and policy experts who had restrictive schedules. Being in the same geographic area as the interview subjects would not necessarily have increased the odds for a face-to-face meeting. Because interviewees were accustomed to press interviews using phone or e-mail, they agreed to time-limited online interviews. Lynn used preinterview e-mail dialogue to answer their questions, to build credibility for her research, and to gain buy-in with initially skeptical participants. In these conversations they set expectations and protocol for the interviews. Dr. Wilson chose a shared Web-based application and **Skype** VoIP calls, so she could simultaneously manipulate data and discuss the process (Wilson, 2006).

Stephen Thorpe's doctoral research about storytelling in online groups involved participants from seven countries and twelve time zones. The only realistic approach to the research was to conduct it online (Thorpe,

2008b). This choice was also based in the fact that online media that were the subject of the study and Thorpe was studying online group interaction and group processes online, choosing a collaborative group method of co-operative inquiry seemed highly appropriate (S. Thorpe, personal communication, August 29, 2008). Synchronous tools included chat, Skype VoIP calls, web conferencing and videoconferencing, and Second Life. Two of the coresearchers in Thorpe's study are dyslexic, so the real-time audio and video provided a level playing field for them when participating in the online research. The research group adopted a "spelling doesn't count" rule in the "group culture" (also known as a group agreement or group norms). As a result, one participant said that the online research group was the first group where she had allowed herself to be fully open about her dyslexia (S. Thorpe, personal communication, August 29, 2008).

Wendy L. Kraglund-Gauthier was a doctoral learner based in Nova Scotia studying at a university in Australia through online learning. When she designed her dissertation research, she selected online methods for reasons similar to those that influenced my own research—she wanted to conduct interviews using the same online media that were the subject of her study. She chose synchronous online interviews in Elluminate because this allowed for a type of interaction not possible in person: playing back ideas from interviews "with participants, about participants." She used reviews of interview sessions as a jumping-off point to deeper probes in follow-up discussions.

Wendy noted an experience similar to Stephen's study group: the online interviews allowed her to reach a sometimes difficult-to-reach population: people with disabilities. "Depending on participants' abilities, the meeting technology easily enable[d] modifications to account for disabilities: visual for hearing impaired, audio for vision impaired, home location for mobility impaired" (W. L. Kraglund-Gauthier, personal communication, July 16, 2008).

Dr. Jon Cabiria chose Second Life as an interview milieu that allowed him to study attitudes and interactions in that immersive environment (Cabiria, 2008a, 2008c). Second Life allowed him to access diverse participants and made accessing the research convenient and flexible for participants. Conducting interviews through his avatar, he found it possible to avoid interviewer effects—potential intimidation participants may have felt when discussing sensitive matters. His study focused on gay men and lesbian women; he observed that the computer-mediated environments allowed participants to say things they might not say face-to-face (J. Cabiria, personal communication, August 18, 2008). At the same time, avatars and the virtual meeting space provided a physical connection missing in a telephone interview. Participants were offered an audio option but chose to chat by text. Text-based interactions provided Jon with an instant transcript.

Dr. Susan O'Donnell uses interviews and focus groups conducted through videoconferences to complement limited on-site work with another difficult-to-reach population: First Nations peoples of Canada. She studies how First Nations organizations are using video communications on **broadband** networks for community, social, and economic development for First Nations people in rural Canada (O'Donnell, Perley, & Simms, 2008). For this participatory research, meetings with researchers and First Nations partners are conducted with four sites connected by videoconference: Fredericton (New Brunswick), Membertou First Nation (Cape Breton, Nova Scotia), Thunder Bay (Ontario), and Sioux Lookout (Ontario). Although travel costs would be prohibitive, Susan has an additional set of considerations since these remote First Nations communities she studies have limited accommodations for visitors.

Dr. Monique Sedgwick faced a similar challenge: the participants in her study were spread across rural western and northern Canada. Participants were located from 1.5 to 16 hours from an urban center where Monique could have traveled by plane. To add to her dilemma, the winter when she conducted her study brought record snowfall, making travel nearly impossible. Because Monique's research is focused on nurses, the participants had access to the Canadian telehealth videoconferencing system at the rural hospitals where they work (Sedgwick & Spiers, 2009). The university videoconferencing system enabled her to carry out the ethnographic research interviews—without having to wait for a spring thaw. Dr. Sedgwick pointed to two additional reasons for favoring videoconferencing for interviews: (1) Researchers and participants are busy people. Taking two to four days for travel is simply not practical. (2) By reducing the need to travel, videoconference interviews leave a small carbon footprint (M. Sedgwick, personal communication, May 21, 2009).

Although all of us looked to cyberspace for practical reasons of cost and convenience, we chose to conduct our research online because we believed the kinds of interactions with target participants offered unique opportunities for robust data collection. I will continue to explore examples from these researchers' work in each chapter's Researchers' Notebook.

Key Concepts

- Researchers choose to conduct interviews online for theoretical and practical reasons.

- Researchers can use synchronous or asynchronous technologies, or a combination of the two, to prepare for, conduct, and follow up on interview research.

- The notion of presence and the possibilities for rich nonverbal and verbal communications are changing with availability of multichannel, interactive technologies.

Discussions and Assignments

Using your library database, find two scholarly articles based on data collected through interviews. Select one example of a study based on data collected in live, face-to-face interviews and one based on data collected online.

1. First, look at the rationale given for selecting online data collection. How did the researcher describe the reasons for taking this approach? Did the researcher make a compelling case? How did the basis for selection given by the researcher align with reasons discussed in Chapter 1?

2. Second, did the researcher use synchronous or asynchronous communications? Do you think the researcher would make a different choice based on technologies that have become available since the research was conducted? If you were conducting the study would you use synchronous or asynchronous communication?

3. Third, look at the article reporting on face-to-face interview research. Could these interviews have been conducted online? Why or why not?

On the Book's Website

You will find the following:

- Descriptions of Researchers' Notebook contributors' studies and links to their work
- Links to articles and materials related to online research
- Updated information

Terms

Asynchronous communication: Communications that involve a delay between message and response, meaning it is not necessary to be online at the same time.

Broadband: High-speed connection that permits transmission of images, audio and video, and large files.

Computer Mediated Communication (CMC): This term refers to human communication that occurs when messages are conveyed by computers.

Digital divide: Term describing unequal access to ICTs across social, economic, and demographic groups.

Forum: A form of asynchronous discussion where original comments and responses are organized by topic. Threaded discussion occurs when one user posts a message that is visible to other users, who respond in their own time. Also known as *threaded discussion*.

Immediacy: Immediacy refers to communicative behaviors that reduce the physical or psychological distance between individuals and foster affiliation (Mehrabian, 1971).

Information and Communications Technologies (ICTs): Umbrella term describing communication devices or applications including the following: cellular phones, computer and network hardware and software, satellite systems, as well as the various services and applications associated with them.

Interactivity: The degree of mutuality and reciprocation present in a communication setting (Kalman et al., 2006).

Mobile access: Ability to connect to the Internet anywhere using computers, cell phones, handheld computers, and personal digital assistants.

Nonverbal communication: Aspects of communication that convey messages without words. Types of nonverbal communication include the following:

- Chronemics communication is the use of pacing and timing of speech and length of silence before response in conversation.
- Paralinguistic or paralanguage communication describes variations in volume, pitch, and quality of voice.
- Kinesic communication includes eye contact and gaze, facial expressions, body movements, gestures, or postures.
- Proxemic communication is the use of interpersonal space to communicate attitudes (Gordon, 1980; Guerrero et al., 1999; Kalman et al., 2006).

Online interviews: For the purpose of this book "online interviews" refer to interviews conducted with CMC. Scholarly interviews are conducted in accordance with ethical research guidelines; verifiable research participants provide informed consent before participating in any interview.

Second Life: A massive multiplayer universe (MMU) set in a 3-D virtual world created by San Francisco–based software maker Linden Labs (Wigmore & Howard, 2009).

Skype: An IP telephony service provider that offers free calling between computers and low-cost calling to regular telephones that aren't connected to the Internet. Included in the free service is a softphone.

Synchronous communication: Communications that occur in real time, meaning it is necessary to be online at the same time.

Voice over Internet protocol (VoIP): A generic term used to describe the techniques used to carry voice traffic over the Internet (infoDev, 2008).

Wiki: A web application designed to allow multiple authors to add, remove, and edit content (infoDev, 2008).

Online Research
With Technology

2

> *Every expansive era in the history of mankind has coincided with the operation of factors . . . to eliminate distance between peoples and classes previously hemmed off from one another. . . . It remains for the most part to secure the intellectual and emotional significance of this physical annihilation of space.*
>
> —John Dewey, 1916

After you study Chapter 2, you will be able to do the following:

- Compare and contrast characteristics of online communication tools;
- Explain ways to use verbal and visual communication features in interviews; and
- Identify four categories of synchronous communication.

Technology = Change

The moment you write about (or worse, buy) any kind of software or hardware, a new option is bound to appear that is smaller, lighter, and faster, with more features. The directions of new technology development represent movement toward increased mobility and convergence of multiple technologies into integrated features and interactivity. These directions combine with trends discussed in Chapter 1: greater interactivity, more access generally, and increased access to broadband. Some emerging features—such as the ability to listen to MP3 files on one's cell phone or

maneuver with touch screens instead of buttons—are not of great consequence for online interviewers. But in general, the fact that more people
can access faster, richer media from any place at any time is advantageous
for their potential research participation.

Programmers, inventers, and technology entrepreneurs who create low-
cost, widely accessible communications tools usually don't have scholarly
research in mind, yet their efforts benefit researchers. Even so, as we learn
new ways to build trusting, authentic dialogue with research participants
we still grapple with the "intellectual and emotional significance of this
physical annihilation of space." John Dewey (1916), educator and philosopher, pointed to the advent of the industrial revolution (p. 85).
Exchanging messages and building relationships are not the same thing.
Chapter 2 will explore ICTs and their potential for tapping the intellectual

and emotional significance of participants' experiences through online
interviews. See the *Online Interviews in Real Time* website for updates on
new trends and options.

Forces for Change

TECHNOLOGY CONVERGENCE: *"TECHNOLOGIES ARE CRASHING TOGETHER"*

Not long ago, communications media were separate, and their services,
deliveries, and uses were distinct. Television broadcasting, voice telephony,
and online computer services were individually received on different
devices: televisions, radio, telephones, and computers. Broadcasts were
received at a given time. **Convergence** describes a major shift in the multimedia environment and/or network where signals, regardless of type
(i.e., voice, quality audio, video, data), are merged and can be accessed
through the same devices, at times convenient to the user (Knemeyer,
2004; Seybold, 2008, p. 11).

In Chapter 1 the concept of media richness was introduced. It distinguished between "lean" and "rich" media based on the number of channels used and the immediacy of feedback (Daft & Lengel, 1986). The
term *convergence* is used here to mean more than simply an increased
level of richness in communication features. Convergence also describes
a new kind of flexibility a user has to make choices about which features
to use for which communication purpose. Where communication by
telephone was once assumed to use voice, we now have the option of text
messaging or sending digital photographs on phones. Where communication by instant message was assumed to be by text, we can now share
files or plug in a headset and voice over Internet to add audio. Users can

watch television on telephones while links to complementary Internet programming appear on television. Convergence makes connectivity more broadly available.

MOBILITY

Since the advent of computers, human-computer interaction has taken place through a now-familiar domain of experience—single users sitting at desks and interacting with desktop computers employing screens, keyboards, and mice for interaction (Dourish, 2004). People accessed the Internet and later the Web from personal computers connected by cables to the telephone jack, with a fairly standardized connection rate and a finite amount of interface and display devices (Knemeyer, 2004). Notebook and netbook computers, personal digital assistants, smart phones, mobile phones, **wireless** Internet connections, public kiosks, and Internet cafés have changed where and how people access the Internet. Extrapolating from current development of a multiplicity of relatively low-cost Internet-enabled devices, ubiquitous computing proposes a digital future in which computer-mediated communication is embedded into the fabric of the world around us and an adjunct to everyday interaction. Anytime, anywhere, Internet and telephone communications are becoming more widely accepted by individuals and intrinsic to the knowledge sharing across organizations.

TECHNOLOGY LEAPFROGGING

Technology leapfrogging is the term used when new digital technologies are adopted in locales where the analog versions are not in place. For example, people now use mobile phone technology even though land-line phones and conventional Internet services are not available. In many countries, mobile phones now outnumber land-line telephones, with 58 percent of these mobile subscribers located in developing countries (Ehrhardt, Gale, McKinlay, & Sethi, 2008). Mobile phones that offer Web and e-mail services enable rich global communications previously unavailable—making online interview participation more widely accessible.

Communication features in smaller, more portable devices allow researchers to develop and study new ways to use technology to solve problems in the developing world. One example comes from Malaysia, where the 1998 Communications and Multimedia Act encouraged new policy objectives and a regulatory framework for the converging industries of telecommunications, broadcasting, and online activities designed to stimulate growth of networks and service providers. The broadband Internet penetration was about 17 percent only as opposed to mobile phone penetration of at least 90 percent (SKMM, 2008). One project enabled by these expanded services is a mobile phone health information system made available to patients in areas where neither Internet access nor land-line telephones are available to everyone. The team of doctors and technology researchers studying this project used mobile phone and online collaborative technologies to conduct an ethnographic action research study (Biswas et al., 2009). The study findings were used to justify funding needed to develop the mobile phone health information system that allows pregnant women, people with diabetes, and other patients the chance to communicate with health care professionals and access databases of health information from their mobile phones. Application of mobile phone/mobile Internet connectivity to other education and public service needs is changing the experiences of people and communities in remote areas of the world.

INTERACTIVITY AND COLLABORATION

The Internet is continually expanding our ability not only to communicate, but to create open or private spaces where we can interact and collaborate. Early online experiences could be characterized as transactional. They consisted primarily of accessing websites and reading materials posted online. Forums, bulletin boards, newsgroups, and e-mail lists enabled text-based exchange between computer users. With next-generation technologies, individuals do more than access materials others have posted; they post comments, pictures, and media and generate material that known or unknown people may view. They have many more choices for communication with colleagues and families and new ways to develop relationships with communities of users they will never meet in person. Users participate in online social contexts, and in the process they change the technologies they use and create new means of exchange.

> [R]ather than taking context and content to be two separable entities ... context arises from the activity. Context isn't just "there," but is actively produced, maintained and enacted in the course of the activity at hand. In this model, context is not something that describes a setting; it is something that people *do*. (Dourish, 2004, p. 22)

Relationships and information are now intertwined. As Hargrove (2001) puts it, "[T]he so-called Information Revolution is, in reality, a Relationships Revolution" (p. 113). Readers and customers can relate directly with the authors or companies who are purveyors of information. We are seeing a change in the flow of information, with individuals both consuming *and* creating content. Such online interaction is intrinsically valuable since "the experience of engaging with the knowledge and views of others is arguably as important as the actual knowledge with which one engages" (Norris, Mason, & Lefrere, 2004). When users experience the creative, generative aspects of online communication, they become more comfortable with tools and approaches that may be used in online research.

Tools and Features for Online Interview Research

ICT features that enable interaction on computers or mobile devices can be categorized as synchronous and asynchronous (see Table 2.1). As noted in Chapter 1, synchronous features require users to be online at the same time while asynchronous features do not. Another way of categorizing features is by the means of exchange: some tools use text only. Others, described here as multichannel, allow for audio or voice, video, or visual exchanges. In the following section some features of ICTs are described.

Table 2.1	ICT Features for Preparation, Interviews, or Follow-up With Participants	
	Text	**Multichannel**
Asynchronous Any Time	*E-mail:* Send and receive questions and answers	*Podcast or Vodcast:* Ask and answer questions by sending audio or video files.
	Forum: Post and respond to questions and answers in secure online threaded discussion area.	*Video:* Post, view, and respond to video clips.
	Weblog (Blog): Personal online journal where entries are posted chronologically. Microblogs allow for very short entries. Blogs can be text only or multichannel, with links to images or media. Viewing may be public or limited to specified group of subscribers or friends.	*Visual Exchange:* Post, view, and respond to photographs, charts and diagrams, and visual maps.
	Wiki: Multiple authors add, remove, and edit content on a website.	

(Continued)

Table 2.1 (Continued)		
	Text	**Multichannel**
Synchronous Real Time	*Text Message:* Send and receive questions on mobile phone or handheld device. *Instant Message or Chat:* Post and respond to questions and answers on computer through secure online website.	*VoIP:* Ask and answer questions using live audio. *Videoconferencing or Video Call:* See interview participants while conversing. *Shared Applications:* View and discuss documents, media, or examples. Log in together and use Web-based software applications, research tools, or forms. Generate responses by writing, drawing, or diagramming ideas on whiteboard or in shared documents. *Immersive Virtual World:* Ask and respond to questions through the physical form and identity of an avatar you create to represent yourself. Experience immersive events or phenomena. View examples or demonstrations.

SYNCHRONOUS COMMUNICATION TOOLS AND FEATURES

Text Messaging, Instant Messaging, and Chat

In real time, people can communicate online by exchanging short written messages. Typically the term *text message* is used when people write back and forth over mobile phones or devices, while *instant messaging* or *chat* refers to the same kind of communication on computers. Chat or messaging may require registration and/or log-in to enter and post; it may be private or open to the public. One-to-one, one-to-many, or many-to-many individuals can converse in writing.

Voice Over Internet Protocol

VoIP and *Internet telephony* are terms used to describe the techniques used to carry voice traffic over the Internet (infoDev, 2008). Using a headset or speakers and microphone, audio conversations can occur online in much the same way a telephone is used. Indeed, some telephone services, using conventional handsets, now use the Internet instead of the usual telephone networks. With VoIP, the customer pays only for the Internet service, dramatically reducing long-distance charges. Skype is one product that allows people to use both VoIP and desktop conferencing features; increasingly, instant or text messaging applications are integrating desktop videoconferencing into the communications package.

Video, Web, or Desktop Conferencing

Videoconferencing is a live session between two or more users who are in different locations. Options include room systems that allow individuals or groups to see each other in an office, meeting room, or studio. Web conferencing, desktop conferencing, or video calls allow users to see each other using a Web camera and computer. Typically the desktop Web conferencing allows viewing participants face-to-face, in contrast to the broader camera range and potential of videoconferencing to show group activities and events, creating a sense of presence and being there. In addition to audio and video transmission, other meeting tools such as whiteboards and shared applications can be used to share visuals, slides, or other documents.

Shared Applications

Connecting over the Internet, a user on one computer can share applications with other invited users. They view, edit, classify, and/or work on documents, media, visuals, or technical applications.

Immersive Virtual World

A **virtual world** is "a synchronous, persistent network of people, represented by avatars, facilitated by computers" (Bell, 2008). Second Life is a popular immersive virtual world. People joining Second Life create their own cartoonlike "avatar" that represents them in the 3-D world and they can create buildings and campuses that may be realistic or based on fanciful imagination (Thorpe, 2008a). Participants travel around the various online environments and interact with each other. Avatars can explore, meet other residents, socialize, participate in individual and group activities, participate in experiential and educational activities, and create and trade virtual items and services with one another. Second Life users can create buildings and campuses that may be realistic or based on fanciful imagination. Participation is free and open to anyone who registers; participants can choose to purchase virtual items or property.

Multichannel Online Meeting Spaces

Some or all of the above features are integrated into online meeting spaces. These spaces can be used for one-to-one, one-to-many, or many-to-many online gatherings. Elluminate, Adobe Connect, and other such platforms allows for dialogue through VoIP two-way audio, text chat, polling, shared applications, Web camera desktop videoconferencing, and shared whiteboard. In addition to exchange and dialogue, the shared whiteboard allows users to record meeting notes or brainstorms, illustrate, use graphic reporting, draw, or create diagrams together. Full versions allow the meeting to be archived for later viewing and transcription. Elluminate and Adobe Connect are commercial services; both offer free rooms for small groups. Other meeting services (free and paid) can be found online.

For the purpose of this book, these synchronous communications tools are organized into four categories, shown in Figure 2.1.

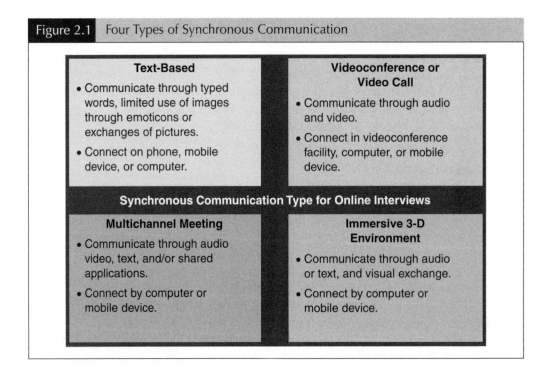

Figure 2.1 Four Types of Synchronous Communication

Text-Based
- Communicate through typed words, limited use of images through emoticons or exchanges of pictures.
- Connect on phone, mobile device, or computer.

Videoconference or Video Call
- Communicate through audio and video.
- Connect in videoconference facility, computer, or mobile device.

Synchronous Communication Type for Online Interviews

Multichannel Meeting
- Communicate through audio video, text, and/or shared applications.
- Connect by computer or mobile device.

Immersive 3-D Environment
- Communicate through audio or text, and visual exchange.
- Connect by computer or mobile device.

ASYNCHRONOUS COMMUNICATION TOOLS AND FEATURES

E-mail

Electronic mail, or e-mail, which can include attachments, continues to be the most widely used form of online communication.

Forum, Threaded Discussion, or Bulletin Board

Post and respond to questions and answers in a secure online threaded discussion area.

Podcasts, Vodcasts, or Video

Podcasts are audio recordings posted online for other users to download and listen to at another time. Vodcasts are video recordings posted online for others to download and view at another time. Other uses of video files could include viewing clips together using shared applications.

Online Questionnaires

Formal online surveys, popular with quantitative researchers, are beyond the scope of this book. However, online questionnaires or surveys can be used to screen participants or solicit demographic or other basic background information from research participants.

Weblog (Blog)

A blog is a personal online journal where entries are posted chronologically. Users create their own weblogs as a way to share thoughts and ideas, and link to other websites and blogs to create families of sites with common interests. Microblogs use the same principle but allow for very short entries. Blogs can be text only or multichannel, with links to images or media. Some are public and others are seen by subscribers or friend lists.

Wiki

Unlike other types of websites that are designed, written, and posted by an individual or company for others' viewing, wikis allow multiple authors to add, remove, and edit content on a website. Users create social context on wikis, where users can contribute to and edit Web pages. Wikis can be public, such as the most global example, Wikipedia, the collaboratively edited global encyclopedia.

Aligning Features With Research Purposes

Researchers using interviews for data collection need several exchanges with research participants in addition to the actual interview. Every stage should be seen as an opportunity to build trust with, and learn about, the research participant. This book focuses on synchronous communications tools for the research interview; nevertheless, a mix of synchronous and asynchronous methods may allow for flexibility, variety, and convenience throughout the stages of the study.

Researchers make choices based on the nature of the study and the options available to the researcher and participant. Some researchers choose asynchronous exchange with research participants and cite many reasons to communicate through e-mail:

- The gap between question and response offers valuable time for reflection for interviewer and interviewee (Bampton & Cowton, 2002; Hunt & McHale, 2007).
- E-mail interviews are iterative (Kitto & Barnett, 2007). Interviewer and interviewee can "explore and revisit insights . . . moving back and forth through their narratives, thinking about their responses, drafting and redrafting what they want to write, creating in effect, a form of enriched interview"(James & Busher, 2006, p. 406).
- E-mail is flexible, allowing researchers to send out all of the questions at once or to start with introductory questions, then respond with replies and further questions (Bampton & Cowton, 2002; Kitto & Barnett, 2007).
- It is convenient since it is not necessary to determine a mutually available meeting time.
- Benefits for the researcher include the ability to manage more than one interview at a time and the ability to maintain day-to-day contact (Mann & Stewart, 2003).
- Because the interview is in writing, an accurate transcript is immediately available with no loss or inaccuracy in transcription.

Different reasons apply to conducting online interviews in real time:

- The researcher is able to approximate aspects of the in-person interview, including verbal and nonverbal cues, while utilizing unique aspects of the Internet.
- Researchers and interviewees can view, share, create, or respond to complex images, diagrams, maps, models, or symbols on shared whiteboards (Blackwell & Clarkson, 2006; Dodge, 2005; Salmons, 2009).
- Researchers and interviewees can observe, participate in, and discuss experiences in an immersive environment such as Second Life. Although the researcher may still need to transcribe the interview, an archive is created for accurate record.

See Chapters 6, 7, and 8 for background and steps for preparing for and conducting interviews with synchronous technologies.

INTERVIEW RESEARCH BUILDS THROUGH MULTISTAGE COMMUNICATIONS

The interview research relationship is initiated with the initial contact, in the sampling and selection of the research participants. (See Chapter 5 for more about sampling and recruiting participants.) Depending on the nature of the study, asynchronous tools such as e-mail lists, posts on blogs, or websites may be useful for communicating announcements for a study and inviting participation. Posted information can provide credibility for the study needed by potential participants such as background on the research, information about the researcher(s), and links to institutions or foundations that sponsor, support, or provide supervision for the study. Online questionnaires can be used as a preliminary step to determine whether the potential participant meets sampling criteria. Researchers and participants can discuss details using synchronous tools such as chat, VoIP calls (especially in multinational studies where telephone is costly), or desktop videoconferencing.

Once the researcher and participant have agreed to proceed with the study, informed consent and preparation are next. (See Chapter 4 for more about ethical research and informed consent.) After participants agree to participate every interaction affords an opportunity to collect data or to develop understanding of the environment and context of the participant's experience. Participants need to fully understand the purpose of the study and expectations; researchers need to communicate fully and in clear terms and be certain participants understand and agree. Background information on the study can be posted on a private, password-protected website or blog where participants can review materials at their leisure. Synchronous tools can be used to ensure that all questions or concerns have been addressed.

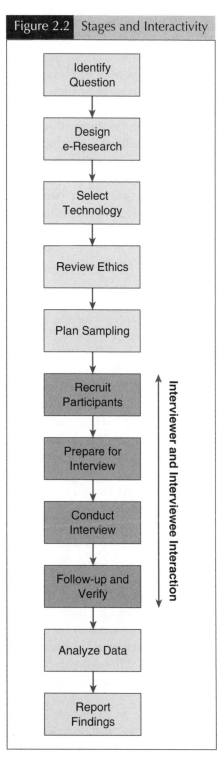

Figure 2.2 Stages and Interactivity

The actual interview (in some cases several interviews) is the formal data collection stage. As noted, some researchers may also choose to conduct some of the entire interview through e-mail. Synchronous tools, the focus of this book, allow for varied types of rich exchange. Data collection using these tools will be explored in detail in coming chapters of this book. (See Chapters 6, 7, and 8 for more about preparing for and conducting interviews with text-based communications, videoconferencing or video calls and meeting space, and 3-D immersive environments.)

After the interview the researcher may choose to design in a follow-up stage, where participants have a chance to review what they have said, elaborate, or correct responses. Asynchronous tools can be used to send documents through e-mail or to discuss any unresolved issues.

Researchers who understand and can use a variety of ICTs are prepared to match communication to stage of the research, needs of the participants, and requirements of the design.

CHOOSING, FINDING, OR CREATING A CONDUCIVE MEETING SPACE

Every researcher needs a safe, neutral location conducive to the interview. A preferred location will be comfortable for the interviewee, with minimal distractions or interference. Few obstacles should prevent the preferred type of interviewee from reaching the location—such as transportation or access for people with disabilities. The setting should not itself become a factor in the interviewee's response because of negative associations or feelings of intimidation. To address these considerations some researchers have chosen to conduct interviews in the field or in settings familiar to the interviewee.

Similar considerations exist when researchers select an online interview setting. Productive, generative interviews require a place to meet where participants feel safe and at ease, and where researchers and participants can focus on the inquiry. It is important to remember that selecting ICTs is about more than simply deciding what tools will be used to transfer messages back and forth between researcher and participant. Technology choices influence the characteristics and feeling of the virtual space that serves as the research setting.

Some questions researchers should consider when making this selection include the following:

- Do people in the target interview demographic generally have access to the type of technology to be used, or will a particular choice of technology exclude many potential participants?

- Will the interviewee feel comfortable, or will additional preparation time be needed to familiarize the interviewee with the setup? Can the researcher be reasonably sure that distractions (noise, family members, others in the office) can be kept to a minimum? (For more on this topic, see Chapter 6.)

- Are interviewees receptive to—or distracted by—creatively presented online environments? Most ICTs take advantage of the graphical nature of the World Wide Web making it possible for the researcher to customize pages or environments used in the interview to create a comfortable, appropriate setting that meets participants' needs. A thoughtful consideration of these elements may involve decisions about inclusion or exclusion of animated graphics, background images, fonts, or colors. (See Chapter 8 for more about visual stimuli in interviews.)

If possible, ask others for feedback on characteristics of the Web interface and impressions it conveys. Take steps as needed to ensure congruence of the online milieu, interface design, and research purpose.

Closing Thoughts

This chapter surveyed some of the technology trends and tools of relevance to researchers who want to conduct online interviews. Designing and carrying out a study entail a complex set of steps and tasks, so any one tool is not likely to be adequate. In considering which tools make sense for the study researchers need to consider the access and ease of use for participants and match for the given tasks. Another question to consider is this: what kind(s) of data do you want to collect? Will verbal, text, or visual data best help you answer the research questions? In addition, researchers need to reflect on their own time and skills. What strengths and skills can you apply to your work as a researcher? Which ICTs are you able to use comfortably to converse? Do you have the time to learn new tools and techniques or to set up new blogs, wikis, or websites? Coming chapters will build on Chapter 2 and explore each step of the interview research and provide guidance for Internet researchers.

Researchers' Notebook: Stories of Online Inquiry

The researchers whose work is profiled in the Researchers' Notebook selected one or more of the synchronous technology types discussed in this book. In addition, all used e-mail for ancillary communications, including planning, sharing documents, and following up the interviews. Although text chat was used in Second Life, none of these researchers conducted text-only interviews.

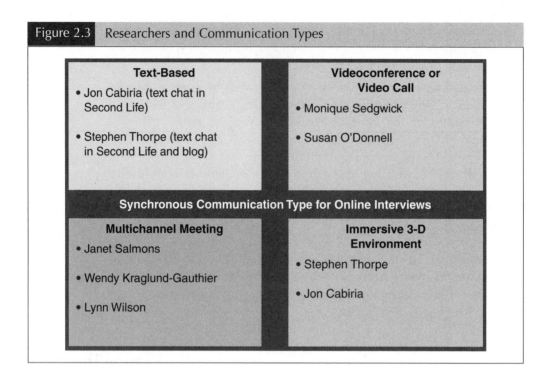

Figure 2.3   Researchers and Communication Types

Text-Based
- Jon Cabiria (text chat in Second Life)
- Stephen Thorpe (text chat in Second Life and blog)

Videoconference or Video Call
- Monique Sedgwick
- Susan O'Donnell

Synchronous Communication Type for Online Interviews

Multichannel Meeting
- Janet Salmons
- Wendy Kraglund-Gauthier
- Lynn Wilson

Immersive 3-D Environment
- Stephen Thorpe
- Jon Cabiria

INTERVIEWS IN A MULTICHANNEL MEETING SPACE

As noted in Chapter 1's Researchers' Notebook, I conducted online studies of online collaboration. I collected data by interviewing instructors and learners in the online meeting space, Elluminate. Each interview participant joined me for a private, one-to-one session. We used VoIP audio, a low-cost alternative for this multinational study. I used my webcam to introduce myself to the participants—none of whom I had met in person.

I used PowerPoint slides to present the questions for the semistructured interview. Because questions were associated with visual images of the model at the center of the interview, this worked very well. Using shared whiteboard tools, participants were able to draw or write on the slides to illustrate points. (See the Researchers' Notebook, Chapter 8, for a detailed description of visual interview approaches.) Given that the purpose of the study was to investigate how participants' experiences correspond to the Taxonomy of Online Collaboration, this multichannel meeting space offered the appropriate set of tools for the study (Salmons, 2010).

Dr. Lynn Wilson used a multichannel approach very differently for her study of communications and decision making involving ocean scientists and policymakers. She used a Q-methods approach. In Q-method, "participants are asked to sort a set of statements representing a broad diversity of opinions and perspectives on the phenomenon being investigated"

(Shinebourne, 2009, p. 94). This is typically accomplished by providing the items on cards which the subject lays out and sorts into horizontally ordered category piles on a desk (Schmolck, 1999).

Lynn generated the set of statements from responses in an initial set of interviews, including face-to-face and e-mail interviews. For the second stage she met with some participants online. She used a shared Web application that allowed for the "Q-sort" process together with a Skype call for the verbal exchange. Participants were interviewed for deeper insights into values and reasoning (Wilson, 2006). Dr. Wilson observed, "Answering questions in the moment allowed for the interviews to flow more naturally and organically. Since I was looking for nuances about why they had made some of the Q-sort choices they did, it required a conversational flow in order to make those discoveries"(L. Wilson, personal communication, June 25, 2008).

INTERVIEWS WITH VIDEOCONFERENCING

Drs. Monique Sedgwick and Susan O'Donnell both conducted interviews via videoconferencing. In both cases the researchers were able to make use of videoconference setups in place to connect rural Canadians to health and other services. The availability of these services meant that research participants did not have to learn to use the technology to participate.

Dr. Sedgwick observed, "For this project we had access to a fully integrated classroom and technical support. All of the participants' videoconferencing sites were located within their local rural hospital, and technical support was offered by local administrative staff trained in the use of the videoconferencing equipment" (Sedgwick & Spiers, 2009, p. 4). Dr. Sedgwick's ethnographic study explored the experiences of nursing students in their rural hospital-based preceptorship. The videoconferencing system, designed for telehealth consults, was set up in a private room with no distractions. It allowed for a close-up view of participants' faces. Because the researcher's setup was similar, she was also visible to participants. Monique found it interesting that participants referred to the videoconference interview as "face-to-face," which they found preferable to a voice-only telephone interview (M. Sedgwick, personal communication, May 21, 2009).

INTERVIEWS IN AN IMMERSIVE 3-D ENVIRONMENT

Stephen Thorpe's doctoral research used co-constructed narratives to study facilitation in online groups. With both one-on-one and group interviews, he included one subproject investigating storytelling using a blog and another subproject to investigate storytelling using the medium of Second Life (Thorpe, 2008a). Thorpe hoped that the 3-D interactive environment would enhance the storytelling by providing a sense of place and a story-telling metaphor for the group and the stories told.

Second Life provided an accessible environment for the research participants to explore the potential of a 3-D environment for group work and the facilitation of storytelling in building online relationships. The group had access to a virtual island attached to the New Media Consortium (NMC) campus[1] that had a range of group environments that could be used for our session.

Nine participants joined in the session from Auckland and Nelson in New Zealand; Sydney, Canberra, and Perth in Australia; Hong Kong; Uppsala in Sweden; and Den Haag in The Netherlands. Participants were asked to create their avatar in advance of the storytelling session. They were invited also to explore the tutorials on the Orientation Island within Second Life to familiarize themselves with the virtual world and navigation.

Participants were invited to share their journeys about becoming a facilitator and to reflect on the experience in the 3-D environment and the use of storytelling. Discussion following the session revealed that participants found the experience emotionally engaging and lots of fun, and many wanted to explore the environment further after the program. Combining storytelling with the interactive 3-D fireplace metaphor meant that participants' connections with each other were on an emotional level. The Second Life experience was described as being very close to what participants experience when meeting face-to-face. It was considered by some a very direct experience with an environment or place.

Jon Cabiria's study took place in Second Life as well, selected to reflect the virtual world effects central to his inquiry. He also intended to use audio originally, to record voice conversations in world. Toward that goal, he installed the program Audacity to record and edit virtual-world conversations. However, in the end, most participants preferred text chat, so he did not use voice recording. The text interviews were saved instead, offering an instant transcript of the conversation. His experience illustrates the need for flexibility on the part of the researcher to respond to the preferences of the interviewee (J. Cabiria, personal communication, September 6, 2008).

SUMMARY COMMENTS

Videoconferencing, Elluminate, Skype, and Second Life are very different kinds of synchronous environments. In the first three, participants and researchers interact as themselves and have rich communication through voice and a variety of visuals. In Second Life participants and researchers interact through avatars and have rich communication through a visual environment and a sense of physical presence. Each has value when aligned with the research purpose and in consideration of research participants' willingness and availability of the tools needed to participate.

Key Concepts

- Technologies change continuously. Forces for change include convergence of features, increased mobile access, and more ways to interact.

- Researchers can use synchronous and asynchronous communications to take care of the tasks associated with planning and carrying out a study. Researchers can choose the most appropriate tools to communicate with research participants through the sampling, preparing for the study, conducting the interview, and following up on the study.

Discussions and Assignments

1. Which ICTs can you demonstrate or teach others to use? Offer peer learning opportunities to improve each other's skills.

2. Which ICTs do you want to learn how to use? Select a technology tool you have not used before. Working with a classmate, try a new communications tool. Ask your peer questions, and record or take notes. Discuss your perceptions of this tool's potential for research interviews. (Note: many software tools offer a free or trial version you can use for this project.)

3. What factors make you feel safe and willing to reveal personal or sensitive thoughts or feelings in online communications?
   - The style or features of the technology?
   - The culture or expectations of the online community or social media site?
   - The personality, style, or credibility of the person with whom you communicate?
   - The ground rules or agreements you state before the interaction?

4. Discuss steps or actions you can take to help others trust you when you communicate online.

5. What strengths and skills can you apply to your work as an online researcher? What skills do you need to develop?

On the Book's Website

You will find the following:

- Links to articles and materials related to emerging ICTs suitable for interviews
- Descriptions of Researchers' Notebook contributors' studies and links to their work

Terms

Convergence: A multimedia environment and/or network where signals regardless of type (i.e., voice, quality audio, video, data, and so on) are merged and can be accessed through the same devices (Knemeyer, 2004; Seybold, 2008, p. 11).

Technology leapfrogging: The implementation of a new and up-to-date technology in an area where the previous version of the technology has not been deployed, bypassing of technological stages that others (other countries) have gone through (Davison, Vogel, Harris, & Jones, 2006; Ehrhardt et al., 2008).

Virtual worlds: Synchronous, persistent networks of people, represented by avatars, facilitated by computers (Bell, 2008).

Wireless: Generic term for mobile communication services that do not use fixed-line networks for direct access to the subscriber (infoDev, 2008).

Note

1. The NMC campus is an experimental effort developed to inform the NMC's work in educational gaming. See http://www.nmc.org/about for details.

Interviews for Scholarly Research

3

> The scientific mind does not so much provide the right answers as ask the right questions.
>
> —Claude Lévi-Strauss, 1983

After you study Chapter 3, you will understand the following:

- Ways to define *in-depth research interview*, roles, and distinctions for the interviewer and interviewee;
- An overview of research epistemologies, theories, methodologies, and methods and how they are interrelated;
- Levels of interview structure; and
- Interviews in qualitative and mixed methods research.

Research: New Knowledge and Understandings

Empirical research is conducted to generate new knowledge and deeper understanding of the topic of study. Research results inform other scholars who may build on the work as well as decisionmakers and practitioners looking for reliable information to guide their work. Researchers use many different interview styles to collect data. The diversity of interview styles pertains to more than simply the preferences of the individual researcher or even to the requirements of the study. Each interview style is rooted in a distinct view of the world, a system of beliefs about the nature of knowledge, and a perspective on the relationships among researcher, worldview, and knowledge. Each has its own language with a corresponding set of definitions. Each expects a slightly different set of attitudes and actions on the part of the researcher and has its own way to describe the person participating in the interview. Selection of interview approach has implications for both theoretical and practical aspects of the study—why, how, and where it is conducted and with whom.

Although each approach to interview research has staunch advocates and critical detractors, it is not necessary to accept an either-or view or to accept any one perspective in its entirety. Given that the interviewer has multiple interactions with the interviewee, different approaches may be appropriate for different phases of the study.

A broad understanding of **methodologies** and **methods** of interview research is essential to online researchers for several reasons. An understanding of interview styles may influence the choice of communications technologies. At the same time, knowledge of available communications technologies may influence choice of research methodologies. These decisions need to be made in a coherent way so researchers can develop thoughtful rationales and proposals that show alignment of interview approach, research purpose, and design.

This chapter surveys major approaches to interview research to provide essential background that researchers need to grasp the relationship between research tradition, purpose, and design (see Chapter 4) on the one hand and technology tools (see Chapters 2 and 7) on the other. **Qualitative research** methods and **mixed methods** are explored extensively in the literature; suggestions for further reading on research foundations are provided.

Defining "Research Interview"

What is an *in-depth research interview?* The word *interview* originates in Latin terms *inter-,* meaning "between, among" or "mutually, reciprocally," and *view,* meaning "the ability to see something" (Soanes & Stevenson, 2004, p. 7). The word *interview* came to English by way of the French word *entrevoir*—"to see each other." A literal interpretation might define the term as "to see something between" people in a "mutual, reciprocal" exchange.

An early, frequently quoted definition calls the research interview a "conversation with a purpose" (Webb & Webb, 1932, p. x). Kvale (2007) says that production of knowledge is the purpose and calls for a particular kind of relationship: "The interview is a specific form of conversation where knowledge is produced through the interaction between an interviewer and interviewee" (p. vii). Holstein and Gubrium (2004) define interviewing as a way to "generate empirical data about the social world by asking people to talk about their lives" (p. 204). Although the interview cannot provide a "mirror image of the social world," Miller and Glassner (2004) point out that it does "provide access to the meanings people attribute to their experiences and social worlds" (p. 126). Holstein and Gubrium (1995) see a story emerging from each interview, which is "an interpersonal drama with a developing plot" (p. 16). Denzin (2001) sees significance beyond the immediate players and their interactions:

> The interview is a way of writing the world, a way of bringing the world into play. . . . The interview functions as a narrative device which allows persons who are so inclined to tell stories about themselves. (p. 25)

The interviewer "starts with the participant's story and fills it out by attempting to locate it within a basic social process" to determine what is happening in the interviewee's world (Charmaz, 2003, p. 314).

Neuman's definition describes the relationship between interviewer and interviewee as one with an intrinsic power differential: "a short-term, secondary social interaction between two strangers with the explicit purpose of one person obtaining specific information from the other" (Neuman, 1994, p. 246). Rubin and Rubin say the interviewer's power entails responsible and respectful actions to "gently guide a conversational partner . . . to elicit depth and detail about the research topic" (Rubin & Rubin, 2005, p. 4).

When trying to define the research interview, writers often wax poetic. But their sometimes flowery characterizations contain practical principles. At the simplest, the **in-depth interview** involves interrelationships among the following:

- *The interviewer,* who, regardless of interview style, is responsible for ethical, respectful inquiry and accurate collection of data relevant to the research purpose and questions. As a *researcher* the interviewer places the interview exchange within a scholarly context.

- *The interviewee,* who responds honestly to questions or participates in discussion with the researcher to provide ideas or answers that offer insight into his or her perceptions, understandings, or experiences of personal, social, or organizational dimensions of the subject of the study. Depending on the nature and expectations of the research, interviewees may also be called *subjects, respondents,* or *research participants.*

- *The research purpose and questions,* which serve as the framework and offer focus and boundaries to the interactions between researcher and interviewee.

- *The research environment,* which provides a context for the study. Depending on the nature of the study, the environment may be significant to the researcher's understanding of the interviewee. Cyberspace is the research environment for online interviews.

A working definition for the purpose of this book is as follows:

> An in-depth interview is a qualitative research technique involving a researcher who guides or questions a participant to elicit information, perspectives, insights, feelings on behaviors, experiences, or phenomena that cannot be observed. The in-depth interview is conducted to collect data that allow the researcher to answer research questions, thus generating new understandings and new knowledge about the subject of investigation.

INTERVIEWS IN AN INTERVIEW SOCIETY

The purpose of the research interview is to collect data—data that will be carefully and critically analyzed to generate credible findings. Interviews are widely used for other business purposes, including hiring, political purposes, opinion polls, as well as for mass media news and entertainment. Another important use of interviews in our society is legal—by police, defenders, prosecutors, congressional investigators. These interviews have interesting parallels with academic research. Indeed, the interview has become so pervasive that the term *interview society* is sometimes used to describe it:

> We see the interview society as relying pervasively on face-to-face interviews to reveal the personal, the private self of the subject. (Atkinson & Silverman, 1997, p. 309)

> Perhaps we all live in what might be called an interview society in which interviews seem central to making sense of our lives. (Silverman & Marvasti, 2008, p. 146)

The researcher's purpose, to generate reliable knowledge, contrasts with the reasons people may have for a casual interview. In a hiring interview, the purpose is clear to both parties, and, in most cases, the interviewer holds the power within the exchange. News interviews are typically conducted to elicit opinions or feelings. Casual interviewers may not see the need to objectively screen for less than truthful, or unrepresentative, views. Indeed, an extreme view may be the one given time on a television program or in print, because it is more likely to stir controversy and attract more viewers or readers. The ubiquity of the casual interview in contemporary media culture places a responsibility on the researcher, who must be able to distinguish scholarly from informal dialogue. Unlike other contemporary interviewers, the researcher must be able to justify and defend methods, data, analysis, and conclusions generated by the study.

Research Epistemologies, Methodologies, and Methods

Although all scholars conduct research in order to generate knowledge and deeper understandings, each scholar thinks about this process in a unique way. Space does not permit full review of the possibilities here, but it is important to establish a basis for **research design** that makes sense for studies that utilize interview methods generally and online interview methods in particular (see Figure 3.1). Four interrelated facets of research—**epistemology, theory,** methodology, and method (Crotty, 1998)—are defined for our purposes as follows:

- *Epistemology* refers to the study of the nature of knowledge, or the study of how knowledge is justified.

- *Theory* refers to an explanation that is internally consistent, is supportive of other theories, and gives new insights. An important characteristic of theory is that it is predictive.

- *Methodology* refers to the study of, and justification for, the methods used to conduct the research (Gray, 2004). Methodologies emerged from academic disciplines in the social and physical sciences and, although considerable cross-disciplinary exchange occurs, choices generally place the study into a disciplinary context.

- *Method* refers to the practical steps used to conduct the study (Anfara & Mertz, 2006; Carter & Little, 2007).

| Figure 3.1 | Interrelated Facets of a Research Design |

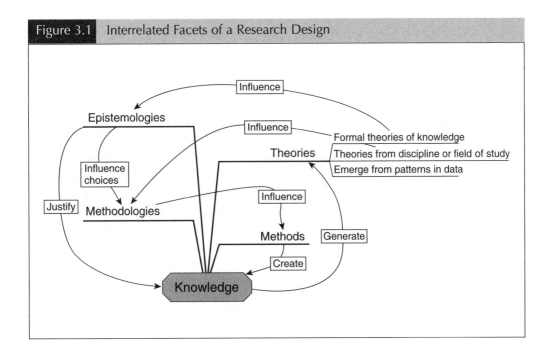

THEORIES AND RESEARCH DESIGN

Theories, whether they are theories of knowledge or theories from the field of study, influence the epistemology that guides the study and will ultimately be used to justify and explain the new knowledge that emerges from the study. Theories also influence the choice and form of research methodology, which in turn influences the methods used to carry out the study.

Theory plays different roles in qualitative and quantitative studies. Some qualitative researchers frame the study in theoretical terms while others aim to discover and "ground" theoretical principles in the data. In **quantitative research,** theory "is an inter-related set of constructs (or **variables**) formed into propositions, or hypotheses, that specify the relationship among variables" (Creswell, 2003, p. 120). Quantitative researchers start with a theory, develop a hypothesis, and collect data to refine or contradict the theory.

Theories from the discipline or field of study may influence not only the choices of methodology, but the nature and questions of the inquiry. Education, sociology, psychology, business, or science researchers will turn to established disciplinary theories—and to previous studies that explored and tested them—when establishing a basis for knowledge and practice in their respective fields.

When researchers choose epistemology, methodology, and methods, they draw on accepted concepts and practices to create their own frameworks to use in designing, planning, conducting, analyzing, and reporting on the study.

(See the template on the book's website to create your own research framework.)

EPISTEMOLOGIES INFLUENCE DESIGN CHOICES

Qualitative researchers often base studies on *interpretivist* or *constructivist* epistemologies. The premise of interpretivism is that we "interpret" our experiences in the social world. It is based on the assumption that knowledge acquisition occurs when people interpret their observations of the world. The premise of **constructivism** is that we construct social reality based on our perceptions of the world. Subjects construct and interpret their own meanings in different ways, even in relation to the same phenomenon (Gray, 2004).

Another set of epistemologies is loosely described as *critical theory.* Researchers who work from these worldviews may have particular concerns in areas such as feminist, lesbian, bisexual, gay, transgender (LBGT) or disability studies. They see research as motivation for change and advocacy. They believe the following:

> [R]esearch [should] contain an integral action agenda that will bring about reform that will change the lives of the research participants, the institutions and communities in which individuals live and work. (Bloomberg & Volpe, 2008, p. 9)

From a view influenced by interpretivism, constructivism, or critical theory, knowledge arises in an individual based on experience and reason or exists in communities of people and defines what they can agree on as common in the individuals' relationships to their environment. The researcher can justify the selection of interview methods based on the desire to uncover the interviewee's knowledge on a topic—or to create new understandings with the interviewee through the research process.

Research justified by interpretivist epistemologies typically uses **inductive reasoning** to come to conclusions. Inductive reasoning works from the specific to the general. Using inductive reasoning, the researcher looks for patterns, relationships, and associations in the data and constructs generalizations. Researchers use inductive reasoning when they examine how people integrate fragmented phenomena into meaningful explanations of experiences. By contrast, **deductive reasoning** works from the general to the specific. When researchers use deductive reasoning, they state a hypothesis, then gather data (evidence) to support or refute the hypothesis. Deductive reasoning is more often associated with quantitative research.

Quantitative researchers often base studies on *objectivist, positivist,* or *postpositivist* views. An objectivist, positivist epistemology describes a worldview that presupposes an objective reality that exists apart from the perceptions of those who observe it. It makes a separation between the consciousness of the observer and the nature of the objects observed. Knowledge is generated by recognizing patterns in the environment that exist independently of individual perception. The goal of research is to discover this objective truth, to better understand this reality (Creswell & Clark, 2007; Schutt, 2006). The positivist view of social reality is that it is "knowable" by researchers using valid forms of measurement (Hesse-Biber & Leavy, 2006).

Social researchers have largely rejected strict interpretations of **positivism** in favor of **postpositivism**. While positivists aim to prove causal relationships, postpositivists rely on deductive logic to build evidence in support of an existing theory (Creswell, 2003; Hesse-Biber & Leavy, 2006). The postpositivist view challenges earlier positivist notions by recognizing that we cannot be "positive" about our claims of the existence of a common objective reality when studying the behavior and actions of humans because of biases and other limitations of researchers (Creswell & Clark, 2007; Schutt, 2006). The scientific method is the foundation of both positivist and postpositivist views. The main distinctions between the two come from the postpositivists' answers to the criticism of positivism that it was based on an artificial separation between the observer and the observed:

> The belief is that there are laws or theories that govern the world, and that these can be tested or verified. Thus, the research begins with a theory and a set of hypotheses, and the intent is to test ideas. (Bloomberg & Volpe, 2008, p. 8)

According to Creswell and Clark (2007), postpositivist researchers make knowledge claims based on the following (p. 22):

- Determinism or cause-and-effect thinking;
- Reductionism or narrowing and focusing on select variables to interrelate;
- Detailed observations and measure of variables; and
- Testing and refining theories.

Mixed Methods, Mixed Epistemologies

When researchers mix methods, they may identify a worldview that encompasses all of their methods. Mixed methods may mean mixed epistemologies; researchers must reconcile seemingly disparate views of the world. They need to identify a worldview that encompasses all of their methods. From a positivist or postpositivist view, they want to understand social reality, while from an interpretivist view, they want to understand the meanings people give to reality.

Mixed methods researchers can draw on the theorist Edmund Husserl who distinguished between "noema," that which is experienced, and "noesis," the act of experiencing in his 1931 book, *Ideas* (Husserl, 1931). This paradigm may be useful for researchers interested in looking through different lenses to explore factual information or realities and at the same time understand people's experiences of the information or circumstances. Data about the phenomenon in question may be collected through methods such as document review, observations, **surveys,** or scientific experimentation. Perceptions and experiences may be explored through interviews with people who have experienced it. Thinking in these terms may allow the researcher to appropriately mix strategies and/or methods as needed to find robust answers for inquiries that encompass multiple dimensions.

Mixed methods researchers can also take a pragmatic stance. The **pragmatic** view is that meaning is determined by the experiences or practical consequences of belief in or use of the idea (Johnson & Onwuegbuzie, 2004). The pragmatic approach looks for plural, rather than polar, positions. Pragmatists take intersubjective attitudes, moving between objective and subjective viewpoints. They rely on **abductive** reasoning by moving back and forth between inductive and deductive reasoning, "first converting observations into theories and then assessing those theories through action" (Morgan, 2007, p. 71). Pragmatic researchers develop models that match their observations, check them for logical consistency, and test them through further observation and action. Because they believe that research approaches should be mixed in ways that offer the best opportunities for answering important research questions, pragmatists mix epistemologies, methodologies, and methods.

The focus of this book is on interview methodologies and methods for online interviews. Researchers from diverse epistemological and theoretical viewpoints may choose to collect data through interviews conducted online. With this premise in mind, *Online Interviews in Real Time* focuses primarily on epistemological influences on interview research methodology and methods and will leave to other philosophers and writers broad questions about the nature of knowledge.

Methodologies and Methods: Key Principles and Distinctions

Research methodologies provide conceptual and theoretical frameworks used to design, organize, and explain a study. *Methods* are the techniques used to conduct the collection and analysis of data.

METHODOLOGIES

The belief that people create, maintain, and live in meaningful worlds is common to most researchers. Literature on the subject describes many ways to collect data about those worlds and meanings by surveying, observing, reading documents, or asking people to talk about them. Scholars offer very different approaches to accomplish this seemingly simple task. Each approach has its own history, development, and disciplinary focus. Doing each methodology justice is beyond the scope of this book. A brief overview of methodologies that are often aligned with interview research is offered here, with references to some major writings for further exploration (see Table 3.1).

METHODS

At its simplest, the interview is a method researchers use to collect data. Critical differences in interview methods center on distinctions between planning and spontaneity, and on roles and expectations of the interviewer, interviewee, and their interactions during the interview. Stylistic choices are influenced by researchers' epistemic views of knowledge and whether they believe knowledge exists apart from, or is created during and through, the interview process. Accordingly, researchers look at the interview as a way to obtain information from *respondents* or construct knowledge with *research participants*. Structure is one pivotal methodological concern that influences the method of interview data collection.

Table 3.1	An Overview of Research Methodologies	
Methodology	**Description**	**Suggested Readings**
Qualitative		
Action research	Action research involves close collaboration between researchers and subjects, who are often practitioners. It often aims to achieve benefits to the school or organization being investigated (Gray, 2004).	Calhoun, E. F. (1993). Action research: Three approaches. *Educational Leadership, 51*(2), 62–66. Gray, D. (2009). *Doing research in the real world* (2nd ed.). London: Sage Publications.
Case study	Case study refers to the collection and presentation of detailed information about a particular participant or small group, frequently including the accounts of subjects themselves (Palmquist, 2008). A setting or group treated as an integrated social unit to be studied "holistically and in its particularity" (Schutt, 2006, p. 292).	Stake, R. E. (1995). *The art of case study research.* Thousand Oaks, CA: Sage Publications. Yin, R. K. (2009). *Case study research: Design and methods* (4th ed.). Thousand Oaks, CA: Sage Publications.
Grounded theory	Theory is "grounded" in the data from participants who have experienced the phenomenon. Situational analysis looks at the social *situation* while grounded theory looks at social *process*.	Charmaz, K. (2006). *Constructed grounded theory: A practical guide through qualitative analysis.* Thousand Oaks, CA: Sage Publications. Clarke, A. (2005). *Situational analysis: Grounded theory after the postmodern turn.* Thousand Oaks, CA: Sage Publications. Corbin, A. S. J. (1998). *Basics of qualitative research: Grounded theory procedures and techniques* (2nd ed.). Newbury Park, CA: Sage Publications.
Phenomenology	Phenomenology is the search for the ways participants experience and give meaning to an event, concept, or phenomenon (Gray, 2004).	Groenwald, T. (2004). A phenomenological research design illustrated. *International Journal of Qualitative Methods, 3*(1). Retrieved August 1, 2009, from http://www.ualberta.ca/~iiqm/backissues/3_1/pdf/groenewald.pdf

Methodology	Description	Suggested Readings
	Phenomenological research methods provide a way to investigate human experience through the perceptions of research participants.	Lester, S. (1999). *An introduction to phenomenological research.* Retrieved August 1, 2009, from http://www.sld.demon.co.uk/resmethy.pdf Moustakas, C. (1994). *Phenomenological research methods.* Thousand Oaks, CA: Sage Publications.
Resources on multiple qualitative methodologies		Creswell, J. W. (2007). *Qualitative inquiry and research design: Choosing among five approaches* (2nd ed.). Thousand Oaks, CA: Sage Publications. Mason, J. (2002). *Qualitative researching* (2nd ed.). Thousand Oaks, CA: Sage Publications. Patton, M. Q. (2002). *Qualitative research and evaluation methods* (3rd ed.). Thousand Oaks, CA: Sage Publications. Ritchie, J., & Lewis, J. (Eds.). (2003). *Qualitative research practice: A guide for social science students and researchers.* London: Sage Publications. Starks, H., & Trinidad, S. B. (2007). Choose your method: A comparison of phenomenology, discourse analysis, and grounded theory. *Qualitative Health Research, 17*(10),
Quantitative		
Experimental	A research methodology based upon cause-and-effect relationships between independent and dependent variables by means of the manipulation of independent variables,	Brown, S. R., & Melamed, L. E. (1990). *Experimental design and analysis.* Thousand Oaks, CA: Sage Publications. Gray, D. (2009). *Doing research in the real world.* London: Sage Publications.

(Continued)

Table 3.1	(Continued)	
Methodology	**Description**	**Suggested Readings**
	control, and randomization (Creswell, 2008).	Sue, V., & Ritter, L. (2007). *Conducting online surveys.* Thousand Oaks, CA: Sage Publications.
Quasi-experimental	A research approach that uses elements of the experimental design, such as use of a control group, but without the ability to randomly select the sample (Gray, 2004).	
Mixed Methods		
Mixed Methods	*Mixed methods* is an umbrella term covering a variety of combinations of qualitative and quantitative methods.	Creswell, J. W. (2008). *Research design: Qualitative, quantitative, and mixed methods approaches* (3rd ed.). Thousand Oaks, CA: Sage Publications. Creswell, J. W., & Clark, V. L. P. (2007a). *Designing and conducting mixed methods research* (2nd ed.). Thousand Oaks, CA: Sage Publications. Creswell, J. W., & Clark, V. L. P. (2007b). *The mixed methods reader* (2nd ed.). Thousand Oaks, CA: Sage Publications.

In this context, *structure* refers generally to the extent to which the questions, order, and process are planned ahead of the interview and the extent of consistency from one interview to another. Does the researcher aim to obtain the same types of answers from diverse interviewees or to make each interview a unique narrative event? On one end of the spectrum, **structured interviews** use predetermined questions in a planned order for interviewers to query respondents. At the other end of the spectrum, no questions are framed in advance, and *unstructured* conversational interviews occur between researchers and participants. Between these extremes, there are many variations. These variations are generally termed *semistructured* interviews: interviews with varying degrees of flexibility in planning and exchange. This Typology of Interview Structures (Figure 3.2) is organized as a continuum to illustrate a breadth of interview types and structures.

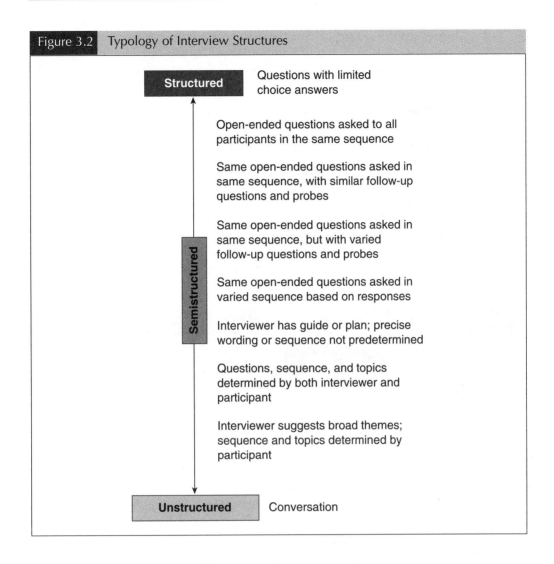

Figure 3.2   Typology of Interview Structures

Structured — Questions with limited choice answers

Open-ended questions asked to all participants in the same sequence

Same open-ended questions asked in same sequence, with similar follow-up questions and probes

Same open-ended questions asked in same sequence, but with varied follow-up questions and probes

Same open-ended questions asked in varied sequence based on responses

Interviewer has guide or plan; precise wording or sequence not predetermined

Questions, sequence, and topics determined by both interviewer and participant

Interviewer suggests broad themes; sequence and topics determined by participant

Unstructured — Conversation

Semistructured

Terminology for structured, unstructured, and especially semistructured interviews is not consistent in the literature. The Typology of Interview Structures will be used to provide a common set of terms and concepts throughout this book.

The Typology of Interview Structures illustrates relationships between the level of structure and flexibility in interview research. Inherent in these distinctions are sets of beliefs about the nature of knowledge and how it is created, and about roles, relationships, and power differentials between interviewer and interviewee. Representative points on the continuum are illustrated by three metaphors—two are terms coined by Kvale (2006, 2007) and a new one, the *gardener,* is suggested here.

On one end of the continuum, the researcher is characterized as a *miner* who digs out facts and feelings from research subjects. The other extreme represents the researcher as a *traveler* who journeys with the participant. Most common interview practices lie between these two extremes. The metaphor of the *gardener* describes these semistructured interviews (see Figure 3.3).

Structured Interviews

Structured and *survey* interviews occupy one end of the continuum with what is essentially a live version of the questionnaire. The metaphor for interaction at this end of the continuum is excavation; the *miner* dispassionately digs for facts in response to a set of questions. "'Knowledge' is waiting in the subject's interior to be uncovered, uncontaminated by the miner" who conducts the interview (Kvale, 2007, p. 19). In structured interviewers the same questions are posed in the same order and maintain a consistent, neutral approach to questioning (Fontana & Frey, 2003;

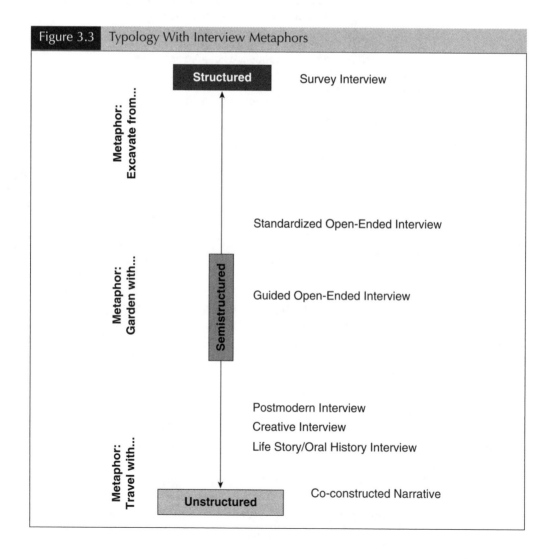

Figure 3.3   Typology With Interview Metaphors

Schaeffer & Maynard, 2003; Schutt, 2006). Options may be limited to multiple choice, yes/no, or three to five alternative responses on a Likert-type scale. Structured interviews may also pose open-ended questions to elicit short narrative answers. Interview respondents do not have the option to redirect questions or embroider on responses.

To prepare for structured interviews, the researcher articulates all questions in advance. Because the role of the interviewer is meant to be as neutral as possible, the researcher may recruit and train others to implement the interview.

Survey interviews usually ask respondents to report on facts or assess attitudes on a product, candidate, or event. The data can be analyzed using either qualitative or quantitative methods. However, structured interviews can serve other research purposes. One type of structured interview, the "laddering interview," is designed to move the discussion from a lower level of abstraction to a higher level of abstraction (Reppel, Gruber, Szmigin, & Voss, 2008). Beginning with an elicitation stage, interviewers use sorting techniques to derive interviewee preferences and develop criteria. Criteria thus derived act as the starting point for "laddering" probes, with the interviewer repeatedly asking questions about why an attribute, consequence, or value is important to the respondent. Each answer serves as the starting point for the next question. The laddering process continues until the respondent either repeats answers or is not able or willing to answer.

Structured interviews can serve as the first or developmental stage of a multistage or mixed methods study. As an initial stage, structured interviews can help the researcher to generate items for exploration using other methods (Gehling, Turner, & Rutherford, 2007). The structured interview may be followed with a survey in a quantitative or mixed methods study or with observations and/or less structured interviews in a qualitative study.

Semistructured Interviews

Semistructured interviews endeavor to balance the organization and framework of the structured approach with the spontaneity and flexibility of the unstructured interview. The researcher prepares questions and/or discussion topics in advance and generates follow-up questions during the interview. In more structured *standardized open-ended interviews,* interviewers may ask the same open-ended questions in the same sequence but with varied follow-up questions and probes. They also may ask a consistent set of questions but vary the sequence based on responses. In more flexible *guided open-ended interviews,* researchers create themes or develop an "interview guide" of topics to discuss, but do not develop precise wording or sequence in advance of the interview (Patton, 2002).

A metaphor for the semistructured interviewer is the *gardener*. The gardener realizes that harvest is not possible without planting the seed. At the same time, many seeds can be sown without results, if contextual conditions of weather, soil, and care are not in balance. The researcher-gardener realizes that the question seeds the participant's thought process. With responsive encouragement the answer will emerge. With it, both the researcher's and the participant's understanding will grow.

Unstructured Interviews

At the other end of the continuum, unstructured interviews are used to collect data through what is essentially a conversation between the researcher and participant. The metaphor for interaction at this end of the continuum is the "traveler on a journey to a distant country whose journey leads to a tale to be told upon returning home." The traveler has conversations with people encountered along the way, asking questions and encouraging them to tell their own stories (Kvale, 2007).

In the unstructured interview, questions emerge from the context and events occurring in the circumstance of the interview. The unstructured interview may be a planned discussion in a formal interview setting. Or, it can be naturalistic, meaning it occurs on site where the participant lives or works, occurring in conjunction with other field or participant observations. Data collected from unstructured interviews are different for each person interviewed and may be different for the same person who is interviewed on multiple occasions (Patton, 2002).

Some forms of unstructured interviews are as follows:

- Life Story or Oral History Interviews

  Researchers interested in the "continuity and wholeness of an individual's life experience" look to narrative forms of inquiry to elicit data (Clandinin & Connelly, 2000, p. 17). Oral histories may tap into the individual's firsthand testimony to historical, community, or social events or processes, or describe "turning-point moments" in people's lives (Denzin, 1989; Smith, 2003). Some interviewers may ask a set of questions to get the story started, while others may simply ask participants to tell their stories in their own way (Clandinin & Connelly, 2000).

- Postmodern Interviews

  The term *postmodern* refers to a set of "orienting sensibilities" rather than a particular kind of interviewing (Holstein & Gubrium, 2003b). These sensibilities may mean blurred boundaries between interviewer and interviewee, new ways of collaborative construction of meaningful narratives in the interview which are often constructed using artistic or electronic media (Fontana, 2003; Holstein & Gubrium, 2003b, p. 5). An important postmodern sensibility points to the **active interview,** a term that signifies the importance of a mutual exchange and highly interactive interview. (Note: the "active interview" does not refer to "action" research.) Meaning is not simply elicited by interviewers' questioning; it is actively and communicatively assembled in the interview encounter. "Respondents . . . are constructors of knowledge in collaboration with interviewers" (Holstein & Gubrium, 2003a).

Two types of active interviews that can be described as "postmodern" are **co-constructed narratives** and **creative interviews.**

- Co-constructed Narratives

  Researchers and interviewees may share stories in collaborative interviews through "co-constructed narratives," which means that the narratives are jointly created. The narrative process is called *mediated* when the researcher monitors the exchange between relational partners, or *unmediated* when a researcher and interviewee, or two researchers, exchange and study their own stories (Ellis & Berger, 2003).

- Creative Interviews

  Jack Douglas' book *Creative Interviewing* introduced a naturalistic, life-story approach to interviews. These unstructured interviews occur on location in situational everyday settings of people in society (Douglas, 1984; Fontana & Frey, 2003). For example, a researcher might observe someone at work and ask him to explain what he is doing, why he did it, and what he has to think about to do the work, in an informal but disciplined exchange (DeVault & McCoy, 2002).

Postmodern researchers "travel with" their participants. They object to the image of interviewees as "passive vessels of answers" for interview questions posed by a neutral interviewer (Gubrium & Holstein, 2003a). Postmodern researchers see interviewees as participants in, rather than subjects of, research (Fontana, 2003; Holstein & Gubrium, 2003a, 2003b). Looking at interviews as generative processes happening in the interactions between researcher and participant "transforms the subject behind the respondent from a repository of information and opinions or a wellspring of emotions into a productive source of knowledge" (Gubrium & Holstein, 2003a, p. 32). The interviewer uses active listening to create a sense of equality and interdependence with the participant (Gubrium & Holstein, 2003a). The *what* (interview purpose and guiding issues) and the *how* (respectful questioning) are fully meshed in the **postmodern interview.** Issues guiding the interview questions and interviewees' responses emerge in the interview (Ellis & Berger, 2003; Gubrium & Holstein, 2003a).

INTERVIEWS IN QUALITATIVE
AND MIXED METHODS STUDIES

The in-depth interview is a method researchers use to collect data for qualitative or for mixed methods studies. *Qualitative research* "aims to produce rounded and contextual understandings on the basis of rich, nuanced and detailed data" (Mason, 2002, p. 3). *Mixed methods* is an umbrella term covering a variety of combinations of qualitative and quantitative methods. Researchers with a predominantly qualitative orientation may decide that some aspect of the study would benefit from numerical measures or statistical analysis. Researchers who come from a quantitative orientation may find that it is not possible to control variables in social research involving human subjects. As well, they may come to the realization that a deeper explanation of the meaning and purpose of participants' behavior would enhance study findings. Such researchers may choose to mix qualitative and quantitative methods. The central inquiry for mixed methods researchers is concisely articulated by Yoshikawa and colleagues (2008):

> How does knowledge gleaned from words complement knowledge gleaned from numbers, and vice versa? How and when does the combination of quantitative and qualitative data collection and analytic methods enrich the study results? (p. 344)

Mixed methods studies collect, analyze, and mix quantitative and qualitative data in a single study or a series of studies (Creswell & Clark, 2007). Data collection and analysis methods can be mixed in a number of ways: qualitative data can be analyzed through either qualitative or quantitative data analysis techniques as can quantitative data. Interview researchers can code responses, then use statistical techniques to analyze data drawn from the transcript codes (Yoshikawa et al., 2008). Interviews also can collect data to clarify, enhance, or follow up on data collected with a quantitative method. One research team remarked that

> [T]he interview method was used to supplement our previous survey findings, and to gather first-hand, self-reported verbal data from our subjects. Interviews provide access to participants' own language and concepts. We expected that the qualitative nature of this study would provide more in-depth and richer descriptions, such as "how" and "why" . . . and would enable us to draw a holistic, and thus more complete, picture of our subjects. (Chin-Sheng & Wen-Bin, 2006, p. 763)

In a mixed methods study, interviews can be conducted as a preliminary step when researchers are defining variables and their relationships.

For example, researchers using **Q-method** may begin with interviews to collect a very large sampling of statements about the questions under investigation (Wilson, 2009). A factor analysis allows researchers to investigate the subjectivity of these statements in a systematic way (Brown, 1980, 1993). Researchers may verify and deepen understanding of the statistical analysis through follow-up interviews.

Mixed strategy is another term that can be used to describe research studies. It is argued here that qualitative and mixed methods studies both use a mix of strategies. Different levels of structure and varied communication modes and technologies may be used to implement each research strategy.

The interview is not usually a single event—the researcher interacts with the interviewee during the sampling process (see Chapter 5), discussion of informed consent or other agreements needed for research participation (see Chapters 4 and 5), explanation of the research purpose and logistics, and then follow-up after the interview (see Chapter 6).

Researchers complement in-depth interviews with other qualitative data collection such as observations, group interviews or focus groups, or review of documents. Document analysis may include the following: review of reports, records, correspondence, diaries, and related items. Observations may include the following: fieldwork descriptions of activities, behaviors, actions, conversations, interpersonal interactions, organizational or community processes, or any other aspect of observable human experience (Patton, 2002, p. 4).

While observers view the subject of the study from the outside, *etic* observation, participant observers adopt an inside view, *emic* observation (Stake, 1995). Participant observers take part in the activity being studied or choose to conduct research on their own activities.

The key to integration of methods—whether within qualitative or with qualitative and quantitative—is to establish a credible rationale for what you are trying to do. In other words, you need to determine and be able to articulate the framework for your inquiry.

Power and Symmetry in Interviews

The researcher defines and designs the study, argues for its scientific merit, and obtains approvals from Institutional Review Boards and other entities. Whether adopting the role of miner, gardener, or traveler, clearly the researcher is in a position of power within the interview. As the one who recruits the participant and asks for a signature on the consent agreement, the researcher has undeniable responsibility for ethical and productive conduct of the interview. The question then is not whether the researcher has power—but how this power is used.

Miller and Glassner suggest that the power differential can be used to advantage or may jeopardize the truthfulness of the data. On one hand, it can add confidence and motivation when "the interviewee can recognize him- or herself as an expert on a topic of interest to someone typically in a more powerful position vis-à-vis the social structure." On the other hand, social distances and distrust can be carried into the interview, and interviewees may purposely mislead interviewers (Miller & Glassner, 2004, pp. 128, 132).

Interviewers minimize the asymmetrical power relationship by promoting a sense of collaboration in a shared task: the production of meaning (Gubrium & Holstein, 2003a). Mutual disclosure helps to level the power differential; this may entail sharing of personal stories or feelings by the interviewer, or simply affirming that there is no hidden agenda (Holstein & Gubrium, 2003a).

Closing Thoughts

This chapter provides a broad overview of profound issues that every researcher must grapple with before beginning the research design. Figure 3.4 is a graphic representation of the concepts discussed in Chapter 2. A researcher's ability to draw useful conclusions as a result of a study will depend, in large part, on thoughtful and coherent consideration of the four basic aspects of the research framework:

- What *epistemic* views justify and guide my choices of methodology and methods?
- What *theories* of knowledge and what disciplinary theories have been applied to explain key principles related to my subject of inquiry in past research?
- What *methodology* corresponds to the purpose of the study?
- What *method* will allow me to collect and analyze the data I need to answer the research questions? For researchers who intend to collect data with interviews, what interview methodology will inform the choice of a structured, semistructured, or unstructured approach?

Coming chapters will build on these ideas and explore ways you can apply them to design and conduct online research.

Researchers' Notebook: Stories of Online Inquiry

The interrelated elements of my study are mapped in Figure 3.5. As this map illustrates, the research took a somewhat circular process. Theories influenced the form and style of the inquiry, and theoretical principles emerged from the results.

Figure 3.4 A Research Knowledge Framework

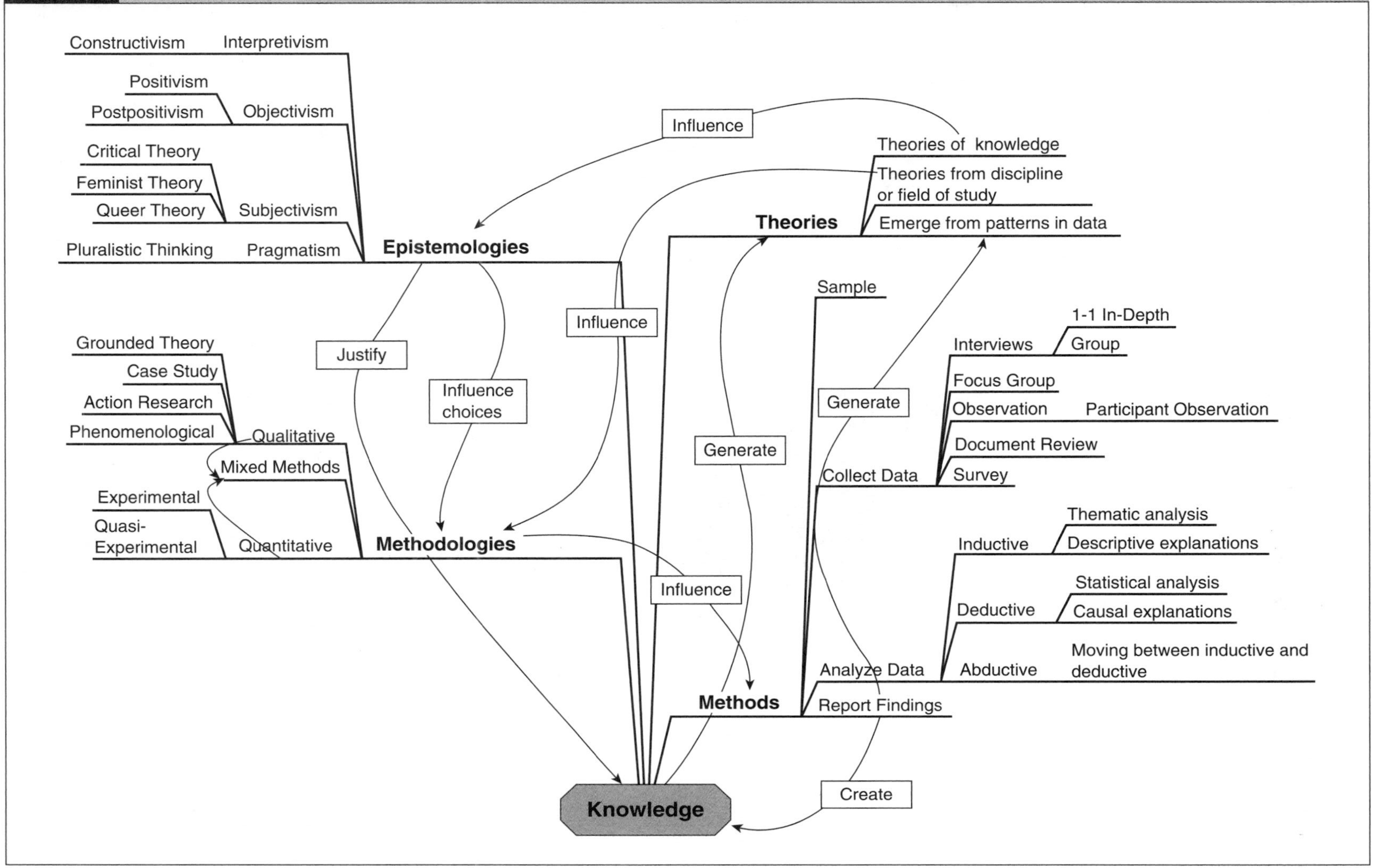

Epistemologies

Constructivism   Interpretivism
        Positivism
Postpositivism   Objectivism
Critical Theory
Feminist Theory
Queer Theory   Subjectivism
Pluralistic Thinking   Pragmatism

Theories

Theories of knowledge
Theories from discipline or field of study
Emerge from patterns in data

Methodologies

Grounded Theory
Case Study
Action Research
Phenomenological   Qualitative
        Mixed Methods
Experimental
Quasi-Experimental   Quantitative

Methods

Sample

Generate

Collect Data
Interviews   1-1 In-Depth
        Group
Focus Group
Observation   Participant Observation
Document Review
Survey

Analyze Data
Inductive   Thematic analysis
        Descriptive explanations
Deductive   Statistical analysis
        Causal explanations
Abductive   Moving between inductive and deductive

Report Findings

Create

Knowledge

Influence
Justify
Influence choices
Generate
Influence
Influence

57

Figure 3.5   Knowledge Map: Salmons' Research

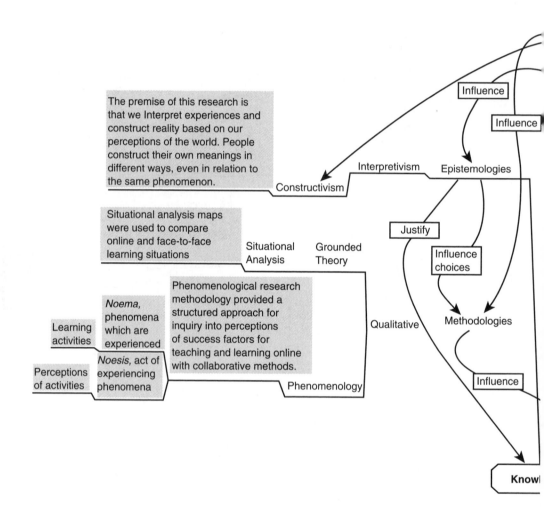

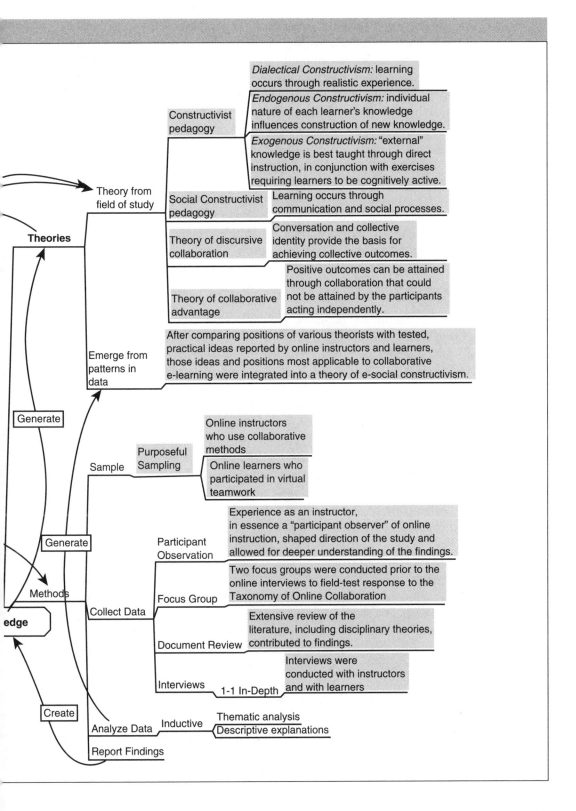

Dialectical Constructivism: learning occurs through realistic experience.

Endogenous Constructivism: individual nature of each learner's knowledge influences construction of new knowledge.

Exogenous Constructivism: "external" knowledge is best taught through direct instruction, in conjunction with exercises requiring learners to be cognitively active.

Constructivist pedagogy

Social Constructivist pedagogy — Learning occurs through communication and social processes.

Theory of discursive collaboration — Conversation and collective identity provide the basis for achieving collective outcomes.

Theory of collaborative advantage — Positive outcomes can be attained through collaboration that could not be attained by the participants acting independently.

Theory from field of study

Emerge from patterns in data — After comparing positions of various theorists with tested, practical ideas reported by online instructors and learners, those ideas and positions most applicable to collaborative e-learning were integrated into a theory of e-social constructivism.

Theories

Generate

Generate

Methods

edge

Create

Sample — Purposeful Sampling

Online instructors who use collaborative methods

Online learners who participated in virtual teamwork

Collect Data

Participant Observation — Experience as an instructor, in essence a "participant observer" of online instruction, shaped direction of the study and allowed for deeper understanding of the findings.

Focus Group — Two focus groups were conducted prior to the online interviews to field-test response to the Taxonomy of Online Collaboration

Document Review — Extensive review of the literature, including disciplinary theories, contributed to findings.

Interviews — 1-1 In-Depth — Interviews were conducted with instructors and with learners

Analyze Data — Inductive — Thematic analysis / Descriptive explanations

Report Findings

The guiding conceptual framework for my study is found in constructivism. Theories related to the field of study, constructivism and social constructivism, were aligned with constructivist epistemologies. Constructivist views influence my research on collaborative e-learning in two ways since the term *constructivism* describes both research and pedagogical theories. In a research context, *constructivism* conveys an assumption that we interpret experiences and construct reality based on our perceptions of the world. In an educational context, *constructivism* conveys an assumption that we learn through the process of interpreting experience and constructing meaning.

All design decisions were made in relation to the theoretical and epistemological principles. **Phenomenological** methodologies provide a way to investigate human experience through the perceptions of research participants—an appropriate choice for a study designed to investigate instructors' perceptions of online collaboration. Participant observation, focus groups, and document review helped me build fundamental understandings of the online environment and the collaborative process in the online environment. However, the main data collection was conducted through interviews.

At the center of my study is the Taxonomy of Online Collaboration (Salmons, 2010). Because this hierarchical model describes a sequence of collaborative processes, I used a semistructured interview method with questions about each level of the taxonomy posed in the sequence they appear in the model. This interview style exemplified the "gardener" metaphor. The initial questions, which were consistent with all participants, seeded the discussion with follow-up and probing questions posed as needed to cultivate the development of ideas from and with each participant. More details about the online nature of these interviews are provided in the coming chapters.

(A template can be found on the book's website so that you can map your own research framework.)

Researchers whose work was introduced in the Chapter 1 Researchers' Notebook chose a variety of styles and levels of structure for their online interviews. Their respective choices cover a continuum and illustrate the fact that the different approaches may fit different kinds of studies or different stages of a study (see Figure 3.6).

Wilson's mixed methods Q study required an initial stage with structured questions to key informants, who helped generate the concourse statements used as the basis for the sorting and quantitative analysis. After carrying out the Q-sort, she used preliminary findings as an interview guide in unstructured interviews to check study results and deepen her understanding of their implications (Wilson, 2006). Similarly, in his qualitative study, Cabiria drew on findings from a preliminary survey to craft interview questions. He alternated between semistructured interviews and unstructured conversations in six stages of the research process (J. Cabiria, personal communications, August 14 and 18, 2008).

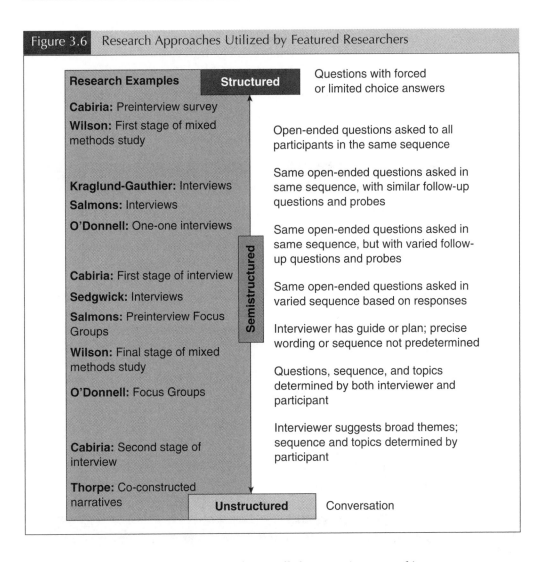

Figure 3.6   Research Approaches Utilized by Featured Researchers

Sedgwick, Kraglund-Gauthier, and O'Donnell chose semistructured interviews for their studies (M. Sedgwick, W. Kraglund-Gauthier, S. O'Donnell, personal communications, June 13, 2008, July 16, 2008, and May 21, 2009). Thorpe's study utilized a cooperative inquiry method and with storytelling as the subject of the study. Unstructured co-constructed narrative interviews and conversations were the appropriate approaches (Thorpe, 2008b).

In coming chapters we will discuss how we designed our studies and collected data using online interviews.

Key Concepts

- Researchers and theorists define *interview* in ways that relate to power, relationships, roles for interviewers and interviewees, and questioning styles. These styles range from unstructured to highly

structured. Many researchers choose semistructured approaches that allow for consistency between interviews as well as flexibility to follow up based on responses.

- Interviews, as a data collection method, are influenced by and relate to research epistemologies, theories, methodologies, as well as other methods.

Discussions and Assignments

Using your library database, find two scholarly articles based on data collected through interviews. Select one example of a study based on data collected in live, face-to-face interviews and one based on data collected through online interviews.

1. Identify the epistemology, main theories, methodologies, and methods used for each study. Assess whether these four elements were aligned in this research design. What would you recommend to improve alignment?

2. Look at the interview approach each researcher used. Which metaphor best describes the interview style and intentions: mining, gardening, or traveling? Did it work, or would you use a different style given the purpose of the study?

3. Compare and contrast the methodologies and methods in the two studies. Do you believe they made the right choices? What would you recommend?

On the Book's Website

You will find the following:

- Knowledge Framework template
- Links and references to additional resources on interview and online interview methodology

Terms

Abductive: A form of reasoning that, along with inductive and deductive reasoning, shows a way to come to a conclusion. Abductive reasoning is used when the researcher has an insight or makes a guess or an assumption that a connection exists in an incomplete or seemingly unrelated set of observations. Philosopher Charles Sanders Peirce (1839–1914) is credited with the origination of this concept and for applying it to pragmatic thinking.

Active interview: In an active interview, both parties to the interview are *active,* putting less focus on the interviewer as the one responsible for the interview process and focus. Meaning is actively assembled in the interview encounter (Holstein & Gubrium, 2004; Kvale, 2007).

Co-constructed narratives: Researchers and interviewees share jointly created stories. Narratives are called *mediated* when the researcher monitors the exchange or *unmediated* when a researcher and interviewee, or two researchers, exchange and study their own stories (Ellis & Berger, 2003).

Constructivism: The premise of constructivism is that we construct reality based on our perceptions of the world. Subjects construct their own meanings in different ways, even in relation to the same phenomenon (Gray, 2004). The term *interpretivism* is often used synonymously with constructivism. The premise of interpretivism is that we "interpret" our experiences in the social world.

Creative interview: Jack Douglas' book *Creative Interviewing* introduced a life-story approach to interviews. These unstructured interviews occur on location in situational everyday worlds of people in society (Douglas, 1984; Fontana & Frey, 2003).

Deductive reasoning: Reasoning used for research in which a specific explanation is deduced from a general premise and is then tested (Schutt, 2006).

Epistemology: A branch of philosophy that considers the criteria for determining what constitutes and does not constitute valid knowledge. In research, *epistemology* refers to the study of the nature of knowledge, or the study of how knowledge is justified (Gray, 2004).

Experimental research: A research methodology based upon cause-and-effect relationships between independent and dependent variables by means of the manipulation of independent variables (Creswell, 2008).

In-depth interview: An in-depth interview is a qualitative research technique involving a researcher who guides or questions a participant to elicit information, perspectives, insights, feelings on behaviors, experiences, or phenomena that cannot be observed. The in-depth interview is conducted to collect data that allow the researcher to generate new understandings and new knowledge about the subject of investigation.

Inductive reasoning: Reasoning used for research in which general conclusions are drawn from specific data (Schutt, 2006).

Methodologies: The study of, and justification for, methods used to conduct research. The term describes approaches to systematic inquiry developed within a particular paradigm with associated epistemological assumptions (Gray, 2004). Methodologies emerge from academic disciplines in the social and physical sciences and while considerable cross-disciplinary exchange occurs, choices generally place the study into a disciplinary context.

Methods: The practical steps used to conduct the study (Anfara & Mertz, 2006; Carter & Little, 2007).

Mixed methods: A research design that combines more than one method of qualitative and quantitative data collection and analysis (Creswell & Clark, 2007).

Phenomenological research: Research method used to investigate the meaning, structure, and essence of human experience (Patton, 2002).

Positivism: A belief, shared by most scientists, that there is a reality that exists apart from our perceptions of it, that can be understood through observation, and that follows general laws (Schutt, 2006). The positivist tradition views social reality as "knowable" and relies on a concept of validity in terms of measurement (Hesse-Biber & Leavy, 2006).

Postmodern interview: "Postmodern" refers to a set of "orienting sensibilities" rather than a particular kind of interviewing (Holstein & Gubrium, 2003b). These sensibilities include new ways to look at theory as "stories linked to the perspectives and interests of their storytellers" (Fontana, 2003; Holstein & Gubrium, 2003b, p. 5).

Postpositivism: A set of "orienting sensibilities" rather than a particular kind of interviewing (Holstein & Gubrium, 2003b). These sensibilities include new ways to look at theory as "stories linked to the perspectives and interests of their storytellers" (Fontana, 2003; Holstein & Gubrium, 2003b, p. 5).

Pragmatism: A worldview that draws on both objective and subjective knowledge (Creswell & Clark, 2007).

Q-method: A structured approach to studying subjectivity. It is self-referential, and it is communicable by the participants (Amin, 2000). More than 2,000 theoretical and applied Q studies have been published in a variety of disciplines including medicine, psychology, and policy (Valenta & Wiggerand, 1997). Invented in 1935 by British physicist-psychologist William Stephenson, Q methodology is frequently associated with quantitative analysis because of its use of factor analysis (Stephenson, 1935). Q can also be used as a qualitative technique because it concentrates on the perceptions, attitudes, and values from the perspective of the person who is participating in the study and relies heavily on qualitative methods in developing the Q concourse. In correlating persons instead of tests, Q-method provides a holistic perspective of a participant's subjectivity in relationship to the research question.

Qualitative research: Methods of inquiry directed at providing an "in-depth and interpreted understanding of the social world of research participants by learning about their social and material circumstances, their experiences, perspectives and histories" (Ritchie & Lewis, 2003).

Quantitative research: Methods of inquiry that analyze numeric representations of the world; the systematic and mathematical techniques used to collect and analyze data (Gray, 2004). Survey and questionnaire data are often analyzed in quantitative units (Yoshikawa et al., 2008).

Quasi-experimental research: A research approach that uses elements of the experimental design, such as use of a control group, but without the ability to randomly select the sample (Gray, 2004).

Research design: A comprehensive strategic plan for the study that "provides the glue that holds the research project together. A design is used to structure the research, to show how all of the major parts of the research project . . . work together to try to address the central research questions" (Trochim, 2006, Chapter 5).

Responsive interview: Rubin and Rubin use the term *responsive interview* to describe their approach that is characterized by a flexible design. They acknowledge the human feelings and common interests that allow interpersonal relationships to form between interviewer and interviewee. Responsive interviews aim for depth of understanding through ongoing self-reflection (Rubin & Rubin, 2005).

Structured or survey interview: Interviewers ask fixed-choice questions and record responses based on a coding scheme. All interviews ask the same questions in the same order, and interviewers are trained to maintain a consistent, neutral approach to questioning and responding to all participants (Fontana & Frey, 2003; Schaeffer & Maynard, 2003; Schutt, 2006).

Survey: An investigation into one or more variables in a population that may involve collection of qualitative and/or quantitative data (Gray, 2004). Data may be analyzed with qualitative or quantitative methods.

Theory: An explanation of a phenomenon that is internally consistent, is supportive of other theories, and gives new insights into the phenomenon. Some qualitative researchers frame the study in theoretical terms while others aim to discover and "ground" theoretical principles in the data. In quantitative research, theory "is an inter-related set of constructs (or variables) formed into propositions, or hypotheses, that specify the relationship among variables" (Creswell, 2003, p. 120).

Variable: A characteristic that is measurable (Gray, 2004).

Design for Credible and Ethical Online Research

4

> *I have always thought that one man of tolerable abilities may work great changes, and accomplish great affairs among mankind, if he first forms a good plan, and . . . make the execution of that same plan his sole study and business.*
>
> —Benjamin Franklin, 1757

After you study Chapter 4, you will understand the following:

- A general overview of research design;

- An exploration of ethical issues important to researchers proposing to collect data through online interviews; and

- Practical steps for designing studies acceptable to Institutional Review Boards (IRBs) or other decisionmakers.

Research Design and Online Interviews

A *research design* is a comprehensive strategic plan for a study. It describes all elements of the study coherently and argues for scholarly and scientific merit. The research design shows how all of the major parts of the research project work together to accomplish the study's purpose and address the research questions. The research design "touches almost all aspects of the research, from the minute details of data collection to the selection of the techniques of data analysis" (Ragin, 1994, p. 191). As noted in Chapter 3, epistemological and theoretical perspectives influence and support the choices made in the research design.

When an organization or business presents a strategic plan that diverges from past practices, strong supporting evidence and proof are needed to validate the soundness of the intentions and new direction. Similarly, when a researcher presents a study design that departs from established approaches, additional care may be needed to substantiate the proposal. **Institutional Review Boards (IRBs)**, Research Ethics Boards, ethics committees, or other review bodies representing potential interviewees or research fellowship staff may be uninformed or misinformed about online data collection. They may have particular concerns about ethical practices in online research. Aspects of research design related to online interview methods are discussed in depth throughout coming chapters. This chapter focuses on design issues and ethical dilemmas particular to studies built around data collected from online interviews. Recommendations are offered to help online researchers design credible and ethical studies.

Research design is a complex process and to cover it comprehensively is beyond the scope of this book. Resources in Table 3.1, An Overview of Research Methodologies, and in the References offer more detailed explanations of research design principles.

Components of a Strong Research Design

A research design connects the purpose of the study, the questions the researcher hopes to answer, and the background that provides context for the study with the practical steps to be used in carrying it out. The research framework described in Chapter 3 is intrinsic to research design because it places the study within an epistemic worldview and explains theoretical influences on methodologies and methods.

Designs for thesis, dissertation, or postdoctoral research, or designs for proposals to government agencies or foundations, follow specific guidelines. However, components of a research design typically include the following:

- A description of the problem the study will address and rationale for the study that explains why the study is important;

- A description of the sample; that is, the subjects or participants for the study (see Chapter 5);

- Information about the method of data collection from the sample (see Chapters 5–8);

- A description of the data analysis techniques to be used—that is, approaches for deriving meaning, findings, or results (see the Appendix);

- Limitations to the study—that is, discussion of the boundaries or scope of the study; and

- Discussion of ethical issues, which are the focus of the current chapter and are woven throughout the book. (See *Ethics Tips* for practical recommendations.)

Ethical Design Considerations for Online Interviews

A study that relies on interviews for data collection depends on the willing participation of interviewees. Any time **human subjects** are involved the researcher has moral and ethical responsibility toward them. Ethical practice is the researcher's central responsibility from the design stage through the final report.

No research involving human subjects should occur without a clear expectation of its benefit, whether it is the advancement of a body of knowledge, new understanding of human experience, or a direct benefit to the research participants. The researcher must make every effort to do no harm and to reduce risks involved in research according to the fundamental principles of research ethics, **beneficence.** The researcher who designs a study using online interviews has four interrelated matters to consider: consent, identity, privacy, and protection of data. Although these four matters are not unique to the online environment, some particular ethical issues are associated with each one when the study entails online interviews.

INFORMED CONSENT

Perhaps the most important ethical principle in research involves actions by researchers to ensure that participation of subjects is voluntarily. The key question researchers need to address is "how to treat individuals as autonomous agents who should decide for themselves if they wish their personal information and interactions to be studied" (Stern, 2009).

The United States Code of Federal Regulations (e-CFR, 2008) mandates that researchers obtain informed consent to do the following:

- Protect human subjects/volunteers;
- Ensure that potential study subjects clearly understand the benefits and risks associated with their participation in a study; and
- Provide the potential study subjects with all information needed to reach a decision on whether or not to participate in a research study.

Ethical researchers disclose any potential risks and clearly explain the nature of the study and intended use of the data, and expectations for the research participant. To protect human subjects' rights to privacy, confidentiality, and autonomy, the researcher needs to approach subjects at the very beginning of the research to ask for consent. The researcher must discuss any data about participants collected prior to consent as part of the agreement.

Participants in any study must understand the researcher's purpose and anticipated commitments, and freely agree to participate—without repercussions if they do not. The onus is on the researcher to ensure that prospective participants understand the information given and that they have capacity to give consent (Loue, 2000). Capacity to consent includes legal age. If the participant is under the age of eighteen or cannot legally sign for other reasons an appropriate individual, such as a parent or guardian, must sign. Depending on the nature of the study, information provided to participants may include the following:

- The purpose of the study;
- The nature of the study and a general description of other participants;
- The expected duration of the individual's participation;
- A description of the procedures;
- A description of the extent to which confidentiality will be maintained;
- A description of who will have access to the data;
- A statement that participation in the study is voluntary and response to a given question is voluntary; and
- A statement indicating that the participant may withdraw at any time without penalty (Gray, 2009; Loue, 2000).

The goals of a research project may shift over the course of the study as emerging patterns suggest new questions. In other cases, the researcher may decide to ask different questions or pursue different directions from what was agreed upon in the original consent form. The researcher may want to describe observations of the participant's avatar, profile, social networking pages, website, or other expressions not originally considered as useful data. With such emergent research design elements, the researcher needs to view consent as an ongoing process throughout the study and renegotiate the agreement as appropriate. To prepare for this possibility, researchers also should include a statement describing the scope of the agreement and indicators for renegotiation in case new research interests or directions emerge.

Ethics Tip: When discussing conditions for consent, let the participant know that you may need to add to or revise the agreement.

The "informed consent" form or letter documents researchers' and participants' agreements based on the information provided. To ensure that all materials describing the study, including all of the implications of the consent agreement, are understood, if the researcher gives any information orally, it should be presented in written form as well. Written materials should be provided in the language best understood by the participant and be written at a reading level that can be understood by the participant. Use alternative mechanisms to convey the necessary information, as appropriate, if the participant has hearing or vision impairments (Loue, 2000).

Informed Consent and Online Research

Open, comprehensive discussion is essential when the informed consent negotiation occurs online. Description of the procedures should include specific technology requirements. Will they need a headset to communicate by voice? Broadband? A Web camera?

Research participants should have a chance to voice any questions or concerns about the study or their participation. In addition to any chat, e-mail, or conversation, written information should be provided to participants through conventional mail.

In online research, the researcher can provide the consent form as an e-mail attachment or download. Depending on institutional or other requirements, the signed form is returned via surface mail, faxed to the researcher, or signed digitally and returned electronically. If the researcher's institution or legal jurisdiction does not require a physical signature, participants can be asked to indicate agreement with a check box ("I accept") in an e-mail returned online to the researcher or on a Web form (Madge, 2006; Walther, 1999).

(Note: You can download sample consent agreements from the book's website.)

Withdrawal From the Online Study

The ability to withdraw from the research at any time is a central tenet of informed consent and should be clearly spelled out in the consent agreement. The researcher should spell this out clearly in the consent agreement. A participant can withdraw from a virtual interview by simply closing the chat window or logging out of the meeting space. During virtual interviews sudden withdrawal of a participant can be disconcerting to the researcher. It may be unclear whether the interviewee no

Ethics Tip: You may want to discuss a withdrawal protocol. Let participants know that, while they can withdraw from the study without penalty, you would appreciate a message confirming a decision to discontinue participation. This can save the researcher from wasting time sending inquiring e-mails, and reduce embarrassment or annoyance at receiving such inquiries.

longer wishes to participate or whether there is simply a technical or connection problem. Researchers may feel some ambiguity about whether to and how to follow up with a participant after contact is lost. To help avoid these potential problems, it is advisable to discuss a withdrawal protocol when negotiating the consent agreement. However, in any study impromptu abandonment is a risk researchers must accept.

Public Versus Private Spaces and Informed Consent

When do researchers need to obtain informed consent? Interview research requires informed consent regardless of the setting when an intentional exchange—no matter how seemingly casual—occurs between researcher and participant and is recorded in some way. Many studies might be enhanced by observational data collected during interviews along with the direct responses of the participants. A researcher who wishes to use such data should make this clear to the participants when obtaining consent.

> **Research Tip:** When designing your research, think about the setting for the online interview and the kinds of information you may want to gather from observation. Discuss your goals and preferences with the participant and include your agreement in the consent letter.

Data collection in "public" settings is typically exempt from informed consent when individuals are not identified. Observing people on the street or noting responses to a civic event could be clearly described as data collection in public. The determination of public versus private space online is not clear cut or universally defined. This creates a dilemma for online researchers: when should a researcher explicitly announce his or her presence and obtain consent?

Researchers disagree on this point. Some suggest that posts in openly accessible forums or social networking sites are public so that there is no need to disclose research activity, particularly when the participants' identities are not recorded. They argue that observing people's activities in a public website is equivalent to observing activities on the street where, as one pointed out, "they would never think of wearing large signs identifying themselves as 'Researcher'"(Sixsmith & Murray, 2001, p. 425). Reading and drawing from postings on a public site may be comparable to reading a newsletter or other informal writing, where proper attribution is accomplished by citing the source.

Others, such as Frankel and Siang (1999), argue that unethical deception can occur when researchers do not identify themselves.

> On the Internet, group discussion formats make it relatively easy for researchers to engage in covert or unobtrusive observation. An investigator can record the online conversations of a community without making

her presence as a researcher known. Alternatively, she can pose as a member of the community, giving false information in order to study the reactions and behavior of community members. (p. 9)

Can a line be drawn between observing public activities and reading publicly available materials and covert participant observation—which may entail conversations with people who do not suspect they are subjects of an inquiry?

Although free and open websites or e-mail lists may appear to be parallel to public places in the real world, the distinction is even more uncertain when access requires some type of membership or registration. Although free and available to anyone willing to sign up, are they "public" in research terms?

The expectations of users of an online resource should be taken into consideration. The researcher must discern whether users expect that communication is confined to the community or whether they expect the general public to observe, read, and/or document their actions, interactions, and postings. Cascio (2009) uses the term *participatory panopticon* to describe a world in which people use digital cameras and transcripts of digital comments to record their own lives as well as the lives of those around them. He points out that "everything is potentially on the record, often from multiple perspectives; not only is privacy a thing of the past but potentially secrecy as well" (p. 1). In this view, everyone should assume that no privacy exists when interacting online. Yet the perception of some level of privacy holds and may vary greatly depending on the user as well as the setting.

The size of the user group is a consideration. Users making a post to a group of ten may have a greater expectation of privacy than a user would when posting to a group of one thousand (Eysenbach & Till, 2001). Perceptions of privacy, norms, and codes are usually spelled out in "frequently asked questions" or "about us" areas of online communities or social networking sites. When such sites require registration for log-in but no fee, users typically assume anything posted will be read by a broad range of people. When a subscription is required or membership fee is paid, researchers may assume that users expect privacy and confidentiality. Subscription-based sites may have community use guidelines or membership policies. Whether an online community is open to all or requires a fee, lurking without participation and collecting data without notice or permission are generally frowned upon (Madge, 2006).

Social networking and online community sites may have stated norms or rules; but e-mail is more ambiguous from an ethical standpoint. Although e-mail can be compared with paper mail, unlike paper mail, e-mail can be archived and/or easily replicated. Messages the writer assumed were private may be passed on to unintended recipients or saved in ways others could access. These characteristics can blur a number of boundaries taken for granted with paper mail. E-mail thus poses a dilemma for the researcher, who must assess whether the writer is the original source of the comments sent by personal e-mail and must determine the appropriateness of citing comments received through an e-mail list.

Elm suggests that when differentiating public from private on the Internet, a continuum is more appropriate than a dichotomy (Elm, 2008). Figure 4.1 expands on and illustrates this suggestion.

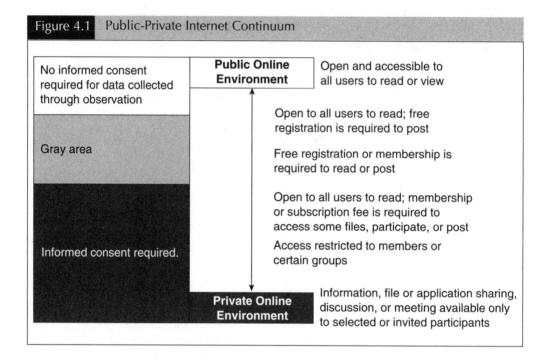

Figure 4.1   Public-Private Internet Continuum

This continuum suggests an approach online researchers can use to distinguish between public and private research settings. On one end of the continuum is the free and open Internet, where no registration or membership is required. On the public Web, *observations* of individuals' behaviors or writings can be collected with proper citation of the source. On sites where access is restricted to members who register and use a secure log-in, informed consent and/or permission should be obtained.

Websites can be defined as "public" when they are online spaces where companies, organizations, or individuals post information about themselves and allow anyone to view or read it. Types of environments in the "gray area" are those that allow anyone to read or view material but require some type of registration to contribute, post, or comment. These might include most blogs, media, or e-commerce sites that offer free content and encourage participation or feedback by consumers. Because the public can read any posts one might assume that people who make comments expect wide readership. Also in the gray area are sites that are free but require membership and approval of the owner of the content before visitors can access the material. Such online communication includes most subscription e-mail lists and social networking sites such as Facebook, MySpace, or Twitter. More clear-cut examples include sites, events, or communications that require a fee, membership, employment in the company, or enrollment in the class to access and participate (see Figure 4.2).

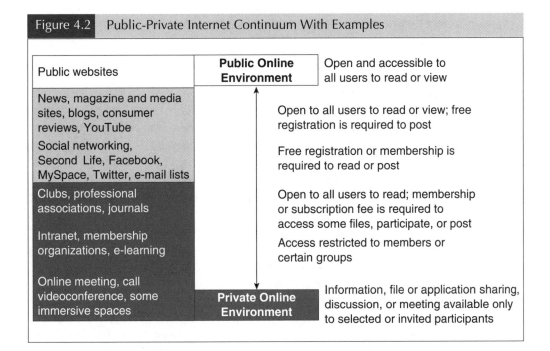

Figure 4.2   Public-Private Internet Continuum With Examples

Public websites	**Public Online Environment**	Open and accessible to all users to read or view
News, magazine and media sites, blogs, consumer reviews, YouTube		Open to all users to read or view; free registration is required to post
Social networking, Second Life, Facebook, MySpace, Twitter, e-mail lists		Free registration or membership is required to read or post
Clubs, professional associations, journals		Open to all users to read; membership or subscription fee is required to access some files, participate, or post
Intranet, membership organizations, e-learning		Access restricted to members or certain groups
Online meeting, call videoconference, some immersive spaces	**Private Online Environment**	Information, file or application sharing, discussion, or meeting available only to selected or invited participants

(Note: As new types of environments come online, updated diagrams will be posted on the book's website.)

Online interviews are typically conducted in a "private online environment" where the interviewer and interviewee are the only participants. In consensual, participatory interview research interviewer and interviewee arrange to meet. They are both aware that they are engaging in online interactions for purposeful data collection. In this type of research, informed consent is unquestionably required.

Researchers must weigh the benefits and risks and make appropriate and ethical decisions for studies in the "gray

Ethics Tip: When you plan observational activities, before you collect data, review any posted terms of membership or behavior, and try to gauge the culture and norms in terms of personal disclosure and privacy. If possible, discuss research goals with moderator and/or members and act accordingly in terms of consent or disclosure of your identity as a researcher.

area"—the online spaces or e-mail lists where membership is required but free to anyone who cares to join. Researchers must decide whether to collect data and remain anonymous or to possibly disrupt or change the course of events by announcing research intentions. Researchers should reflect on two key questions: What risks to the observed subjects may be associated with the study? Would the credibility of the study be jeopardized without consenting participants? To be on the safe side, the researcher should consult with the host or moderator or active members in a community setting before collecting data from individuals' postings or conversations.

IDENTITY AND PRIVACY

Many research ethics issues are comparable online or off, but identity may generate unique issues online. As the saying goes, no one knows if you are a dog on the Internet. How does the researcher know whether a potential research participant is the proverbial dog? In some cases, research participants have verifiable identities. Researchers may be able to corroborate identity through academic or other affiliations. In other cases identity may be ambiguous since online, people commonly go by first names, nicknames, and/or avatar names. Association of data to the interviewee raises questions such as: Will the material be attributed to a specified person? Referred to by his/her real name, a pseudonym, or an avatar's name? Should the name and identity used on the Internet be protected in the same way as the name and identity used off the Internet?

These issues are under debate and online research protocols are not yet clearly defined. In the meantime, there are some clear guidelines all researchers should observe when it comes to identity. First, ethical researchers must begin by being honest about their own identities throughout all stages of the research. Just as research subjects can be cloaked in anonymity and pseudonymity, so can researchers, raising the potential of deception. "Deception can occur when a researcher intentionally misinforms or does not fully disclose relevant information to subjects in cases when informed consent is required" (Frankel & Siang, 1999, p. 9). Ethical researchers are careful to introduce themselves. Where possible, academic e-mail addresses or other evidence of institutional affiliation should be used to affirm trustworthiness and inspire confidence.

> **Ethics Tip:** Avoid any confusion about your identity as a researcher. Use an institutional, corporate, or foundation e-mail address. Create a research site or blog where participants and others can verify the researcher's identity and learn more about the study.

Second, researchers must verify that the potential interviewee is over the age of eighteen or the age of consent in the country where the research is conducted. If there are any doubts about age, corroborating records or copies of photo identification should be requested as part of the informed consent process. Third, researchers must respect participants' privacy.

📖 **Research Tip:** Is there publicly accessible information about you online that could undermine your credibility as a researcher? If so, to the degree possible, remove it before you begin recruiting participants.

Privacy in the research context refers to steps taken to safeguard interviewees' right to integrity and self-determination. This means research participants have the right to decide what kind of information to share with the researcher and under what conditions (Elm, 2008). Carusi (2008) feels it is important to distinguish between information on "thin identity" or "thick identity":

> Thin identity is the identity of a particular individual as a re-identifiable identity. Proper names pick out particular individuals and have to do with thin identity. Thick identity is a matter of that individual's experience of their own personhood, their own subjective or psychological sense of who they are. [T]hick identity can be a matter of ethical concern even when it has been detached from thin identity. (p. 41)

Carusi illustrates the distinction with this example: if *thin* identity has to do with a particular individual and the fact that she has a certain medical condition, then *thick* identity concerns her representation as a victim, a fighter, or survivor of that condition (Carusi, 2008). An online researcher may breach the participant's confidentiality by appropriating images, quotations, stories, or other representations even if the researcher removes any personal information and thick identity has been detached from thin identity. Search engines allow people to enter phrases and locate the original post, with the writer's name (Carusi, 2008; Eysenbach & Till, 2001). This means researchers can easily and unintentionally violate the privacy of individuals by quoting the exact words of an e-mail list or online community posting—even though they have not attributed it directly.

Ethical dilemmas described in this chapter can be further complicated by the fact that online research—with easy access to participants across the globe— may cross cultural as well as geographic boundaries. Sensitivities about privacy,

⚖ **Ethics Tip:** Respect both thick and thin identity of participants when data are collected from public sites.

identity, the types of information to be shared, and the conditions for the exchange may vary widely. In addition, crossing geographic boundaries may mean different legal jurisdictions must be considered, with their own rules about privacy as well as about protection of human subjects in research. For example, when data are transferred from a European Union (EU) to a non-EU country, data must be adequately protected under EU regulations. Researching groups, such as indigenous peoples, may mean notions of harm, risk, privacy, and confidentiality have to be considered at the level of the community, not just the individual (O'Hara, 2005). A uniform standard is not possible and clearly, researchers must honor the codes and expectations that are in place in the culture or community where the participants reside or interact.

PROTECTION OF DATA

For many Internet studies, potential breach of confidentiality may be the gravest risk the participant could face. Researchers must be aware of the vulnerability of the data at every stage of the research process. Data are vulnerable during collection, transmission, and storage. Given the ease with which researchers can digitally manipulate data, the agreed use of data must be honored.

Mann and Stewart (2000) describe a set of Principles of Fair Information Processing Online that can help prevent ethical lapses:

- Personal data should be collected for one specific purpose;
- People should have access to the data collected about themselves;
- Personal data should be guarded against risks such as unauthorized access, modification, or disclosure;
- Data should be collected in a context of free speech; and
- Personal data are not to be communicated externally without the consent of the subject who supplied the data.

Bakardjieva and Feenberg (2001) use the term **alienation** to describe "the appropriation of the products of somebody's action for purposes never intended or foreseen by the actor herself, drawing these products into a system of relations over which the producer has no knowledge or control" (p. 206). As noted earlier in the chapter, if the purpose of the study or the kinds of data the researcher wants change in the course of the study, then the consent agreement must be updated. The research design should include a feedback loop— the person interviewed should be about to see, review, and clarify information in the data. With these safeguards in place, the researcher can honor fairness and respect for research participants' preferences.

> **Ethics Tip:** Consider implications of the Principles of Fair Information Processing Online when articulating the consent agreement.

Another ethical minefield for electronic data involves the researcher. When words, paragraphs, or entire documents can be easily (and selectively) copied, re-arranged to alter the meaning, or deleted altogether, the researcher's own integrity is essential to maintain the verbatim raw data and use them properly. Davis (1999) elucidates situations in which lapses in integrity can occur:

- "Smoothing out" reported data by dropping certain results because they show weaknesses in research design or implementation;

- Suppressing data clearly inconsistent with one's conclusions ("cooking");

- Fabricating of data ("forging"); and/or

- Keeping incomplete records of research, discarding records after research is complete, or denying others access to data on which published research relied.

Ethical researchers spell out the standards they will uphold—and stick with them. Although the data itself must be kept private, the process and procedures of research should be transparent to reveal honesty at all stages of the study.

Ethics Tip: Create a checklist that articulates your own standards of values and ethics before you start collecting and analyzing data. Keep it handy and consult when you confront sticky situations.

Ethical Frameworks

Traditional ethical concepts offer today's researchers varied ways to think about their studies. Ethical frameworks relevant to researchers include deontological, consequentialist, and virtue ethics. Brief descriptions of each are provided here:

THE DEONTOLOGICAL APPROACH

Deontological ethics, building on the philosophies of Immanuel Kant (1785), has at its simplest views morality in terms of duties and principles. Deontologists have less regard for the outcomes resulting from following their principles, believing that some choices are morally wrong, no matter how good the consequences (Baggini & Fosl, 2007; Zalta, 2008).

Deontology has respect of the individual as a tenet; individuals are not seen as a means to an end. "Informed consent becomes a way of operationalizing that tenet, through an acknowledgement of an individual's values and choices that are freely made" (Loue, 2000, p. 97). Deontological researchers are concerned with following ethical rules, codes, or formally specified guidelines (Berry, 2004). *The Belmont Report,* which is the basis for protection of human subjects regulations in the United States, and the Association of Internet Researchers' professional codes of ethics have their origins in Kantian deontological theory (Ess, 2002; Pedroni & Pimple, 2001). As noted at the beginning of this chapter, researchers proposing new approaches may need to show review bodies that they can follow established guidelines for research even when the study is conducted using new techniques.

THE CONSEQUENTIALIST OR UTILITARIAN APPROACH

Consequentialism, building on the philosophies of John Stuart Mill (1861), is concerned with moral rightness of acts. It emphasizes that ethical action provides the most good or does the least harm, so whether an act is morally right depends only on the consequences of that act (Baggini & Fosl, 2007; Zalta, 2008).

Because Utilitarianism seeks to maximize good, involvement of individuals in research without their understanding or their permission or against their will would be considered clearly unethical (Loue, 2000). Consequentialist researchers might prioritize the potential of research findings to add to the greater common good over strict adherence to established rules or guidelines. For Internet researchers this could mean taking a flexible approach to applying principles, believing that the value of the study outweighs adherence to rules they perceive as outdated. They may believe that by doing so they can advance more appropriate ground rules for future Internet researchers: a positive consequence. Alternatively, consequentialism could be used to justify deception, in that informative research findings would outweigh covert online observation (Berry, 2004).

THE VIRTUE ETHICS APPROACH

Virtue ethics is grounded in ideas from Plato and Aristotle. This approach suggests that ethical actions ought to be consistent with certain ideal virtues that provide for the full development of our humanity (Velasquez et al., 2008). These virtues enable us to act in ways that demonstrate values like honesty, courage, compassion, generosity, tolerance, and fairness. People are best able to practice virtue ethics when they possess *phronesis,* moral or practical wisdom (Zalta, 2008).

Virtue ethics emphasizes the qualities of respectfulness and benevolence, which again argue for the recognition of and respect for an individual's freely made choice and informed consent (Loue, 2000). Using virtue ethics, a researcher relies on his or her personal value system and moral code and character to make the right decisions and to treat the research subject with fairness and integrity.

TOWARD AN UNDERSTANDING OF INTERNET RESEARCH ETHICS

Ethical Internet researchers must somehow reconcile elements of these frameworks. Berry (2004) argues that "they are all necessary components of a dialogical and relational process of ethical responsibility" (p. 330). Whether or not researchers see themselves as adhering to deontological positions, they need to be accountable to some degree to rules established by the relevant academy or agency. Whether or not they see themselves as consequentialist, they must subscribe to the principles of beneficence and aim to maximize possible benefits and minimize possible harm. Whether or not they see themselves as virtuous, they will need to use fairness and honesty to achieve credible research findings. If the researcher believes that all persons have an inherent capacity for self-determination, this belief provides the grounds for an obligation to avoid interfering with participants' actions and decisions by withholding relevant information (Pedroni & Pimple, 2001). During research, all these positions argue that questions should be raised: "Is the researcher responding to the needs of others? Do they care about the activities of members of online groups as people with feelings like themselves?" (Berry, 2004).

Research Design, Ethics, and Review Boards

Faculty members and graduate students typically submit proposals for research with human subjects to an IRB, Research Ethics Board, or similar entity. While each researcher should consult his or her own institution's guidelines, this section discusses IRB reviews and offers suggestions for proposals that include online interview data collection. Additional suggestions about selection of subjects and IRB reviews will be made in Chapter 5.

RISK/BENEFIT ANALYSIS

The IRB will try to determine whether research subjects could be exposed to physical, economic, or social harm. Even small risks will be of concern to the IRB if the population is vulnerable, especially children or people who are incarcerated.

Most online research entails little or no physical risk. Psychological harm is typically minimal or transitory. It is the job of the IRB to discern whether risks are such that long-term harm could occur. IRB reviewers realize the following:

> Stress and feelings of guilt or embarrassment may arise simply from think-
> ing or talking about one's own behavior or attitudes on sensitive topics such
> as drug use, sexual preferences, selfishness, and violence. These feelings may
> be aroused when the subject is being interviewed. (Penslar & Porter, 2009)

Questions reviewers will ask include the following:

- Are both risks and anticipated benefits accurately identified, evaluated, and described?

- Are the risks greater than **minimal risk**? Has the proposal taken into
  account vulnerabilities among prospective subjects that might be
  relevant to evaluating the risk of participation?

- Has due care been used to minimize risks and maximize the likelihood of benefits?

- Are there adequate provisions for a continuing reassessment of the
  balance between risks and benefits? Should there be a data and safety
  monitoring committee (Porter, 1993)?

Because the IRB committee may not have evaluated many proposals for online interviews, the researcher should offer either sample questions or interview themes so reviewers can be assured that research participants will not be deceived and psychological stress will be minimized. See the sections in this chapter about interviewer deception and articulate your approach for disclosing your presence and stating the purpose of the study.

Informed Consent

This chapter explored issues and ambiguities related to public and private settings and the need for informed consent. Adequacy of information to the participants and credibility of their voluntary agreement to participate are subjected to scrutiny in the IRB review. In the United States, researchers are required to inform participants of information, including the following:

- An explanation of the purposes of the research and the expected
  duration of the subject's participation, a description of the procedures to be followed, and identification of any procedures which are
  experimental;

- Description of any reasonably foreseeable risks or discomforts to the
  subject;

- A statement describing the extent, if any, to which confidentiality of records identifying the subject will be maintained;

- An explanation of whom to contact for answers to pertinent questions about the research and research subjects' rights, and whom to contact in the event of a research-related injury to the subject;

- A statement that participation is voluntary, refusal to participate will involve no penalty or loss of benefits to which the subject is otherwise entitled, and the subject may discontinue participation at any time without penalty or loss of benefits to which the subject is otherwise entitled; and

- Anticipated circumstances under which the subject's participation may be terminated by the investigator without regard to the subject's consent (HHS, 2005).

Researchers must consult the laws and regulations governing the institution as well as the laws and regulations governing the country where research participants reside. Institutional Review and International Research Regulations governing research to be conducted outside of the United States by U.S. investigators may require that the protocol be reviewed and approved not only by a review committee based in the United States, but also by the appropriate review committee in the country hosting the research.

Generally the agreement to participate based on these terms should be signed by the participant. This requirement can be waived in some situations where risks are associated with a breach of confidentiality concerning the subject's participation in the research. If the nature of research participation can potentially change mid-study, reviewers may want to know how consent will be renegotiated during the course of the research (Porter, 1993). They may or may not require resubmission to the IRB board, depending on the extent of the changes.

The IRB is concerned about the possibility of psychological harm when reviewing behavioral research that involves an element of deception, so reviewers will look at evidence of honesty and disclosure. Reviewers will want to know whether researchers intend to withhold information about the real purpose of the research or to give subjects false information about some aspect of the research, meaning that the subject's consent may not be fully informed (Porter, 1993). Questions reviewers may ask about the proposal include the following:

- Is the language and presentation of the information to be conveyed appropriate to the subject population? (Consider the level of complexity and the need for translation into a language other than English.)

- Are the timing of and setting for the explanation of the research conducive to good decision making? Can anything more be done to enhance the prospective subjects' comprehension of the information and their ability to make a choice?

- Who will be explaining the research to potential subjects? Should someone in addition to or other than the investigator be present (Porter, 1993)?

To pass this part of the review, online researchers will want to plainly spell out the ways they will provide information participants need before agreeing to be interviewed. In addition, researchers need to discuss ways to verify that participants fully understand the expectations and requirements of the study. If an emergent design anticipates that another phase may be added to the study, then the researcher should outline the frequency and/or events that will trigger the sharing of additional information about the study or another signed consent form.

PRIVACY AND CONFIDENTIALITY

IRB reviewers want to be sure that adequate safeguards for privacy and confidentiality are in place for the proposed study. Reviewers want to be sure that participants have control over the extent, timing, and circumstances of sharing information. They look for ways confidentiality will be handled. Confidentiality refers to treatment of information that an individual has disclosed and protections to prevent that information from being divulged in ways that are inconsistent with the understanding of the original disclosure without permission (Porter, 1993).

Questions reviewers may ask about the proposal include the following:

- Does the research involve observation or intrusion in situations where the subjects have a reasonable expectation of privacy? Would reasonable people be offended by such an intrusion? Can the research be redesigned to avoid the intrusion?

- Will the investigator(s) be collecting sensitive information about individuals? If so, have they made adequate provisions for protecting the confidentiality of the data through coding, destruction of identifying information, limiting access to the data, or whatever methods that may be appropriate to the study?

- Are the investigator's disclosures to subjects about confidentiality adequate? Should documentation of consent be waived in order to protect confidentiality (Porter, 1993)?

Online researchers need to answer these questions and thoroughly explain how they will protect confidentiality, and protect the data in order to pass this section of the IRB review.

Closing Thoughts

Research design is a complex and often lengthy process. In addition to the typical elements every researcher must address, the online researcher must also consider implications related to the online milieu. This chapter focuses on the ethical dilemmas inherent in the evolving online environment. Addressing real ethical issues, as well as fears of ethical pitfalls in little-known online research settings, must be addressed to meet institutional demands. Attention to ethical practice is needed at every stage of the research process (see Figure 4.3). Ultimately, the quality of the design and attention to ethical conduct allow the researcher to generate credible findings.

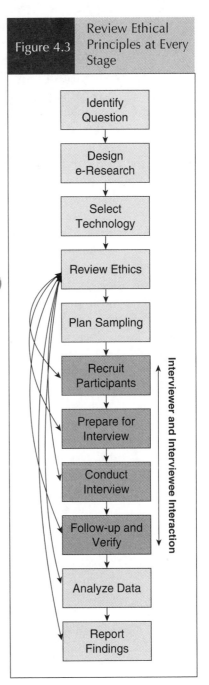

Figure 4.3 — Review Ethical Principles at Every Stage

Identify Question

Design e-Research

Select Technology

Review Ethics

Plan Sampling

Recruit Participants

Prepare for Interview

Conduct Interview

Follow-up and Verify

Analyze Data

Report Findings

Interviewer and Interviewee Interaction

Researchers' Notebook: Stories of Online Inquiry

The Researchers' Notebook for Chapter 4 contains four very different success stories of committee and **IRB approval** of online research designs.

Dr. Sedgwick planned to conduct her interviews in person—before the thirty-year record snowfall dropped a very physical obstacle between her and her geographically dispersed participants (Sedgwick & Spiers, 2009). When she described what "face-to-face" interview would mean in this case, her doctoral committee paused for a long moment before approving the change of venue to the videoconference. The committee applauded Monique's trailblazing approach (M. Sedgwick, personal communication, May 21, 2009). A committee member, Jude Spiers, subsequently coauthored an article with Dr. Sedgwick: "The Use of Videoconferencing as a Medium for the Qualitative Interview" (Sedgwick & Spiers, 2009).

The technician who assisted with Dr. Sedgwick's videoconferenced interviews signed a confidentiality agreement, even though the technician was not present at the interview.

My qualitative research designs involved online interviews with instructors who teach online and learners who study online. Their identities were verifiable, even though I conducted my purposeful sampling online. The research design spelled out preinterview communication about and preparation for the interview. The interviews were semistructured. Preliminary questions, and the model that we would be discussing, were provided in advance. This assured reviewers that participants were adequately informed about the nature of the study before they signed the consent form. The design also included follow-up communication with each participant, who had the opportunity to review the reporting from their interview. This step assured reviewers that participants had control of the information they shared about themselves.

The consent form (see the book's website) asked participants to agree to the terms of archival for the data captured in the online interview. It allowed participants to choose the level of anonymity in any reporting of the study, with options for direct, attributed quotations or to have input aggregated with other data and presented anonymously. All participants provided a signed (paper) form.

The pre- and postinterview communications took place by e-mail, and the interviews were conducted in a private Elluminate meeting space. No one else had access to the meeting space or to the archive of the interview meeting. As the only person working in my office, I was able to assure the reviewers of secure protection of the data.

There were no known risks for participation, and the topics of the study—teaching and learning online—were not sensitive. I conducted two parallel studies (instructors and learners) that entailed IRB approval from two institutions; both were granted without hesitation from the respective boards.

Dr. Thorpe encountered something unique in his research project: like other research in New Zealand, consideration of the Treaty of Waitangi, a treaty signed in 1840 with the indigenous Maori people during colonization, was a factor (S. Thorpe, personal communication, August 29, 2008). Essentially researchers are encouraged to consider who might be affected by the project, to identify any possible social consequences (particularly for Maori, but also for other cultures), any consultation issues, and any partnership issues ("partnership" is a component of the treaty). Special areas of consideration in the project were around cultural difference and protecting the rights of coresearchers to their research within the project and encouraging full participation in group processes and research decision making.

Thorpe's emergent research design called for co-constructed narratives through unstructured interviews. Decisions around information gathering and recording were especially important as these were aspects of the method that the researcher wanted the coresearchers to choose by group consensus.

At times data were captured through the online software used, such as screen shots, images, audio, and video. At other times differing members of the research group took initiative and leadership around the collection and processing of research data and information. This meant that the privacy and confidentiality of some information could not always be preserved with the collection of visuals such as images and video.

The unstructured nature of the research method was challenging for some in the group who simply wanted to be told the plan and led through the process. Coplanning, cocreating the research design, coinvestigating, and coanalyzing the research were very new ways of researching and working for some in the group. However, others were intrigued and happy to engage in learning a new collaborative and co-constructed approach to research.

No similar studies were found that used the cooperative inquiry method in an online setting. Examples tended to come from small group management, medical, and counseling and social ecology fields. A few research participants had previously used the cooperative inquiry method when they facilitated face-to-face settings. Without previous successful examples, the researcher and participants learned together throughout the study.

Dr. Thorpe and coresearchers, who are all facilitators, were guided by their common professional ethics code: the "Statement of Values and Code of Ethics for Group Facilitators" from the International Association of Facilitators. Thorpe received ethics committee approval for the project under his university's research ethics, guidelines, and procedures, which are accredited to the Health Research Council of New Zealand (which serves the same role as an IRB). Given the unusual, groundbreaking nature of the study, Dr. Thorpe found that meeting both the faculty research representative and the head of the Auckland University of Technology Ethics Committee in an informal setting aided approval by allowing him an opportunity to articulate research ideas and to receive feedback on critical areas to address (S. Thorpe, personal communication, August 29, 2008).

Dr. Cabiria's study offers yet another variation of online research design and IRB approval. His qualitative study of attitudes toward experiences of gay and lesbian life involved multiple interactions with participants through online surveys and interviews. All of these interactions occurred between Cabiria and the avatars that represented his study participants. The study participants agreed to participate in the study using the identities of their avatars and all communications were anonymous.

Dr. Cabiria observed, "Although my interactions were with avatars, which are graphical representations, I was deeply aware that they were being operated by human beings through a mediated environment" (Cabiria, 2008b). He let participants know that he understood the potential stress involved in recalling developmental aspects of being a lesbian or gay person.

The biggest concerns were how best to protect participants from harm. As in traditional research, the goal was to protect the participants who were offering very personal, and potentially harmful information about themselves and their relationships. In the virtual world environment, people use pseudonyms, which acted as one line of defense to protect their anonymity. I them gave them my own fictitious names in order to protect their virtual world identities. My feeling was that even fictitious identities in virtual worlds have relationships and sense-of-self that also need to be protected from harm. (J. Cabiria, personal communication, September 6, 2008)

To alleviate any discomfort, he offered to meet with them to discuss results and ask any questions. At the time Cabiria was designing the study, Linden Labs, which operates Second Life, had no specific policies regarding data collection for research in Second Life, just Terms of Service and Community Standards.

The biggest hurdle was that Second Life no longer has a formal research policy, which many academic, corporate, and governmental institutions want to see. Researchers will want to get explicit information, often through forums, about how each virtual world handles research requests. The interviews themselves would need to be conducted with, not only the same care as one would take in real life, but pay attention to the extra considerations in virtual world interviews, such as the presence of Griefers, casual passersby, and virtual stationary objects that are actually avatars. Interview interactions need to be hidden, preferably by using multiple layers of obstacles to deter unwanted observers. These layers can include interviewing at the upper limits of the virtual world where others tend not to go, creating an off-limits, invitation-only space, using private chat, conducting interviews in glass-walled spaces or open spaces (to view the presence of others), using other communication tools not native to the virtual world (such as Skype) while having an avatar presence in the virtual world. (J. Cabiria, personal communication, September 6, 2008)

Because of the sensitive and confidential nature of the interview topics, Dr. Cabiria was able to convince his university's IRB of the preference for informed consent by the avatar rather than the individual represented by the avatar. He made a compelling case on the basis of human subjects' regulations that allow for cases "where a signed informed consent document may pose a risk to subjects" (HHS, 2005).

The only ambiguities had to do with whether avatars are people or cartoons. We had to wade through thoughts about where real-world identity ends and virtual world identity begins. In the end, I decided to treat all as real-world identities and to apply the same protections. It was clear in the research that there is a great deal of real-world–virtual-world identity blending and transference. (J. Cabiria, personal communication, September 6, 2008)

Cabiria supported his case by designing a study that drew the sample from trustworthy user groups of professors and educators. The multistage design, which required a five-week commitment, discouraged impostors. He used an online survey tool to create questions for the consent, with a protocol that allowed participants to indicate agreement by submitting the online form.

As these examples show, research designs that spell out ethical relationships with participants take many forms. Those in the position of advising and approving such studies are learning along with the researchers where to draw the line in innovative online studies. At the same time researchers must take care in creating ethical designs that respect the privacy, confidentiality, and fairness and beneficence.

Key Concepts

- Attention to ethical online research begins with the research design and continues throughout the study;

- Simplistic either-or explanations will not be adequate for researchers who want to propose online research. They must navigate the dichotomies such as public versus private definitions of online space, deontological versus consequentialist thinking about ethics to find workable approaches; and

- Robust justifications may be needed for review boards who lack experience with online research—especially in the areas of privacy, confidentiality, and informed consent.

Discussions and Assignments

1. Create a checklist for ethical online research that articulates your own standards of values and ethics before you start collecting and analyzing data. Compare and contrast your checklist with your peers' lists. Discuss similarities and differences; refine based on new insights.

2. Justify your choices using principles from one or more ethical theories.

3. Compare and contrast your ethics checklist with the ones your peers develop. Were your priorities the same? Were your theoretical justifications the same or different?

4. Review at least two studies conducted with data collected online (observation, participant observation, interviews, or focus groups).

5. Do you feel the researchers acted ethically? Why or why not?

6. Where would you place research setting on Figure 4.1: Public-Private Internet Continuum?

7. What advice would you give the researcher to improve ethical practices with the research participants?

8. Reflect on the ethical risks for researchers. Discuss the steps you will take to conduct research in a transparent, honest way.

9. Use the following case, "Two Researchers: Ethical or Not?," as the basis for discussion or present your analysis as an essay.

Two Researchers: Ethical or Not?

A researcher plans to study citizen journalists and their blogs. For the first phase of the study the researcher intends to observe dialogue between bloggers and their readers. After observing a number of blogs for several months, the researcher plans to identify key themes and questions to guide online interviews with a sample of the bloggers and regular commenters. The researcher chooses a number of blogs to observe on a daily basis for a month. She makes notes about the length, frequency, and content of the postings by the bloggers and contributors. She remains an anonymous reader; like any number of other visitors she does not post any comments on the blogs or complete the registration form that would enable her to make such posts. She does not solicit consent or announce her presence as a researcher. After reviewing her notes and reflecting on her observations, she identifies some criteria she will use to select interview participants. She contacts those individuals to introduce herself and discuss the purpose of her study. The bloggers and contributors who are willing to participate in the study sign a consent agreement and arrange to meet in a private online space for the interview. The agreement spells out terms of the interview as well as the scope of information the researcher can use as data.

A researcher with the same general study in mind could choose a number of blogs to observe on a daily basis for a month. Like the first, she plans to do so without obtaining consent. This researcher completes the registration using a pseudonym and posts comments to the blogs to elicit responses on topics of interest to her research. Because the other visitors assume a public readership, the researcher believes it is acceptable to take notes on the content of the responses. With registration, she can access a profile of the blogger, including other affiliations. She finds other sites and e-mail lists where these bloggers are members and joins to track participation and view their profiles, posts, and comments. These steps allow her to gain more information about the bloggers' interests and background. She continues to participate and take notes on any responses made to her postings. She believes her actions are consistent with the role of a participant observer in a public environment. She does not solicit consent or announce her presence as a researcher.

After reviewing her notes and reflecting on her observations, she identifies some criteria she will use to select interview participants. She selects posts the bloggers have made to use as the basis for further discussion during the interview. She contacts those individuals to introduce herself and discuss the purpose of her study. The bloggers and contributors who are willing to participate in the study sign a consent agreement and arrange to meet in a private online space for the interview.

If you were advising these two researchers about ethics, what would you say and why?

On the Book's Website

- Sample consent forms
- List of research ethics codes and resources from various disciplines

Terms

Alienation: "The appropriation of the products of somebody's action for purposes never intended or foreseen by the actor herself, drawing these products into a system of relations over which the producer has no knowledge or control" (Bakardjieva & Feenberg, 2001, p. 206).

The Belmont Report: The basis for protection of human subjects regulations in the United States.

Human subject: A living individual about whom an investigator (whether professional or student) conducting research obtains the following:

- Data through intervention or interaction with the individual, or
- Identifiable private information (HHS, 2005).

Institutional Review Board (IRB), Research Ethics Board: Body responsible for verifying that the research design protects human subjects.

IRB approval: The determination of the IRB that the research has been reviewed and may be conducted at an institution within the constraints set forth by the IRB and by other institutional and federal requirements (HHS, 2005).

Minimal risk: The probability and magnitude of harm or discomfort anticipated in the research are not greater in and of themselves than those ordinarily encountered in daily life or during the performance of routine physical or psychological examinations or tests (HHS, 2005).

Sampling

Selecting Participants for Online Interviews

5

> *The ideal interview subject does not exist—different persons are suitable for different types of interviews.*
>
> —Steiner Kvale and Svend Brinkman, 2009

After you study Chapter 5, you will be able to do the following:

- Describe sampling issues in qualitative research;
- Compare and contrast sampling types;
- Relate sampling types to a design for online interview research; and
- Apply recommendations for online sampling plans and recruitment.

A Critical Decision: Who to Interview?

Every researcher must make a variety of conceptual and practical decisions about how to conduct the proposed study. Every researcher must consider ways theoretical stances and principles influence approaches to data collection and analysis. Because all aspects of the research design are interrelated, each design decision a researcher makes has implications for the entire study. Ripple effects of each decision impact other areas of the research design and may have subtle or radical effects on the outcomes of the study. Researchers must assess and balance risks and opportunities and determine what is to be gained or lost with each choice.

Nowhere are researchers' choices more critical than in determining how they will identify and select the individuals who will contribute relevant thoughts and experiences as research participants. Interview researchers depend on interviewees to generate high-quality data. As noted in Chapter 3, the interviewee's role is to respond honestly to an interviewer's questions or to participate in discussion with the researcher. Interviewees' responses ideally offer insight into perceptions, understandings, or experiences of personal, social, or organizational dimensions of the subject of the study. Once a researcher decides on the purpose of the study and the style of interview, including the technology to be used for the interview (see Chapter 2), level of structure and type of interaction (see Chapter 3), and potential ethical dilemmas or risks (see Chapter 4), it is possible to clarify the expectations for interviewees and characteristics they will need to possess to participate. Gaining participants' consent and preparing for the interview are described in Chapter 4 and Chapter 6, respectfully.

How does a researcher find the right people who have the ability, experience, and willingness to serve as research participants? In addition to the issues every researcher must consider, the online researcher also must think about potential consequences of the interview technology and the virtual milieu for the conduct of the study and the nature of its results. Online sampling for online research is a new area without established conventions. General approaches to sampling for qualitative research can be adapted to structure and organize the process. However, new approaches are needed when researchers use the Internet to locate and recruit participants.

This chapter provides an overview of key issues in qualitative research sampling generally and a discussion of significant issues in sampling specific to online interview research. The chapter recommends ways that the online researcher can creatively address common expectations reviewers of a research proposal may hold for online sampling and in the process strengthen the research design.

Sampling in Qualitative Research

If research interviews are "conversations with a purpose," then sampling is the systematic process for determining who can serve the purpose of the study. The qualitative research interview is conducted to describe a particular experience and/or context in-depth with as much nuance and complexity as possible. The researcher needs to locate individuals who can and will provide honest, robust information about themselves and/or the phenomena of interest, and fully participate in an interview and related communications about the study.

The term **sampling** originated in quantitative research methodology where researchers look for participants who are a "sample" of a larger population. In what is sometimes called **probability sampling,** members of the research population are chosen at random and have a known probability of selection. Quantitative methods use standardized measures so that the varying experiences of participants in the sample can be fit into a limited number of predetermined response categories to which numbers are assigned (Patton, 2002). With a quantitative approach it is possible to "measure the reactions of a great many people to a limited set of questions, thus facilitating comparison and statistical aggregation of the data" (Patton, 2002, p. 14). Quantitative researchers are concerned with minimizing bias in the group so the sample represents groups in their proportion to the population at large, thereby producing a statistically representative sample (Koerber & McMichael, 2008). This enables the researcher to test hypotheses and make generalizations from a small population to the whole population (Wilmot, 2008, p. 3).

Qualitative research typically uses a nonprobability basis sampling. Probability sampling is inappropriate for qualitative interview research, or for research that integrates qualitative interviews into a larger mixed methods study. Qualitative studies tend to entail a deeper, more detailed exploration with a smaller number of research participants. The goals do not include producing a statistically representative sample or drawing statistical inference. Qualitative researchers have other goals and means for ensuring rigorous sampling appropriate to the study, including triangulation and cross-checking, discussed later in this chapter.

Qualitative researchers often use what is broadly defined as **purposive** or **purposeful sampling** when selecting people to interview because the sample is intentionally selected according to the needs of the study (Coyne, 1997). Mason suggests that there are two kinds of purposes the sample should satisfy: the empirical purpose, which is to provide data needed to address the research questions, and the theoretical purpose, which is to generate ideas that advance your understanding of, prove, or develop a theory (Mason, 2002).

To align with empirical purposes the researcher seeks participants because they typify a circumstance or hold a characteristic that may have salience to the subject matter of the study (Ritchie & Lewis, 2003, p. 82) and are experienced, are knowledgeable, and offer diverse perspectives (Rubin & Rubin, 2005). To align with theoretical purposes, the researcher seeks participants on the basis of how their characteristics or experiences relate to theoretical positions and the explanation or account the researcher is developing (Mason, 2002). According to Miles and Huberman (1994), the researcher wants to see different instances of theoretical principles, at different moments, in different places, with different people. The qualitative researchers' concern is with the *conditions* under which the construct or theory operates, not with the generalization of the findings to other settings (Miles & Huberman, 1994, p. 29). In grounded theory studies, the theoretical purposes for sampling take priority. In grounded theory, the data provide the basis for describing the theory, whereas in other studies, the theory provides the basis for explaining the data. When grounded theory researchers see a new phenomenon in the data, they purposely look for new research participants who can confirm it or raise relevant questions about it (Charmaz, 2006; Koerber & McMichael, 2008).

Sampling decisions may be motivated by different goals and purposes—empirical and theoretical—sometimes in the same study. These decisions should be articulated in a systematic and well-defined sampling plan (Lee & Lings, 2008, p. 213). The sample plan lays out the approach(es) to be used and explains how they align with the research purpose and questions, epistemology, and methodology. Interrelated questions the researcher answers in the sample plan include the following:

- What type or combination of types of sampling will I use?
- What are the sample criteria?
- How much detail will be needed to adequately describe how the study's purpose aligns to the sample (Koerber & McMichael, 2008)?
- How much detail on the sample criteria should be developed in advance of the study?
- To what degree do the research methodology and design permit the researcher to introduce new criteria that might emerge during the study?
- What is the target population?
- How much diversity is needed to represent the variations known to exist within this population (Koerber & McMichael, 2008)?
- What is it about this population that interests me (Mason, 2002)?
- Am I interested in people as individuals, groups, or collectives (Mason, 2002)?
- How should I classify people for the purpose of the study (Ritchie, Lewis, & Elam, 2003)?
- By characteristics such as age, sex, class, ethnicity, occupation, social class?
- By specific life experiences, feelings, perceptions, behaviors?
- With time parameters such as era of the experience or life stage of the experience?
- Who should be excluded from the sample?
- "What relationship do I want to establish, or do I assume exists, between the sample or selection I am making, and a wider population" (Mason, 2002, p. 123)?
- What, besides agreement to informed consent, is required of participants?
- What is the time commitment? How long will the interview be?
- In addition to the actual interview, what are other expectations for preparation and follow-up (see Chapter 6)?
- How many people need to be sampled? Should the sampling strategy take a planned or an iterative approach to determining sample size and selecting participants before or during the study?

- What is the budget?
- What is the time frame for recruiting participants?
- What data collection methods should be employed?
- How are the data to be analyzed? (See the Appendix.)

The online researcher begins the process of developing a sample plan by reflecting on these questions, in concert with consideration of issues that relate specifically to sampling for data collection through online interviews.

TYPES OF SAMPLING

The online interview researcher first selects the sampling type that aligns with the purpose and methodology, and then customizes it to the online milieu of the study. Researchers have found many ways to meet the specific research purposes they have identified. A number of approaches are presented in the Sampling Typology, Table 5.1.

SAMPLE SIZE

How many research participants are appropriate given the research design and type of sampling selected for the study? Sampling procedures for qualitative research do not follow standardized guidelines, and guidelines for sample size are no exception. Phenomena need only appear once to be included in the findings, so statements about incidence or prevalence are not the concern of qualitative research (Ritchie et al., 2003). Without suggesting specific numbers, a "small" sample is the norm in qualitative interview research.

> [T]he type of information that qualitative studies yield is rich in detail. Interview data is rich in detail with "many hundreds of 'bites' of information from each unit of data collection." (Ritchie et al., 2003, p. 83)

> With a purposive non-random sample the number of people interviewed is less important than the criteria used to select them. (Wilmot, 2008, p. 4)

> [T]he sample size is not determined by the need to ensure generalizability, but by a desire to investigate fully the chosen topic and provide information-rich data. (Higginbottom, 2004, p. 16)

> The validity, meaningfulness and insights generated from qualitative inquiry have more to do with the information richness of the cases selected and the observational/analytical capabilities than with sample size. (Patton, 2002, p. 245)

Table 5.1	Sampling Typology	
Type	**Description of Approach**	**Advantages**
Combination or mixed purposeful	More than one sampling approach is used to address different aspects of the research design or purpose.	Triangulation, flexibility, meets multiple interests and needs (Patton, 2002).
Convenience	The researcher selects participants who are readily available and easy to contact.	Saves time, money, and effort, but has the lowest credibility; yields information-poor cases (Patton, 2002).
Criterion	Participants are chosen because they meet a predetermined set of criteria (Patton, 2002).	Useful for quality assurance (Miles & Huberman, 1994); enables the researcher to explore and understand central themes of the study (Ritchie et al., 2003).
Critical case	The researcher selects cases seen as "critical" to an understanding of the subject of inquiry (Patton, 2002; Ritchie et al., 2003).	Permits logical generalization and maximum application of information to other cases; what's true of the critical cases is likely to be true of all other cases (Patton, 2002).
Deviant or extreme	Participants are chosen because they are unusual or uniquely manifest the phenomenon (Miles & Huberman, 1994; Ritchie & Lewis, 2003).	Researchers can learn from highly unusual manifestations of the phenomenon of interest, such as outstanding success/notable failures, top of the class/dropouts, exotic events, or crises (Patton, 2002).
Emergent	Participants are chosen as opportunities arise during the study (Patton, 2002).	Useful in fieldwork or when there can be no a priori specification of the sample; it cannot be drawn in advance (Lincoln & Guba, 1985, p. 201).
Heterogeneous	A deliberate strategy to include participants who have widely different experiences of the phenomena of interest (Ritchie & Lewis, 2003).	(See maximum variation.)
Homogeneous	Participants are chosen to give a detailed picture of a particular phenomenon or experience they have in common (Patton, 2002; Ritchie et al., 2003).	Focuses the study on common characteristics, reduces variation, and simplifies analysis (Miles & Huberman, 1994).

Type	Description of Approach	Advantages
Intensity	Select participants who manifest the phenomenon intensely but not extremely (Patton, 2002).	Although similar to deviant or extreme, intensity sampling allows the researcher to focus on participants that strongly manifest or have deeply experienced the phenomena of interest rather than participants who are unusual (Ritchie & Lewis, 2003).
Maximum variation	Purposefully picking a wide range of variation on dimensions of interest . . . documents unique or diverse variations that have emerged in adapting to different conditions. Identifies important common patterns that cut across variations (Patton, 2002).	Researcher can document unique or diverse variations and identify important common patterns in the data (Creswell, 1998; Patton, 2002).
Nominated	Potential participants are recommended by other participants or by knowledgeable experts (Roper & Shapira, 2000).	Researcher's choices can be confirmed by input or recommendations from a third party.
Opportunistic	The researcher takes advantage of opportunities that arise to find participants (Ritchie & Lewis, 2003).	(See convenience and emergent sampling.)
Politically important	Participants are chosen because they connect with politically sensitive issues in the study (Miles & Huberman, 1994).	Attract desired attention or avoid undesired attention to politically sensitive studies or findings (Miles & Huberman, 1994).
Snowball or chain	Identify people who know people who are good interview subjects (Patton, 2002).	Snowball sampling can be used to access hard-to-reach populations or "individuals and groups often 'hidden' because openly identifying with specific factions or lifestyles can result in discrimination" (Browne, 2005, p. 47).

(Continued)

Table 5.1	(Continued)	
Type	**Description of Approach**	**Advantages**
Stratified purposive	A hybrid approach used to select participants in subgroups.	Illustrates characteristics of particular subgroups of interest; facilitates comparisons.
Theoretical sampling	"Theoretical sampling is the process of data collection whereby the researcher simultaneously collects, codes and analyzes the data in order to decide what data to collect next. Deciding where to sample next according to the emerging codes and categories is theoretical sampling" (Coyne, 1997, p. 625).	Grounded theory researchers conduct interviews with an initial sample of participants selected using criterion sampling. In analysis of this initial set of data, they identify categories of experience or perspectives. To gain insight into these categories they select additional research participants on the basis of how participants' characteristics or experiences help them to explicate the data (Charmaz, 2006).
Theory-based sampling	Finding manifestations of a theoretical construct of interest so as to elaborate and examine the construct (Patton, 2002).	To get to the theoretical construct, "we need to see different instances of it, at different moments, in different places, with different people. The prime concern is with the conditions under which the construct or theory operates, not with the generalization of the findings to other settings" (Miles & Huberman, 1994, p. 29).
Total population	The researcher studies an entire population of people who share a particular characteristic or experience.	Appropriate for studies of a publicly experienced phenomena, event, or crisis or situations where a small group constitutes the "total" population.
Typical case sampling	Illustrates or highlights what is typical, normal, or average (Creswell, 1998; Miles & Huberman, 1994).	What is "typical" must be known in advance; useful in mixed methods study where participants are selected based on responses to a survey (Patton, 2002; Ritchie & Lewis, 2003).
Volunteer	The researcher studies people who volunteer to be a part of the research.	Useful when the researcher is studying a common experience or phenomenon.

Although the literature does not offer a straightforward protocol for determining the number of participants, key questions will help the researcher think through the most appropriate sample size: heterogeneity or homogeneity of the population. If the population is diverse in nature, a larger sample will be needed; the more homogeneous the sample population, the smaller the sample.

- *Number of selection criteria.* The more different criteria, the larger the sample (Ritchie et al., 2003).

- *Multiple samples within one study.* If it is necessary to have more than one sample within a study for reasons of comparison or control, then a larger sample will be needed (Ritchie et al., 2003).

- *Interview length.* The intensity and therefore the length of the qualitative interview will also impact on the design of the qualitative sampling strategy and the decision of sample size. Longer interviews may provide more data than shorter interviews. A decision may be taken, depending on the nature of the study, to conduct a larger number of shorter interviews or a smaller number of longer interviews (Wilmot, 2008, p. 4).

- *Emerging factors in data.* Unexpected generalizations may lead the researcher to seek out new research participants who can add to or contradict the data (Silverman & Marvasti, 2008). Researchers using snowball, chain, or nominated sampling expect this to occur. Researchers using other sampling strategies need to decide whether or not they are open to an increase of sample size while the study is in progress, or whether they prefer to make a note of the emerging factors for consideration in a follow-up or future study.

- *Saturation or redundancy.* Saturation occurs when the researcher begins to hear the same or similar responses from interviewees. "If the purpose is to maximize information, the sampling is terminated when no new information is coming from the new sampled units; thus redundancy is the primary criterion" (Lincoln & Guba, 1985, p. 202).

Like the storied Goldilocks, the interview researcher needs a sample size that is not too big—so as to be unwieldy to manage with a risk that quality standards are difficult to maintain. At the same time, the sample should not be too small, thus risking the possibility of missing key constituencies or lacking enough diversity to show important influences. The researcher must weigh all factors and determine what size is just right for the proposed study.

SAMPLE FRAMES

Fundamental to the sampling strategy is the choice of a **sample frame**. The term *sample frame* refers to a list or grouping of people from which the sample is selected.

There are two broad types of frames:

- *Existing Sample Frames.* Existing frames usually consist of records previously constructed for administrative purposes. They could include membership lists for organizations or associations or lists of students or program participants (Ritchie & Lewis, 2003; Wilmot, 2008). In mixed methods studies where a quantitative research instrument is administered as the first step, the survey sample can be used as a frame from which interview participants are selected for the qualitative stage of the study.

- *Constructed or Generated Sample Frames.* Where an existing frame or list is not available, researchers may have to create their own. In some cases, researchers can construct a frame from partially adequate or incomplete existing frames. Another way to construct a frame is by working through organizations that provide services to or represent a population of potential participants. Researchers can generate sample frames by approaching people in a particular organization, location, setting, or meeting. This method is best used to identify people who are willing to consider taking part in the study, seeking their permission to contact them privately to discuss the study in detail (Ritchie & Lewis, 2003).

Fortunate researchers find an existing frame and can move directly into creating a sampling plan and recruiting participants. More often researchers encounter issues in the selection and use of a sampling frame that may require significant time and attention. The researcher may discover that relevant information about the population relevant to the study is inadequate. Available information may be out of date or simply incomplete (Mason, 2002). The researcher may find that not all representatives of the target population are included in the available lists. Sections of society missing from the frame may have different characteristics and indeed different behaviors, opinions, and attitudes from those covered by the frame (Wilmot, 2008). In such situations, the researcher may need to augment or build on the existing frame to develop an appropriate pool of potential participants.

Sampling for Online Interview Research

The integrity and authority for any study results depend on the quality of the data. Obtaining the best data means finding the best research participants for the study. The credibility of the research participants is, quite simply, essential to the credibility of the study. As Markham (2009) observes, "[I]n the world of academic knowledge production, 'quality' is a state granted and recognized from the outside. One's work is assessed by various audiences who have their own sets of standards and context-specific criteria for evaluation" (p. 192). Lincoln and Guba (1985) point specifically to the need to establish confidence in the "truth value" of the research participants in the context of the inquiry (p. 290).

Reviewers unfamiliar with online research—whether they are committee members, grantmakers, or peers—may scrutinize online sampling plans more closely to assess the "truth value" of the research participants. Chapter 4 pointed to common areas for concern: age and identity of the research participants and whether they voluntarily consent to share information and participate in the study. Although the ability to generalize results from the sample to the general population is less relevant in qualitative than in quantitative research, reviewers may want to know whether the target population has adequate access and technology literacy needed for a worthwhile sample. Are Internet access and the skills needed to engage in online communications common throughout the target population or limited? Does a known limitation in access and/or ICT skills within the target population correlate to factors being studied in such a way that they might skew the results of the study?

A challenge the researcher will confront is this: no generally accepted standards, approaches, or guidelines exist for sampling research participants for online interview research. A typology of sampling approaches and a set of recommended practices are presented here to guide those who are designing studies with online interview data collection.

DESIGN DECISIONS INFLUENCE SAMPLING PLANS

Whether to interview online or whether to sample and recruit online are two different decisions. A researcher could use online sampling and recruiting for interviews conducted in person, or use face-to-face approaches for sampling but conduct the interviews online. The research purpose, rationale for deciding to interview online, geographic scope of the study, and the researcher's access to the target population are determining factors for the decision to use online or other sampling approaches. One important distinction: whether the digital environment serves as means for exchange or part of the subject of inquiry. Researchers who conduct online interviews to collect data fall into two broad categories:

- Those who choose to conduct interviews online to study online or technology-mediated behaviors, culture, practices, attitudes, or experiences, and

- Those who choose to conduct interviews online to study phenomena that occur in the face-to-face world.

More and more activities in the fields of business and sales, education and training, government and civil society, culture and entertainment, as well as in personal and family life that once occurred face-to-face and locally can now occur online, without regard to geographic location. Researchers whose purpose is to study online behaviors may find an online sampling strategy the logical choice based on the principle that "research questions that explore an online phenomenon are strengthened through the use of a method of research that closely mirrors the natural setting under investigation" (Geiser, 2002).

However, researchers have diverse motivations for choosing to collect data through online interviews, as discussed in Chapter 1. Some researchers choose online interview methods to study behaviors or phenomena that occur face-to-face because such methods allow for flexibility of timing and location for the interview, or because they permit the use of shared applications or visual methods (see Chapter 8). For these researchers the online environment is the meeting venue, not the subject of inquiry. They may take either an online or a more conventional approach to the sampling strategy.

For example, consider a hypothetical study designed to improve understanding of community college instructors' attitudes toward methods of instruction for at-risk learners.

- *Researcher A* is interested in the attitudes of instructors who teach in face-to-face classrooms but chooses to conduct interviews online to work around teachers' erratic schedules. Researcher A could use an online sampling plan or a hybrid approach to sampling, including both online and face-to-face strategies to recruit participants.

- *Researcher B* wants to compare attitudes of instructors who teach in face-to-face classrooms of urban, suburban, and rural community colleges in different parts of the United States. Researcher B chooses to interview online to gain access to perspectives from geographically diverse communities without the need for extensive travel. Researcher B uses an online recruiting strategy to locate participants who meet the sampling criteria.

- *Researcher C* is interested in the online, e-learning experiences of community college instructors. Researcher C may use online sampling strategies similar to those of Researcher B, but Researcher C has a greater interest in the digital culture(s) and context of the interactions with potential interviewees. For Researcher C preliminary observations of online teachers' communities and types of e-mail lists or newsletters they share may inform not only approaches to sampling and recruiting, but the questions and themes of the interview itself.

The following examples show how a similar pattern of choices might apply across different disciplines:

- In business research, Researcher A is interested in experiences of business owners in the local community, but chooses online interviews that allow flexibility and ease of recording; Researcher B is interested in experiences of business owners in different markets and chooses online interviews to broaden access to participants; and Researcher C is interested in experiences of business owners that sell products and services online through e-commerce, so is interested in the digital milieu where the business operates.

- In social sector research, Researcher A is interested in the experiences of leaders in agencies that serve the local community; Researcher B is interested in experiences of leaders in agencies in locations beyond reach for face-to-face interviews; and Researcher C is interested in experiences of leaders whose agencies provide services online.

The empirical purpose of these studies is similar, yet the sampling strategies they could use and the way they will describe those strategies in the sampling plan may vary greatly. All of the sampling plans will need to answer the questions listed earlier in this chapter. In addition, Researchers B and C should address the following questions:

- What sampling approaches are appropriate for online interview research and why?

- How will the researcher assess whether the target population has access to the technology the researchers intends to use, and the capability and willingness to use it as a research participant?

- How can the researcher locate credible research participants? How will the researcher verify the identity and age (or other relevant criteria) of research participants recruited online?

- How will online recruitment be carried out?

No two researchers will answer such questions in the same way. Still, some common principles for online sampling can be identified. Some of these principles are not unique to online research. However, these principles are applied differently in practice for online research in large part because the researcher needs to counter potential communication gaps or breakdowns that are more prevalent in online communication. Considerations for each question and recommendations are offered here.

WHAT SAMPLING APPROACHES ARE APPROPRIATE FOR ONLINE INTERVIEW RESEARCH AND WHY?

If research interviews are "conversations with a purpose," then the first step is to clearly determine the specific purpose for each research participant. What indicators will signal the researcher that a potential research participant can meet the purpose of the study? These indicators should be defined and articulated as criteria for sample selection. Precision and clarity are important in any project involving online communication. When communicating the study's purpose and information needed to answer the research questions, clear criteria are beneficial to potential participants who may need to decide whether to click on a website button or respond to text or e-mail. Clear criteria will be valuable in cases where relationships are needed with others who might suggest or introduce potential participants, or promote a call for participation.

Criterion sampling is based on the researcher's identification of specific characteristics that serve as the basis for selection of research participants. The researcher sets some parameters or priorities for the kind of participant who can contribute data needed to answer the research questions by participating in an online interview. By stating criteria, the researcher also creates additional factors that can be independently verifiable from other sources besides the research participant's own statements.

> **Research Tip:** Criterion sampling should be a core component of an online sampling plan.

> **Research Tip:** Mesh criterion sampling with other approaches as needed to devise explicit sampling plans.

Criteria can be refined by using other types of sampling to further align with the purpose and research questions guiding the study. See Table 5.2 for suggested ways to think through and select the best approach for the study at hand.

Table 5.2	Sampling Typology: Define Criteria to Describe Scope and Focus of Sample
Type	**Kinds of Criteria**
Convenience	Define specific factors that would make the participant someone "convenient" to interview online, such as same time zone, member of a group familiar to researcher.
Critical case	Define "critical" in the context of the study and articulate criteria for being included in the sample.
Deviant or extreme	Identify which characteristics are within the norm and state criteria defining what qualifies as "extreme."

Type	Kinds of Criteria
Emergent	Identify the known characteristics desired in the sample population, and, where possible, identify the kinds of characteristics the researcher may hope to find.
Heterogeneous	Identify range of diversity desired for specific characteristics in the target sample population, for example, different experiences of the same phenomena, different educational levels, or different cultural backgrounds.
Homogeneous	Identify the characteristics members of the target sample population should have in common, for example, experience of a phenomenon, race, or occupation, and state criteria accordingly.
Intensity	Identify which characteristics are within the norm, and state criteria defining what qualifies as "intense."
Maximum variation	Identify range of variation desired for specific characteristics in the target sample population, and articulate the maximum acceptable in the interview sample. For example, state the maximum age range of sample.
Politically important	Define "political" in the context of the study and differentiate between "important" and "unimportant." On this basis, articulate criteria for sample appropriate for the study.
Snowball or chain	Identify criteria for initial participants, then state criteria to be communicated to those interviewees who might be able to recommend other people appropriate for the study.
Theoretical sampling	Identify criteria for initial interviewees; based on theoretical constructs that emerge from the first round of interviews, state criteria participants will need to exemplify to be included in study.
Theory-based sampling	State criteria describing what participants will need to manifest in relationship to the theoretical construct of interest to be included in study.
Total population	Determine the characteristic or experience that defines the population.
Typical case sampling	Define "typical" in the context of the study; on this basis, articulate criteria for sample appropriate for the study.
Volunteer	Determine criteria volunteers will need to meet to participate in the study.

Clarifying the expectations and requirements for the research participant is a step related to setting criteria. The kinds of individuals the researcher can find and their agreement to participate may depend on what it is the researcher expects them to do. The time required for one or

Research Tip: Clarify your expectations for research participants.

Ethics Tip: Be open and disclose unknown factors that could result in changes in expectations, scheduling, and so on that could affect the research participant.

more interviews and the period of time for multiple interactions through the course of the study should be defined as closely as possible in advance.

Some interview types may necessitate participant preparation in advance of the interview (see Chapter 6), multiple stages of interaction with the participant, and/or follow-up during data analysis to substantiate the researcher's understanding of participant statements (see Chapter 7).

As discussed in Chapter 1, a participant may drop out by simply closing the interview window or deleting the e-mail. In this digital milieu, the researcher should specify expectations from the beginning of the relationship to ensure persistence.

When you consider the Typology of Interview Structures, it is apparent that the requirements and level of commitment for participation may vary greatly depending on the type of interview. It makes sense that the more the researcher views the interview as a knowledge-generating interaction, the more time he or she will need to build trust, relationships, and understanding of the study's purpose.

These design decisions should be spelled out in the sample plan and included in the IRB, Research Ethics Board, or other reviews. Otherwise, the researcher may find that other interactions outside the approved study are needed, or that potentially illegitimate data were collected. Either case may precipitate a return to the review process for approval of additional interactions with the interviewees and/or a revision of the consent agreement to allow inclusion of all data (Garg, 2008).

HOW WILL THE RESEARCHER ASSESS PARTICIPANTS' TECHNOLOGY ACCESS AND ICT LITERACY?

In addition to specifying expectations for the time and nature of potential research participants' commitment to the study, online researchers need to specify technology access and skills involved in research participation. What combination of online communication tools does the researcher intend to use for preparation, interview, and any follow-up communication? Will routine communication such as arranging times to meet for the interview or discussing the purpose of the study be carried out through e-mail, text or instant messaging, or telephone? Will the synchronous interview require a microphone, a Web camera, or other specialized hardware or software? What can the researcher provide? Does the researcher need to seek funds to subsidize participants' acquisition of technology? Can the researcher arrange for interviewees to participate from a computer lab or another setting?

Participant access is a fundamental question that influences any research design. Researchers who intend to interview people in person are concerned with geographic access to the desired meeting place and access for people with disabilities or

> **Research Tip:** Identify means of communication for each stage of the study; do not assume that the ICTs the researcher wants to use are best for sample populations. Change if possible—or offer a practice session—if the participant objects to using a particular ICT.

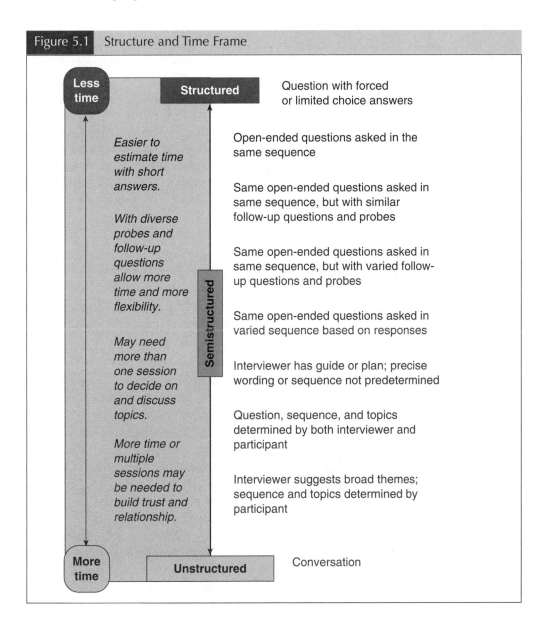

Figure 5.1   Structure and Time Frame

other restrictions. Researchers consider possible effects of the setting on interview responses—will participants be intimidated or influenced by the room arrangement or by associations with the institution, power, or authority reflected in the meeting space? Online interviewers must ask similar questions when selecting the data collection methods and tools. Will potential participants who fit the sample demographic have access to the online tools the researcher intends to use? Will they feel comfortable responding to questions in the selected online meeting space?

ICT literacy, technology adoption, and census studies mapping rates of Internet access by people in various demographic categories and geographic areas provide researchers with useful background about the target sample population. In addition, the researcher can look on the signs of online presence of the target population. Are there websites on topics of interest to this population? Are online communities or social networking sites by and for them up-to-date and active? This kind of broad exploration may help the researcher answer the general questions; specific questions will need to be posed to individuals as part of the initial discussion of needs and requirements for participation in the study. Based on the hypothetical example presented earlier, researchers A and B are more concerned with questions of access and ICT literacy than researcher C, who is exploring Internet-related behaviors, transactions, events, or cultures and can assume that participants are comfortable with various forms of online communication.

HOW CAN RESEARCHERS ENSURE THAT RESEARCH PARTICIPANTS ARE CREDIBLE?

Once the researcher has developed a clear and specific set of criteria and identified the ICT-related issues, the next step is to devise a way to locate people who fit the study's purpose and requirements. Strategies to verify potential research participants' identities and ensure that they authentically meet the study criteria are important to any online sampling plan but critical when the researcher intends to recruit in public online environments. Researchers who have access to private, members-only online spaces have less concern for identity and consenting age of potential participants and can proceed in a similar style any researcher might use. Once again, the Public-Private Internet Continuum illustrates the differentiation and points to the fact that the issues are not black and white (see Figure 5.2). Researchers will have to use their own judgment, based on the nature of the study, the target population, and the norms and culture of the online environment where they hope to find information-rich cases for research participation.

> **Research Tip:** Determine where online the target population can best be reached; assess whether it is a public or private space.

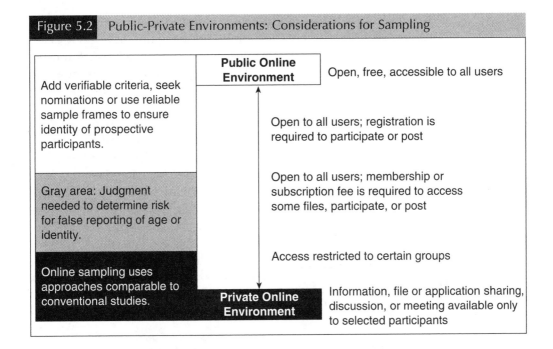

Figure 5.2   Public-Private Environments: Considerations for Sampling

Two approaches are suggested here as the basis for locating credible research participants online: *nomination* and *existing sample frames.* The first relies on verification of identity by another person who knows the potential participant; the second relies on verification by membership in a group, organization, or reliable administrative list. These approaches suc-

> ⚖ **Ethics Tip:** Err on the safe side if you have any reason to doubt age or identity of potential participant, and seek additional verifiable evidence before selecting the individual to participate in the study.

ceed when the researcher is very specific about desired characteristics—another reason why criterion-based sampling has added value online.

Participant Is Nominated by Trustworthy Third Party

Can someone else recommend potential participants who meet sampling criteria? In the act of nomination the identity of the potential participant is verified. A nomination from a known person or organization deflects the question: "How do you know the participant is who he says he is?" The use of this approach does add another step for the researcher, who must explain the study and ask for assistance from others who can make the nomination. Online, nomination could be accomplished with an e-mail request to colleagues, program directors, or others in a position to know individuals who meet the sample criteria.

Nomination can be meshed with a snowball or chain approach. Research participants whose identities and credibility have been established may be asked to nominate others who share characteristics or experiences. A crucial element of successful nomination by research participants is trust.

> Trust and networking, and the role of the professional relationship, have an impact on the nature, strength, and numbers of further nominations in this type of recruitment and retention. Researchers rely on the truth and fidelity of information received from their contacts, and perhaps more importantly, contacts must feel they can trust the fidelity of the researchers. (Streeton, Cooke, & Campbeii, 2004, p. 45)

Research Tip: Triangulate information; build in cross-checking and verification by involving third parties.

In the sample plan, the researcher should explain the nomination strategy and specify kinds of people the researcher will count on to nominate potential interviewees.

Existing Sample Frames

Fundamental to any sampling strategy is the choice of sample frame, the list or grouping of people from which the sample is selected. As discussed earlier in this chapter, some researchers construct sample frames while others rely on existing frames. Constructing a sample frame online is possible but adds more layers of information or identity the researcher must verify. Thus, constructing a new sample frame online may be too time-consuming to be practical.

Existing frames can serve the online researcher because they are aggregate pools of individuals who have verified their identities (and perhaps even credit card numbers) to qualify as members. With the advent of online communities and social networking websites, and the movement of professional associations and clubs to the Internet, many potential sample frames exist online. In some cases faculty, employee, or membership lists may be posted on a website or published in a directory. What groups or affiliations would attract and engage the target sample population, and what appropriate means can be utilized to communicate the study's call for participation?

By using nomination or existing frames researchers avoid a time-consuming recruitment process of filtering out potential participants who will not or cannot contribute to the success of the study. Nomination or existing sample frame approaches can be combined or used together with other tactics as needed to meet the purpose of the study.

Practical Steps: How Will Online Recruitment Be Carried Out?

Locating the right people and recruiting them to participate in a study is a challenge for any researcher. Central to the challenge for online researchers is the avoidance of sending or receiving unwanted messages, commonly known as spam. If the researcher posts a recruitment message or advertisement on a public website, networking community, or e-mail list, a deluge of unwanted responses may result. On the other hand, if the researcher sends unsolicited e-mail requests to potential participants, the message may be perceived as spam. Ethical issues related to types of online communication were discussed in Chapter 4.

> **Research Tip:** Create a recruitment statement so all posts or requests use consistent language to describe the study and convey the same message to potential participants.

It is important to create a statement that explains the researcher's approaches and expectations on the matters discussed in this chapter. One benefit of such a statement is consistency of language and message, so all potential nominators or potential research participants begin from the same common view of the study. The statement can be summarized when a briefer post is needed, or in the case of a heterogeneous or extreme case sample, the researcher may refine some elements of the statement to appeal to diverse audiences. A succinct but comprehensive recruitment statement may include these elements:

> **Ethics Tip:** Keep ethics and privacy issues in mind when communicating online.

- **Purpose of the study:** Research questions, reasons for conducting the study, and the researcher's goals for the results should be outlined. Is the researcher conducting dissertation or thesis research? If so, note the institution. Such academic purposes assure potential participants of some level of faculty oversight of the study. Is the researcher assessing needs for programs or services? Creating the basis for a larger survey research project? How will the researcher disseminate the findings? What aspects of the researcher's goals will draw in potential participants and motivate them to contribute?

- **Ethics and privacy:** Offer assurances about ethical conduct of the study, confidentiality, protection of privacy, and private data storage. Indicate appropriate ethics, institutional, or other review board approvals granted for the study. If the study anticipates an international sample, indicate how you will address multiple sets of requirements.

Ethics Tip: Keep in mind that when interviewing people internationally, different principles or regulations may be in place. For example, when data is transferred from a European Union (EU) to a non-EU country, data must be adequately protected under EU regulations.

- **Incentive for participation:** Discuss reasons target population members should participate. Appeal to sense of altruism, and point out that they will be creating new solutions to a problem, improving understanding about an issue, adding to the body of knowledge on a topic.

- **Criteria:** State key sampling criteria, including characteristics, scope, and focus of the desired sample.

- **Expectations:** Time frame of study, time commitment, and technology tools needed for participation.

- **Screening and selection process:** Provide sample size information and explain how the researcher will choose participants.

Researchers can create an online space where the recruitment message can be posted online: a website, blog, or virtual space in immersive environments. In addition to text description of the call for predication, the researcher can create a video clip or audio excerpt of the recruitment message to increase interest and make more personal contact with site visitors. Links to the researcher's academic institution or other publications can convey integrity and authenticity of the study. Provide means for contact, such as a link to an e-mail or messaging address. (Avoid using the researcher's primary or personal e-mail address to avoid excessive spam or privacy violations for the researcher. Free e-mail services are ideal for this purpose.)

Because online posts will reach a very general audience, a very specific recruitment message should be used to better reach the target population. The researcher can direct the call to potential participants or ask for nominations of research participants. Links to the message can then be posted in briefer announcements in relevant online spaces or communications with colleagues.

The researcher can share a recruitment statement or link to recruitment site through e-mail discussion lists. If relevant to the topics of the list, the researcher can initiate a discussion about the nature and importance of the study. Similarly, the researcher can interact with others in a social networking space. The best practice is to approach the moderator of the list or discussion group directly to get permission for the recruitment posting and respect any norms or guidelines.

Another way is by using the networking possibilities of the digital milieu: the researcher can offer a **webinar** or host an online event or discussion on issues related to the study. The researcher creates an opportunity to interact with individuals who are interested in the subject of inquiry and may be potential participants or people who can nominate participants.

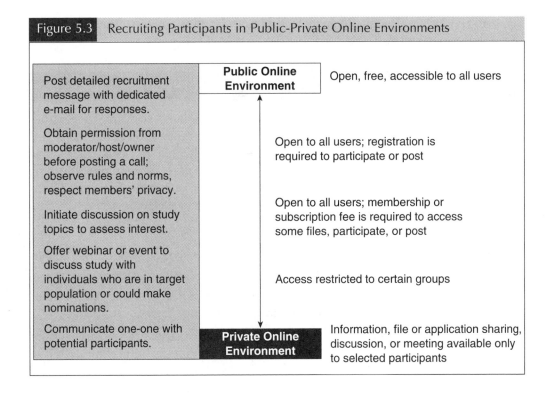

Figure 5.3   Recruiting Participants in Public-Private Online Environments

Post detailed recruitment message with dedicated e-mail for responses.	**Public Online Environment** — Open, free, accessible to all users
Obtain permission from moderator/host/owner before posting a call; observe rules and norms, respect members' privacy.	Open to all users; registration is required to participate or post
Initiate discussion on study topics to assess interest.	Open to all users; membership or subscription fee is required to access some files, participate, or post
Offer webinar or event to discuss study with individuals who are in target population or could make nominations.	Access restricted to certain groups
Communicate one-one with potential participants.	**Private Online Environment** — Information, file or application sharing, discussion, or meeting available only to selected participants

Closing Thoughts

Selection of the type or combination of types of sampling, decisions about sample size, and recruitment are essential steps in the research design, proposal development, and planning process. Although researchers using observation or documents for data collection also must make hard decisions about sampling, interview researchers have a more delicate task since they are choosing people with whom they will communicate personally. Interview researchers will have before them a human being—not simply an information-rich data source. If the sampling was successful, trust and rapport will develop so the researcher gains the information needed to answer the research questions, in an interchange characterized by mutual respect. Sampling is a complex and sensitive process for any interview researcher, regardless of experience or research design. The online researcher has some additional considerations—and some additional options.

A researcher may seek help from an online community with shared interests, such as a professional association, to characterize the subjects of a study and to find participants. The potential for interacting informally with members of the target population means researchers can gain insights that may help in determining sampling and recruitment strategies best suited to the study.

Researchers' Notebook: Stories of Online Inquiry

In purposeful sampling participants are chosen because they have particular characteristics that will enable detailed exploration and understanding of the central themes of the study (Ritchie & Lewis, 2003). The research design for my online interview research on collaborative e-learning was best served by a small, purposeful sample of information-rich cases. A criterion-based approach was used. Research participants were selected on the basis that they represent a set of criteria:

- *Criteria 1:* College- or graduate-level instructors who value collaboration as a part of academic online study and practice.
- *Criteria 2:* College- or graduate-level instructors who teach leadership or management topics.
- *Criteria 3:* College- or graduate-level instructors who use two or more online collaborative teaching methods in their classes.

Although it sounds paradoxical, I used aspects of both homogeneous and heterogeneous sampling. Common, homogeneous characteristics included requiring that all participants had online teaching experience at the college level, within comparable subject areas of leadership and management. All were expected to have used a minimum of two different instructional techniques in support of collaborative e-learning.

In looking for research participants, I sought heterogeneity in participants with experience in as many different instructional approaches as possible to enhance the richness of the data. I also wanted as global a representation as possible; indeed, global access was a big reason for selecting online interview methodology.

Because the IRB had never reviewed a proposal for real-time online interview data collection, I decided that a snowball or emergent sampling plan might introduce too many unknowns into the process. Instead, I relied on several existing sample frames. In the year prior to the study, I participated in numerous online conferences, belonged to professional e-mail lists, and took an online class. Teaching and Learning in Virtual Learning Environments was cosponsored by five European universities for educators worldwide. Course, meeting, and attendee lists served as fertile sample frames for the study. By participating in these events and meetings and observing other participants, I was able to identify active contributors. The presentations, writings, and/or comments of these contributors were reviewed. Those with interests and experience relevant to the study were contacted to introduce the study and discuss possible participation. The recruitment message was sent primarily in the context of one-to-one e-mails, and in one members-only e-mail list. Research participants' identity information could be readily triangulated with information from other sources; there were no questions about whether the interviewees were who they said they were.

Dr. Jon Cabiria similarly immersed himself in the environment he intended to research; in his case that meant Second Life. He also used a criterion-based sampling approach. He used an online questionnaire, posted in Second Life, to convey criteria and make a preliminary determination of participant match. He also distributed notices about the study and sampling questionnaire to a professional group with general characteristics of his target population. Given the nature of his study—focusing on the experiences and identities of gay and lesbian individuals—he emphasized the confidentiality of all potential and selected research participants.

Of the 130 people who completed the initial questionnaire, thirty were selected for participation, and fourteen completed the entire research process through a five-week time commitment.

As noted in the Chapter 4 Researchers' Notebook, Dr. Cabiria had to develop his own approach for a Second Life context where at present no formal research policy is in place beyond Terms of Service and Community Standards (J. Cabiria, personal communication, September 6, 2008). He operated within these formal terms and informal cultural norms in Second Life as well as the terms of the professional group where he distributed his recruitment messages.

Dr. Thorpe used the International Association of Facilitators, of which he is a member, as an existing sample frame. He contacted the seven regional representatives and asked them to forward an e-mail to their local facilitator networks canvassing for interested coresearchers. Twenty facilitators contacted him, and after Thorpe provided information about the study, seventeen of them joined the project. Dr. Thorpe used a snowball approach as well: "As many were working with groups online, either in a facilitation or training role, other participants came into the study indirectly from the groups that coresearchers were working with. Sub-projects were often created with these groups" (S. Thorpe, personal communication, August 29, 2008).

Dr. Wilson used a primarily face-to-face approach to recruiting participants for research about face-to-face phenomena conducted both online and face-to-face. She used a snowball approach, with referrals from selected participants. She worked within existing sample frames of the professional fields of interest. She selected interview subjects from referrals by professional contacts at meetings and from contacting other individuals identified from process documents as likely to have significant roles as ocean scientists, policymakers, and other pertinent stakeholders. Other subjects were contacted at meetings related to local and regional ocean policy issues during which they agreed to interviews; some were contacted directly first by e-mail or telephone to set up interviews (L. Wilson, personal communication, January 18, 2009).

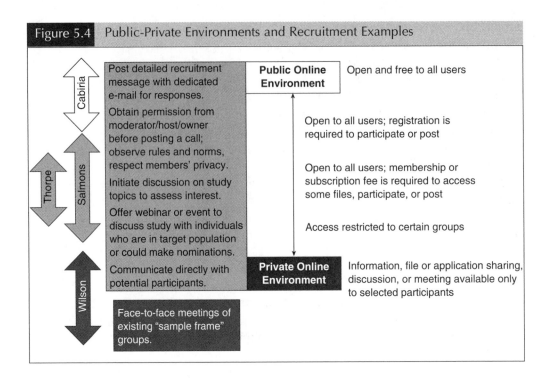

Figure 5.4   Public-Private Environments and Recruitment Examples

These examples illustrate diverse ways that researchers can use the Internet while aligning sampling and recruitment strategies with the purpose of the study. All three used purposive sampling with criterion-based approaches. As online researchers try new ways to reach potential participants—and study the significance of online sampling on the research methodologies and findings—we will undoubtedly see a great variety of approaches emerge.

Key Concepts

- Before the researcher seeks out people to interview, a sampling plan is needed.

- Qualitative researchers use nonprobability sampling. Although a combination of sampling approaches can be used in online research, developing specific criteria will help the researcher locate and verify potential interviewees. Thus criterion-based sampling is recommended as a component of the online sampling plan.

- Online interviewers may recruit participants through online or offline approaches. Nomination and existing sample frames offer ready verification of the identity of participants recruited online.

Discussions and Assignments

1. In assignments for previous chapters, you located articles describing interview studies. Look at those articles again.

   - What kind of sampling did they use? Look at Table 5.2 and identify the approach. Do you feel the researcher made the best choice? Why or why not?

   - Did any of the studies discuss online recruitment of participants? Where on the Figure 5.4 continuum would you place their strategies? What other recruitment strategies would you suggest?

2. Discuss issues of identity in online culture. Do you believe people are more, or less, honest about their identities online? Support your perspective with specific examples.

On the Book's Website

   - Models and templates for creating plans for sampling and recruiting participants for your study

Terms

Existing sample frame: Existing lists or collections of information about groups of people such as membership rolls or administrative records.

Probability sampling: A sampling method that relies on a random or changing selection method so the probability of selection of population elements is known (Schutt, 2006).

Purposive or purposeful sampling: A nonprobability sampling method in which participants or cases are selected for a purpose, usually as related to ability to answer central questions of the study.

Sample frame: Lists or collections of information about groups of people, either already existing or constructed by the researcher for the purpose of selecting the sample.

Sampling: Procedure for selecting cases or participants to study.

Saturation or redundancy: The point at which selection is ended; when new interviews seem to yield little additional information (Schutt, 2006).

Webinar: A workshop or lecture delivered over the Web. Webinars may be a one-way webcast, or there may be interaction between participants and presenters. VoIP audio, shared whiteboard, and shared applications may be used.

Preparing for a
Live Online Interview

6

If you begin tasks with the end result in mind, you will be more productive.

—Stephen Covey, 2004

After you study Chapter 6, you will be able to do the following:

- Understand steps needed to plan an online interview;
- Outline specific preparations needed based on technologies, and the type and research context of the online interview; and
- Describe the essential preinterview groundwork needed by online interviewers.

Planning to Interview

Once the researcher has divined a research purpose designed the study, considered ethical issues, obtained approval, planned for sampling, and recruited sample participants, it is time to move to the practical steps of interview planning and preparation. It has been shown in preceding chapters that online interview researchers can and should draw principles from relevant qualitative research methods and methodologies and adapt them as appropriate for use in online interview research. Interview preparation is no exception. This chapter draws relevant suggestions for interview preparation from research theorists and points to additional considerations for online interviewers.

Eliciting descriptions of experiences and perceptions of interviewees is the goal of any research interview. In-depth interaction with research participants should occur at each stage of the process: preparing to collect data, collecting data (see Chapter 7), and analyzing data (see the Appendix). Researchers are wise to see all communications conducted throughout the planning process, both informal and formal, as opportunities for building the relationship, comfort with the process, and trust in the interviewer.

This chapter explores three interrelated areas of interview preparation: preparing questions or discussion themes, preparing to use the interview technology, and individual preparation for the interviewer.

Preparing the Questions

Questioning is central to any interview. Whether the interview is structured, semistructured, or unstructured, the interviewer must discern how the interviewee can contribute insights needed to understand the research questions the study was designed to answer.

Researchers planning for structured or semistructured interviews will articulate all or most of the **main interview questions** in advance and plan the sequence for asking them. Open-ended questions solicit participants' stories, thoughts, and feelings. Researchers planning for structured or semistructured interviews may also ponder ways to encourage interviewees to dig deeper and determine how far they want to go with any particular question. Is it worth possibly sacrificing breadth and leaving some questions unasked if the interviewee wants to keep talking on one topic? If not, how will the interviewer encourage the participant to move on? Rubin and Rubin (2005) spell out a number of kinds of **probes**:

- Continuation probe encourages the interviewee to keep going with the current response.
- Elaboration probes ask for more explanation on a particular point.
- Attention probes ("Okay, I understand," etc.) let the interviewee know you are listening.
- Clarification probes ask for better definition or explanation if the researcher is confused or could not follow the thread of the story.
- Steering probes intend to get the story back on topic.

The sequence of main questions may be predetermined or arranged as the interview proceeds. Although subquestions, **follow-up questions,** or probes can be outlined in advance, the researcher will refine or add to the planned list as needed based on interviewee responses.

Researchers conducting semistructured interviews may develop an **interview guide**, a kind of "cheat sheet" to remind them of the key points to cover. Guides can be very detailed or simply list or outline the subject areas to be covered and key words the researcher wants to make sure to use when posing the question. Researchers can modify Moustakas' (1994) suggested list of questions to fit their own research designs (p. 116):

- What dimensions, incidents, and people connected with the experience stand out for you?

- How did the experience affect you? What changes do you associate with the experience?

- How did the experience affect significant others in your life?

- What feelings were generated by the experience?

- What thoughts stood out or are memorable?

- Have you shared all that is significant with reference to the experience?

Researchers at the unstructured end of the continuum approach the interview with the larger purpose for the inquiry in mind; they develop specific topics and articulate questions as the interview unfolds.

Whether the interviewer spells out each question or maps out key topics, if the interview is to be conducted online, the nature of the technology will influence the options for conveying the question, and receiving and responding to the answer. Will the participant be typing responses using text on a mobile device or chat software on a computer? Will the participant be speaking? Will the participant and interviewer be able to see each other's natural visage or an invented persona? Will they be able to observe and respond to visual examples or media? (See Chapter 8 for more about online visual methods.) Each is a distinctively different communication experience. This means selection of interview technology relates specifically to the kind of planning the interviewer needs in advance of the interview (see Figure 6.1).

Synchronous Technologies and Online Interview Preparation

CONSIDERATIONS FOR ICT SELECTION REVISITED

Synchronous communication allows interviewers and interviewees to interact in real time. Chapter 2 offered an overview of some types of ICTs researchers

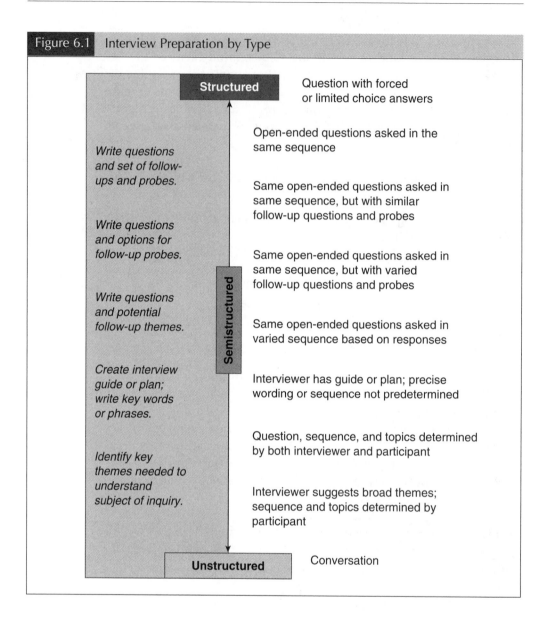

Figure 6.1   Interview Preparation by Type

can use for synchronous interviews. This book focuses on four main types of synchronous ICTs: text-based, videoconference or video call, multichannel meeting space, and 3-D immersive environment (see Figure 6.2).

The selection of technologies to use in the interview, and in other communications between researcher and participant, may depend on a variety of considerations. Besides the obvious practical matters of cost and access, technology selection may also be influenced by the research design and sampling plan.

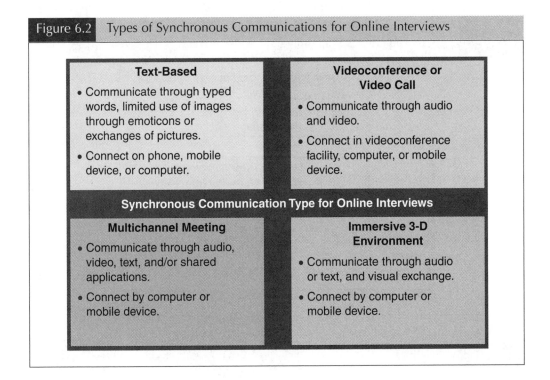

Figure 6.2   Types of Synchronous Communications for Online Interviews

When online interviews are conducted to investigate face-to-face phenomena then, as noted in Chapter 5, the online environment is the meeting venue, not subject of investigation.

Such a researcher may have limited opportunities to introduce unfamiliar technologies, and the participant may have limited interest in learning new ICTs. In this type of interview, access to and comfort with the tool might be the critical factors for success.

A different set of factors may influence technology choices for online interviews to investigate online behaviors, events, transactions, or experiences. Researchers may want to use the same tools the participants are using in the circumstances being studied. Would a researcher who wants to understand ways facilitators stimulate discussion in online meetings want to carry out the interview in the same meeting space? Using the same example, does the researcher also want to conduct some observations of the facilitator in action? Might the researcher find that conducting interviews in a variety of spaces positive or might it be impractical? Considering that each type of communication medium needs a slightly different preparation, researchers may want to offer a limited selection from which to choose.

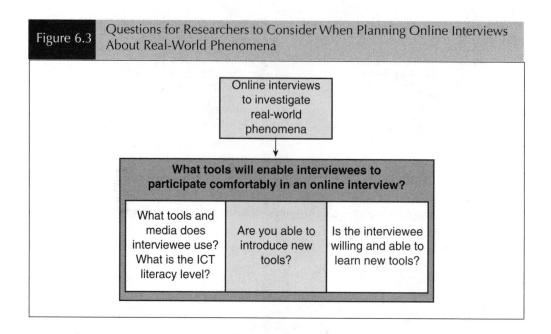

Figure 6.3   Questions for Researchers to Consider When Planning Online Interviews About Real-World Phenomena

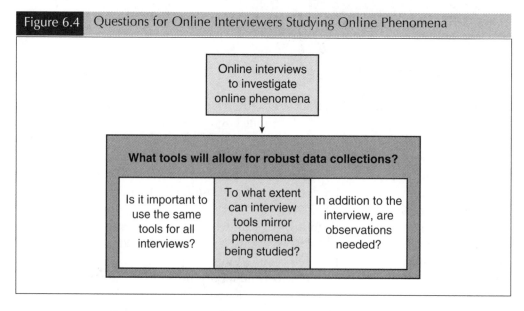

Figure 6.4   Questions for Online Interviewers Studying Online Phenomena

LEARNING THE ICT

Some ICTs require researchers to be actively involved in the management of the tool during the interview. Others, like text chat, are simple to operate or, like videoconferencing in a facility, involve technicians who manage the equipment. Researchers must be fully cognizant of the operation— and perils—of selected interview technologies. Communicating in the medium should come naturally by the time the first interaction with a participant occurs.

Practice interviews are essential, whether or not the researcher is familiar with the ICT. The ideal practice partner is candid and generous with constructive feedback. Researchers may benefit from practicing both roles: interviewer as well as interviewee. By taking the research participant's side the researcher may gain new insights about how to proceed.

It is important to anticipate types of technical problems and either learn to fix them, work around them, or find alternatives that could be quickly made available. Support information or troubleshooting tips must be reviewed. Technical support service phone numbers, links to live chat help, and turnaround time for assistance should be explored. User groups or forums may be helpful for finding solutions to common problems. Implications of last-minute changes must be considered. For example, if it is necessary to switch from VoIP to telephone, will a different recording mechanism be needed?

Preinterview communications with the research participant must include an assessment of the experience and comfort level with the selected technology or technologies. If possible, arrange a time when you can meet using the interview technology as part of the preparation. A brief online planning session and orientation to the software will reduce the pressure on both researcher and participant in the interview. This planning session can be used to reiterate expectations spelled out in the recruitment statement (Chapter 5) and to answer any remaining questions. Such informal dialogue is valuable for building the trust and relationship needed for productive and open dialogue in the interview.

Interview Preparation by Information and Communications Technology Type

Some preparation steps common to all and specific to ICT type are outlined here.

COMMON TO ALL ONLINE INTERVIEWS

- Establish protocols for the interview, including basic logistics. These may include agreement on signals to indicate need for more time to answer or time for a break.

- Confirm time frame, anticipated length for interview.

- Schedule time as needed to try the ICT prior to formal data collection.

- Schedule interview(s).

> **Ethics Tip:** Make sure all plans are consistent with the protocols laid out in preinterview discussions and verified in the consent agreement signed by the research participants.

PREPARING FOR A TEXT-BASED INTERVIEW

Text-only synchronous interviews use text messaging or chat. Text-based interviews are a good choice when the following are true:

- Social cues of the interviewee are not important information sources for the interviewer (Opdenakker, 2006);

- Visual anonymity is desired by interviewers (Fielding, 2007; Joinson, 2001);

- The sample population has closed or limited access (such as hospitals, religious communities, prisons, the military, and cults) (Opdenakker, 2006);

- The sample population is comfortable with and/or prefers mobile text-based communication;

- The nature of the research questions makes short responses an acceptable form of data; and

- A written record of the exact interview comments is beneficial.

Text communications have evolved from computer to mobile devices and mobile phone use, creating a nearly ubiquitous means of communication. Text-messaging systems began as basic exchanges of ASCII characters but have evolved to include a variety of fonts, text colors, emoticons, sound, as well as the capacity to attach, embed, or link to nontextual elements. Texters can have some limited visual exchange by sharing images—either photographs on file or those taken in the moment using camera features on the mobile device. (See Chapter 8 for more on visual artifacts in online interviews.) O'Sullivan and colleagues' (2004) research showed that participants gave higher ratings for immediacy when researchers used first-person pronouns, informal and casual language, and graphics, bold fonts with varying sizes, and colors in the text formatting. "The artifacts of the channels themselves are appropriated by users as expressive devices, and are applied to interpersonal purposes, in ways that become a language in and of themselves" (O'Sullivan et al., 2004, pp. 467–468).

To hurry along the slow process of typing conversation, texters use various shortcuts. Electronic paralinguistic expressions such as *lol* meaning "laugh(ing) out loud" or *ttyl* meaning "talk to you later" have evolved as part of a large system of shorthand. Text users allow emoticons as substitutes for social cues 😊. However, like facial expressions or gestures, they do not have universally shared meanings 😊. When an interviewer conducts a text-message interview with an interviewee with another cultural background or communication style, the interviewer must pay careful attention to the use of emoticons. It cannot be assumed that emoticons will be interpreted in a manner as meant by the interviewer 😨 (Opdenakker, 2006). Miscommunication can occur during a text interview when a participant is more competent in the use of emoticons or text abbreviations than the interviewer (O'Connor, 2006).

Even with the use of shortcuts, online interviews in the synchronous mode are slow. In one study, researchers reported that text-based synchronous interviews took about twice the length of in-person interviews and produced far fewer words. "A 120-minute online interview produced about seven pages of text. A 90-minute face-to-face interview produced 30 to 40 pages of text. The exchange of questions and responses was clearly influenced by the reading, reflection and typing skills of the respondents" (Davis, Bolding, Hart, Sherr, & Elford, 2004, p. 947). To adapt, they resorted to short, closed questions that fostered simple question-and-answer sequences (Davis et al., 2004).

Although the medium has limitations, Davis and colleagues (2004) observed the following:

> [T]he typed dialogue of online interviews can be seen as textual performance. As such, there is cause to argue that online interviewing is a distinctive social practice and should not be simply equated with FTF interviews. For example, data derived from online interviews are not properly represented as speech. Online interview data is textual performance mediated by the social and technical aspects of the Internet. (p. 949)

Another research team, Chen and Hinton (1999), similarly concluded that the text-based interview bridged an oral/written divide. Although clearly in written format, the type of interactions were very oral in nature, resembling a "written conversation" (Chen & Hinton, 1999). Researchers find this informal style promotes a fruitful exchange.

Variations on the text-only interview include using text chat in conjunction with other communication technologies. Text chat also can be used for interviews conducted in several episodes. Easy on-location access, without the need for special equipment, makes it possible for researchers and participants to check in and report on observations or experiences. For example, the interviewer and participant could log in for a couple of short questions on a daily or weekly basis, allowing data collection at strategic times relevant to the purpose of the study.

To prepare for a text-based interview, one should do the following:

- Select a text interview technology with which participants are familiar; discuss platform choice as part of consent agreement.

- Familiarize yourself with communications options in that setting; review archiving function for saving transcript.

- Familiarize yourself with electronic paralinguistic expressions, emoticons, or other communication shortcuts or slang used by the target population. Decide how you will use these shortcuts to save time and keep the conversation moving.

- Articulate a greater number of questions that elicit shorter responses; break big questions into a series of subquestions.

- Write out questions or key phrases in advance so you can cut and paste them into the text window to save time and keep interview flowing.

- Provide any background information in advance so you can move quickly into a dynamic exchange.

PREPARING FOR A VIDEO INTERVIEW

Not long ago studios with costly setups were the only way to meet via video-conference. However, desktop and even mobile videoconferencing options are emerging with the advent of low-cost Web cameras and free online services. Facilities, including videoconference/integrated classrooms, offices, and meeting rooms offer high-quality options for research purposes. Multiple cameras and assistance of trained technicians mean videoconferencing facilities enable either close-up or room visibility, can accommodate groups, or allow for complex interactions or the presence of observers. Many multisite businesses, governmental agencies, and educational institutions have invested in such videoconferencing systems. Per-session rentals are available at commercial sites such as office and business services.

Movement toward greater access and flexibility for desktop videoconferencing is advantageous for interview researchers with small budgets or those without access to such facilities. Many text messaging and chat services now allow users to plug in a Web camera; others such as Skype offer two-way audio, video, and chat in free Internet calls. Depending on whether the technology is a videoconference facility or video call, the researcher will need to decide whether a close-up, waist-up, or wider picture of the person in the room will work best. Testing the setup and communications options is a crucial part of preparation. Additional points include the following:

- Experiment with setup and camera positioning options.

- Review other features, such as text chat or areas for presenting visuals, and determine whether or how to use them in the interview.

- Decide how you want to present yourself. Just as in a face-to-face live interview, the background, your attire, and style all convey messages.

- Carefully review questions or interview guide so you can minimize the need to look down at notes. Take the time, before looking down to read notes, to make the best "virtual eye contact" possible.

- Discuss options and parameters for participant's Web camera. Is it acceptable for the participant to turn the camera off and use audio only?

- If using a facility where others (technicians, camera operators) will be present, determine policies for confidentiality. Depending on the setting and policies, you may decide to ask intimate questions in another way.

PREPARING TO INTERVIEW IN A MEETING SPACE

Online meeting or conferencing platforms integrate text chat, audio, and videoconferencing functions with various combinations of tools that may include shared applications and shared whiteboard. To prepare for an interview in an online meeting space, the researcher reviews the various communication features to determine which to use to convey questions, and what options to make available to interviewees. How will visual, verbal, and/or text options be utilized? (See Chapter 7 for more discussion of communication during the interview and Chapter 8 for discussion of visual methods in online meeting spaces.) The entire interaction is captured and archived, thus providing a data record for the researcher to review and analyze.

Such software suites are typically used for online meetings in business or for instructional purposes. Some are fee-based or subscription services such as Elluminate, Adobe Connect, Live Meeting, or WebEx. These services often offer free or low-cost versions for personal use. Other ad-supported or nonprofit services also are available.

When people log in to an online meeting space, they typically see a screen divided into different areas, with space for text chat, various toolbars for drawing and writing, and icons linking to other services. These links allow researchers and participants to view and comment on websites, documents, media, or applications. A central workspace can be used to show PowerPoint slides, diagrams, photographs, or other visual elements. Text and videoconference applications have been discussed earlier in this chapter, and the visual research potential for the shared whiteboard is addressed in Chapter 8. Three other components found in most online meeting platforms are considered here: the central workspace, shared applications, and the Web tour.

The central workspace can be used to share written or visual details about the study. Key points about the study's purpose or background can be reviewed and discussed by researcher and participant. Interview questions or themes can be presented in the workspace, one by one. For a structured or semistructured interview, questions or key discussion topics can be written on PowerPoint slides in advance of the interview. This allows the interviewer to focus on the conversation, without the need to cut and paste from another document or type during the interview.

For less structured interviews, themes for discussion can be written, diagrammed, or illustrated on the shared whiteboard during the interview. Because questions are communicated both verbally and in writing, participants who are more visually or aurally oriented can grasp them.

In addition to straightforward questions and answers, the shared applications or Web tour features enable the interviewer and/or interviewee to share and discuss media clips, websites, software applications, documents, or other artifacts that illustrate the phenomena under investigation. All elements the researcher intends to share must be selected and tested in advance of the interview. Any intellectual property issues, such as permissions for use of images or media, should be obtained before finalizing the interview plans.

The main issue that is both an advantage and a disadvantage of the meeting space is the diversity of tools, which some researchers may find overwhelming. With a little practice, researchers can overcome this potential challenge. Highly engaged participants may be less likely to exit out of the interview prematurely. Diverse options for communication make the online meeting environment an ideal choice for the interviewer who wants to cultivate answers from and with participants as the metaphorical gardener or explore answers by traveling through the interview with the participant.

Once the tools, process, and approach have been selected, steps to prepare for the interview include the following:

- Check audio features. If the space allows for only one speaker at a time, determine protocols for turn-taking in conversation and include in preinterview run-through.

- Check recording/archiving features.

- Select or develop relevant diagrams, illustrations, examples, photographs, visual maps, and so on that can be used to show, rather than ask or tell, the participant what you want to discuss. (See Chapter 8 for more discussion of visual methods in online interviews.)

- Some platforms allow for PowerPoint slides, while others allow for shared documents. In addition to posing questions using audio, questions or key topics can be written out on the shared whiteboard. If this approach will be used, develop the slides and documents.

- Some platforms allow media, such as video clips, to be shown. If you are using media, make sure you can easily access, run, and close out of the media and back into the main discussion area.

- Review interactive features of platform; can any of them be used in the course of the interview? These could include asking participants to draw or diagram answers to some questions.

If the meeting space allows for a webcam option, add the following preparations:

- Follow preparatory steps for videoconferencing.

- Practice using the webcam.

- Adjust the webcam to allow for close-up view.

- Determine whether you want to use the webcam during all or part of the interview. For example, you could use the webcam to make contact in the introduction and then turn it off.

- Decide who gets to choose when and how to use the webcam. This decision may be one to discuss in advance of the interview.

PREPARING TO INTERVIEW IN A
3-D IMMERSIVE ENVIRONMENT

Preparing for an interview includes creating (or updating) an avatar that represents the researcher. Williams (2007) calls the avatar a "graphical pseudo-presence." The avatar "explicitly communicates a wealth of information upon the observer's online identity. The choice of pseudonym for the day and the dress and stature of the avatar chosen impact on how the observed react to the observer" (Williams, 2007, p. 11).

Messinger's research team draws on earlier theories by Hull (1943), Kaplan (1975), Swann (1987), and Swann, Pelham, & Krull (1989) to analyze whether people act more in accordance with motives for *self-enhancement* or *self-verification* when creating avatars. Self-enhancement theory is based on the notion that individuals are motivated to promote a positive self-concept and solicit positive feedback from others. People with negative self-views tend to distort personal information in a positive direction, referred to as *compensatory self-enhancement.* In contrast, self-verification theory contends that people are motivated to maintain a consistent self-concept, preserve the truth about them, and seek objective feedback from others. People are motivated to self-verify because portraying one's self-concept in a stable, self-congruent manner bolsters a person's confidence in predicting and controlling the world, and facilitates social interactions (Messinger, Ge, Stroulia, Lyons, & Smirnov, 2008). Messinger et al. (2008) found that people generally balance motives for self-verification and self-enhancement, customizing their avatars to bear similarity to their real selves, with moderate enhancements. Researchers need to decide how to present themselves as an avatar. Additional preparation points include the following:

- Test your "image" with colleagues or friends to assess whether you convey the persona you intend to present to research participants.

- Familiarize yourself with Second Life functions and protocols, including teleporting and sharing items with other avatars.

- Decide where and how to conduct the interview. If you create a space, consider making it private and requiring permission to enter (make sure space is large enough so that audio exchanges are out of range of others who could eavesdrop).

- If it is not your own property, make arrangements to use it for interview purposes. Make sure to schedule and plan to minimize the likelihood that others could be present and eavesdrop.

- If you select a place like a library or academic meeting area, determine what ethical expectations are established by the setting.

> **Ethics Tip:** If you want to collect data through observation, the style of avatar chosen by the participant, or the space built by the participant, make sure you have asked for permission in the consent agreement.

> **Ethics Tip:** If you want to collect data on the participants' activities, group memberships, and so on by reviewing their profiles or other information, make sure you have asked for permission in the consent agreement.

- Make sure participant has all information needed, including meeting place.
- Offer to meet ahead of the interview, so both researcher and participant are familiar with the location and features. If you decide to meet on the participant's property, ask to visit in advance of the interview.
- Decide whether to use text chat or audio features for dialogue in the interview.
- If you are using text, see suggestions for text-based interviews.
- If using VoIP or telephone, check audio operations. Arrange for audio recording.

Getting Ready to Interview

As noted, the online interviewer has three kinds of preparation to make: one is related to preparing questions or discussion themes apropos to the empirical and theoretical basis of the study; a second is related to preparation for use of selected technology; the third is the personal preparation needed to serve as guide and facilitator of the interview—the person behind the monitor in a human-to-human conversation with a purpose.

DEFINING ROLES

Earlier sections have explored researchers' roles in terms of the miner who excavates information, the gardener who cultivates exchange, or the traveler who journeys with the participant (see Chapter 3). Researchers need to have clear intentions in mind. They also need to consider how participants perceive them. Rubin and Rubin (2005) point out that people relate to one another through culturally understood roles in which obligations and responsibilities are known to both parties. In establishing an acceptable role as researcher, it is important to decide how you want to present yourself and how much of your own experience you want to share. In the online interview, unless a full videoconferencing system is used, your visual image may be limited and as a result may seem even more significant. What image do you want to convey as it relates to your role in this study?

EPOCHE, SELF-REFLECTION, AND PREPARING TO LISTEN

As researcher it is important to approach each interview with a clear and fresh perspective; this is what phenomenological researchers call **Epoche** (Moustakas, 1994). Whatever methodological tradition guides the study, starting with an open mind is important for data collection through interview research.

Moustakas (1994) points out that Epoche is "preparation for deriving new knowledge" by listening without expectations for any particular outcome (p. 85). "In the Epoch, we set aside our prejudgments, biases, and preconceived ideas about things" (p. 85). It is of course impossible to pretend that researchers have no biases and can listen to answers without sifting through their own experiences and cultural lenses. Rubin and Rubin (2005) suggest that self-reflection is essential; researchers need to continually examine their own understandings and reactions" (p. 31). Moustakas (1994) calls this being "transparent to ourselves" (p. 86).

The attitude of Epoche emerges when the researcher is self-aware and sets aside time to mentally refresh before beginning an interview. The attitude of Epoche emerges when the researcher has sense of deep respect and appreciation for the unique contribution of each participant. When online researchers are confident about the intended direction for questioning and the smooth application of the ICTs, they enter the interview ready to listen deeply and respectfully to the participant.

With ongoing self-reflection and Epoche, each new interview is a fresh experience. This kind of preparation is needed before each interview. Once the interviewer has conducted several interviews certain responses to particular questions may be anticipated; the interviewer who has made a conscious effort to set preconceived notions aside may hear subtle or profound nuances that might otherwise be overlooked.

Closing Thoughts

Preparing for an online interview involves personal, theoretical, and technical steps for the researcher and participant. The exchanges throughout the process—whether routine or substantive—should be seen as meaningful aspects of the overall research relationship. The exchange begins when the researcher describes the study, clarifies expectations, and obtains informed consent agreements (see Chapter 4). The process of planning for the interview offers additional opportunities to communicate and build trust, which are foundational to the successful research interview.

In Chapter 3's discussion of interview structure, a range of very structured to very unstructured interviews were defined. Some interviewers prefer an unstructured conversational style of interviewing. Online, even these interviewers will do best by writing out key phrases or themes in advance if text will be used in the interview.

Although new tools for communication will undoubtedly appear, the basic distinctions of synchronous and asynchronous, visual, and text-based will likely persist. Decisions about the ICT and means of communication are closely interwoven with the research purpose, methodology, and theoretical framework. There is no simple recipe for how to mix them; finding the right synergy will be part of the learning and new knowledge to result from the study.

Researchers' Notebook: Stories of Online Inquiry

Interviews for my study on collaborative e-learning took place online in a virtual meeting space. The Elluminate platform allows for dialogue through VoIP two-way audio, text chat, and shared whiteboard. To prepare for these interviews, I took several important steps. In advance of data collection, three informal focus groups were conducted with educators. These focus groups were not part of the data collection; they were intended as a test for both content and process prior to the actual research interviews. I also carried out preinterview discussions with each research participant.

A TEST RUN: FOCUS GROUPS

The sessions each lasted from forty minutes to one hour. Each session involved three to five participants. Participants self-selected based on notices posted in the online communities where educators with a shared interest in technology congregate. Participants were comparable with the target group of research participants in regard to key criteria; that is, they were all experienced online educators with an interest in collaborative methods. Similar to the research participants, the focus group participants represented an international mix.

The sessions utilized the same approaches planned for the interviews. The working definition of collaborative e-learning and the Taxonomy of Online Collaboration (Salmons, 2010) model and conceptual framework were presented through visual images on PowerPoint slides with verbal descriptions. Open-ended questions were posed to participants, who were able to respond by text message, VoIP, and by writing or drawing on the shared whiteboard.

The preresearch focus groups accomplished two important objectives:

- They allowed me the opportunity to practice in the role of questioner and facilitator on the Elluminate platform.
- They allowed me to introduce the definition of collaborative e-learning, the prototype Taxonomy of Online Collaboration, and some of the interview questions and themes to educators.

It was possible to discern that the conceptual framework of the design was understandable to people with no previous exposure to it. Participants did not request additional explanations of the taxonomy elements or levels. Comments such as "These categories or levels are great and well articulated" and "I agree with your dual focus on the content objectives and the ICT goals and process you have laid out" indicated that the description of the taxonomy and its purpose were clear. The interactive, participatory exchange among participants showed effectiveness of the Taxonomy of Online Collaboration as a stimulus for discussion of collaborative teaching methods. This conclusion was verified by the fact that additional sessions were requested so others could attend. These sessions allowed for experimentation with interactive features of the platform; some of them, including the shared whiteboard, were later used to enhance interview dialogue.

PREINTERVIEW DISCUSSIONS

Prior to the interviews, selection criteria and agreements were discussed with research participants and any questions about the process were answered. Research participants were provided with the working definition of collaborative e-learning, the prototype Taxonomy of Online Collaboration, interview topics, and questions. Research participants were encouraged to select a course or program of study to discuss in the interview that best demonstrated collaborative methods of teaching and learning, where more than one level of collaboration was practiced.

The organization and intended purpose for the taxonomy were discussed with research participants. I emphasized that while like most taxonomies, it is organized systematically from simple to complex, with increasing complexity at each level, the sequence presented in the prototype was not fixed. I also emphasized the organization of the Taxonomy of Online Collaboration should be changed depending on research participants' recommendations. The preinterview included a discussion of the ethical framework of the research. All research participants signed the informed consent form.

These preparatory steps resulted in greater confidence on my part and readiness on research participants' part for lively and generative online interviews.

Key Concepts

- Quality of interview research outcomes depends on data contributed by research participants. Establishing productive communications using online technology requires careful planning.
- Whether the inquiry is designed to study online behaviors or face-to-face behaviors may shape the choice of technology tool for conducting online interviews.
- Regardless of technology, the interview researcher must be self-aware and take time to reflect on his or her role as well as biases or presumptions that could influence the way participants' remarks are understood.

Discussions and Assignments

1. Identify an ICT you are interested in using for an online interview. Discuss the specific options available for communicating, how you would use them, and steps you would take to prepare.

2. Create a planning timeline and checklist for an online interview using the ICTs you plan to use.

3. Discuss the concept of Epoche. What could you do to clear your mind in readiness for an online interview?

4. Discuss the point made by Rubin and Rubin (2005): people relate to one another through culturally understood roles in which obligations and responsibilities are known to both parties. When the interview occurs online, how do people know "culturally understood roles" and agree to obligations and responsibilities? Identify any steps researchers (or participants) should make in the planning phase.

On the Book's Website

- Checklists and materials to help you prepare for your interviews

Terms

Epoche: "Setting aside prejudgments and opening the research interview with unbiased, receptive presence" (Moustakas, 1994, p. 85).

Follow-up questions: Follow-up questions build on interviewee responses to get a clearer or deeper understanding of the interviewee's response.

Interview guide: A list or outline of key themes to cover during the interview.

Main interview questions: Main interview questions are articulated to elicit overall experiences and understandings.

Probes: Probes encourage the interviewee to provide detail to flesh out and expand on the answer.

- A continuation probe encourages the interviewee to keep going with the current response.
- Elaboration probes ask for more explanation on a particular point.
- Attention probes ("Okay, I understand," and so on) let the interviewee know you are listening.
- Clarification probes ask for better definition or explanation if the researcher is confused or could not follow the thread of the story.
- Steering probes intend to get the story back on topic (Rubin & Rubin, 2005).

Conducting the Synchronous Online Interview

7

The important thing is not to stop questioning. Curiosity has its own reason for existing. One cannot help but be in awe when he contemplates the mysteries of eternity, of life, of the marvelous structure of reality. It is enough if one tries merely to comprehend a little of this mystery every day. Never lose a holy curiosity.

—Albert Einstein, 1879–1955

Always be suspicious of data collection that goes according to plan.

—Michael Q. Patton, 2002

After studying Chapter 7, you will be able to do the following:

- Summarize roles and responsibilities of the interviewer during the interview;
- Describe essential practices for conducting a productive research interview; and
- Conduct a research interview using synchronous technologies.

After contemplating options for technology in Chapter 2, interview approach in Chapter 3, ethical issues in Chapter 4, sampling and recruiting in Chapter 5, and preparation in Chapter 6, you are ready to explore practical steps for conducting an online research interview in this chapter. Such interviews use tools that allow interviewer and participant to communicate with text, audio, visual, or immersive technologies. Chapter 8 continues the discussion of data collection with a focus on conducting online interviews that involve highly visual interactions and visual artifacts to collect visual data.

The Interviewer and the Interview

The moment comes when dreaming, training, practicing, and rehearsing are through. The athlete stands poised at the end of a diving board with an Olympic audience's attention, the actor takes the stage, the nervous lover pulls a ring from his pocket—and it is time for action. Similarly, the researcher moves from intellectual exploration of literature and theory to the moment when the very real research participant is there, anticipating a question that will launch the interview. At that moment the researcher must begin to actualize the purpose of the study and, as Denzin (2001) describes it, "Bring the world into play" (p. 25). The way the researcher proceeds is guided by design decisions and interview structure and approach—and by the researcher's own relational style.

Interview research success depends on the interviewer's personal and professional, affective and cognitive skills. Clandinin and Connelly (2000) observe that the "way an interviewer acts, questions, and responds in an interview shapes the relationship and therefore the ways participants respond and give accounts of their experience" (p. 110). Mason (2002) warns that "it is all too easy to orchestrate a pleasant social encounter whose content has little or no bearing on the intellectual puzzle which the research is designed to address" (p. 67). Clearly a skilled interviewer balances content and process, and active or neutral stances when collecting data through interviews.

Each research methodology associates slightly different expectations for the interviewer. In general, those working in the more structured interview genres expect the interviewer to mine for data and "avoid shaping the information that is extracted. . . . Interviewers are generally expected to keep their 'selves' out of the interview process" (Gubrium & Holstein, 2003a, p. 31). These interviewers aim for a greater degree of neutrality. Patton (2002) defines neutrality as follows: "The person being interviewed can tell me anything without engendering either my favor or disfavor with regard to the content of her or his response. I cannot be shocked; I cannot be angered; I cannot be embarrassed; I cannot be saddened. Nothing the person tells me will make me think more or less of the person" (p. 365). This is not an insignificant matter. Interviewers want to draw out stories that interviewees are reluctant to share with others. As a result they may find themselves called upon to move into "realities that are not only different from one's own but also surprising, alien, uncomfortable, a direct challenge to one's thinking, disgusting, horrifying, anxiety-provoking, boring or otherwise difficult" (Rosenblatt, 2003, p. 229). Maintaining some level of nonjudgmental openness can be a challenge for interviewers who are studying cultures or circumstances greatly different from their own.

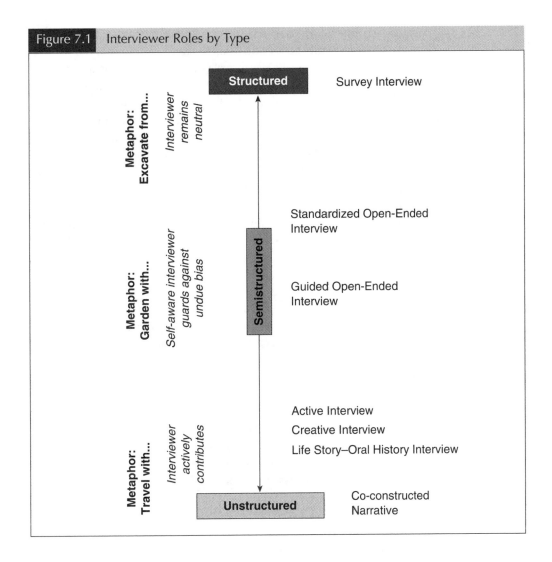

Figure 7.1   Interviewer Roles by Type

Interviewers who want to cultivate exchange in semistructured interviews, using the "garden" metaphor, should be self-aware enough to listen without "sifting answers through their own experiences and cultural lenses" (Rubin & Rubin, 2005, p. 31). Rubin and Rubin (2005) suggest active interviewer involvement balanced enough with care to guard against allowing emotions or empathy with the interviewee to influence questioning—or interpreting answers. To achieve this balance—being involved but not too involved—researchers must engage in continuous honest reflection not only to identify biases and assumptions, but to think about how this background shapes the research focus and show how those reflections lead to insights (Baym, 2009). This clear-minded openness was described as "Epoche" in the Chapter 6 description of interview preparation.

Postmodern interviewers who aim to cocreate narratives by traveling with research participants believe neutrality is neither desirable nor achievable. As Fontana and Frey (2003) observe, "Asking questions and getting answers is a much harder task than it may seem at first. The spoken or written word always has a residue of ambiguity, no matter how carefully we word the questions" (p. 697). Postmodern interviewers look for ways to work with participants to generate knowledge from positions within the interview (Gubrium & Holstein, 2003a). Interviewers need to consider the nature of the research and characteristics of the sample population and to adopt an approach that suits the design and nature of the study.

Regardless of methodological approach, the core activity is the same for any interviewer: to engage in dialogue with the research participant with the purpose of data collection. And regardless of epistemological or methodological stance, the interviewer is responsible for the interview and must take this role seriously. Kvale (2006) argues the following:

> It may be concluded that a research interview is not an open and dominance-free dialogue between egalitarian partners, but a specific hierarchical and instrumental form of conversation, where the interviewer sets the stage and scripts in accord with his or her research interests. The use of power in interviews to produce knowledge is a valuable and legitimate way of conducting research. (p. 485)

Some researchers may chafe at this description of the power dynamic of the interview. But undoubtedly identifying clear research questions and an appropriate design are the job of the researcher, as are the steps involved in preparing for, carrying out interviews, and ultimately analyzing the data to answer the research questions. Given the power inherent in the role comes responsibility for self-awareness, fairness, and respect for the research participant.

Research participants are not without power in the interview. Kvale and Knapik offer these observations:

> The interview subjects have their own countering options of not answering or deflecting a question, talking about something other than what the interviewer asks for, or merely telling what they believe the interviewer wants to hear. (Kvale, 2006, p. 485)

> Although participants do have fewer opportunities to explain what is salient for them when interactions are more structured, it does not make sense to assume that responsiveness is eliminated. Answers might still be chosen in response to what is salient for them in the moment or for their anticipated futures (e.g., cherished self-descriptions, perceived goals of the research, what the question is really asking). (Knapik, 2006, p. 6)

Knapik (2006) studied the perceptions of the interview from the perspectives of participants, whose comments are useful for those considering interviewer styles and approaches. Participants in Knapnik's study observed that the way they reported their experience of the phenomenon of interest in their research interviews was influenced by "continually updated understandings that resulted from their active monitoring of researchers' reactions" (Knapik, 2006, p. 6). In one example, the researcher's expression of surprise indicated to one participant that he was providing an account that ran contrary to her expectations. The participant described how "subsequent back-and-forth exchanges supported his growing sense that his unexpected account was more problematic than interesting for the researcher" (p. 5). Two of her participants expressed a concern that becoming aware of the possibility that their account would contribute to existing stereotypes—a concern that their comments might be misrepresented and too easily categorized. In both cases, this perception had a dampening effect on the participants and limited their willingness for greater self-disclosure (p. 7).

Knapik observed that we can compromise both quality and ethics when we make interviewees' spontaneous reactions a problem to be managed. She warns that the interviewer needs to be flexible and open to the possibility that what might be seen as the participant derailing the interview may actually be an opportunity to collect data on new aspects of the phenomena. She said, "I do not wish to negate the importance of developing guidelines for researchers; focusing on imperatives can leave unacknowledged the level of improvisation that is inevitably needed and ultimately desirable" (Knapik, 2006, p. 6). Gubrium and Koro-Ljungberg (2005) make a similar point:

> [Q]ualitative researchers are dependent on participant engagement—silences, pauses, refusals to answer, and misunderstandings. On one hand, some engagements can limit the involvement of the participant, thus violating the interactiveness of the interview, but on the other hand, these engagements are the participants' means to share or take over control and power during interviews. . . . [F]rom the social constructionist perspective, if researchers do not relinquish some control during the interview, they limit their data and research process. (p. 696)

Awareness of these issues is essential for the online interviewer because, as was noted in Chapter 1, research participants can withdraw from an online interview with one click. Online interviewers have a narrower margin of error when it comes to engaging—or alienating—research participants.

To collect data through a purposeful interview Ritchie and Lewis (2002) and Mason (2002) point out that a researcher must do the following:

- *Establish credibility* so the interviewee is assured of the professionalism and legitimate uses intended for the data.

- *Demonstrate respect for the interviewee* to engender trust and comfort needed to reveal personal views or experiences.

- *Listen* actively and reflectively, and decide whether to dig deeper or move on to another topic. Find a balance between talking and listening.

- *Think clearly, logically, and in the moment.* The less structured the approach, the more decisions about the content and sequence need to be made spontaneously within the interview. Flexibility and willingness to change from prepared questions and going with the interview flow is essential.

- *Remember* what has been said and make a mental note so it is possible to make a timely return to points made earlier in the interview.

- *Be curious* and show interest in the topic of inquiry.

The online interview researcher demonstrates all of these skills and attitudes in communications carried out using selected ICTs. The online interviewer's role as the curious, respectful active listener further emphasizes the importance of developing social presence with the research participant. According to Ross (2001):

> Social presence is an individual's ability to demonstrate his/her state of being in a virtual environment and so signal his/her availability for interpersonal transactions. Social presence is the means by which online participants inhabit virtual spaces and indicate not only their presence in the online environment but also their availability and willingness to engage in the communicative exchanges. (p. 94)

Shin (2002), drawing on the work of Lombard and Ditton (1997), points out:

> Presence, as social richness, involves the degree to which media are capable of making users perceive other users' sociability, warmth, sensitivity, personality, or closeness in a mediated communication situation. (p. 124)

Online interviewers will most likely use a mix of written, audio, and visual communications so will need to consider how to develop social presence in each respective medium. Participants' willingness to follow the researcher's agenda or their interest in exerting control over the interview in different directions may be influenced to some extent by their expectations for online participation generally. Bakardjieva (2005) characterizes two distinct orientations toward the social character of the Internet: the consumption model and the community model. The consumption model emerged when online libraries and publications began to offer Internet consumers an unlimited supply of data and media. Such users see the social Web as a place to access and share information. The community model emerged when users found ways to build online networks and use interactive capabilities for communicating and collaborating with families, friends, and colleagues

(Bakardjieva, 2005, p. 165). They see the social Web as a place where they can contribute user-generated information. They seek affiliation with others who share common interests, rather than efficiency in finding answers (O'Sullivan et al., 2004). Understanding whether the study's sample population are more likely to see their relation to the Internet as either consumers or generators of Web-based resources may help the interviewer plan accordingly and be more successful at engaging participants.

Self-presentation and impression formation can influence research relationships, and thus take on new significance in the online environment. The face-to-face interviewer might think about issues of identity and credibility when deciding how to present him- or herself. What to wear—will professional or casual dress create the appropriate impression? Should the researcher aim to appear as similar as possible to the research participants and emphasize their common characteristics? The online interviewer must decide whether, when, and how to share his or her pictures. O'Sullivan and colleagues' 2004 research on Dimensions of **Mediated Immediacy** in online communications points to similarity, informality, and self-disclosure as important "approachability cues" that signal to others that "you can approach me" (p. 472). Their findings showed that people were perceived online as friendly and open when they self-disclosed some personal information and shared photos portraying experiences outside their official role in informal postures or settings (p. 473).

When considering what kinds of pictures to share—still, moving, graphical—it is important for interviewers to clarify the intended purpose and desired impression. Researchers may want to share their pictures in order to establish credibility and reinforce the fact that a responsible, caring human exists on the other side of the monitor. Pictures can help build a more personal relationship, establish rapport, and create social presence. On the practical side there are numerous ways to share pictures online. A research website, blog, or wiki could offer photographs of the interviewer. The researcher should be aware that informal photographs (and personal information from the nonprofessional side of life) posted online may be accessed by curious research participants.

Photographs could be shared as part of preinterview preparation or when introducing the study during the interview. Any medium chosen for dialogue, even text-based channels, offers file-sharing for digital picture exchange. Multichannel meeting groupware or videoconferences allow interviewers to share live, real-time images. Interviewers working in immersive virtual environments have an additional challenge when determining what avatar characteristics are appropriate given the context and culture of the setting for the interview. No firm guidelines exist for such interviewers. Observations of avatars in similar environments or observations of representations used by the target population may offer some clues about whether more realistic or fanciful images would best serve the research purpose.

Although some interviewers believe using visual images (whether real or graphic) adds to the richness of the exchange, other researchers report that lack of visual identification can have advantages. "[Visual] anonymity in text-based CMC [Computer Mediated Communication] can encourage response in research on sensitive topics" (Fielding, 2007, p. 20). Another researcher made a similar observation: "CMC discussions proved to have higher levels of spontaneous self-disclosure than face-to-face discussions. And visually anonymous participants disclosed significantly more information about themselves than non-visually anonymous participants did" (Joinson, 2001, p. 23). Some welcome the opportunity for online social spaces that are "free of the constraints of the body, (so) you are accepted on the basis of your written words, not what you look like or sound like or where you live" (Kitchen, 1998, p. 387).

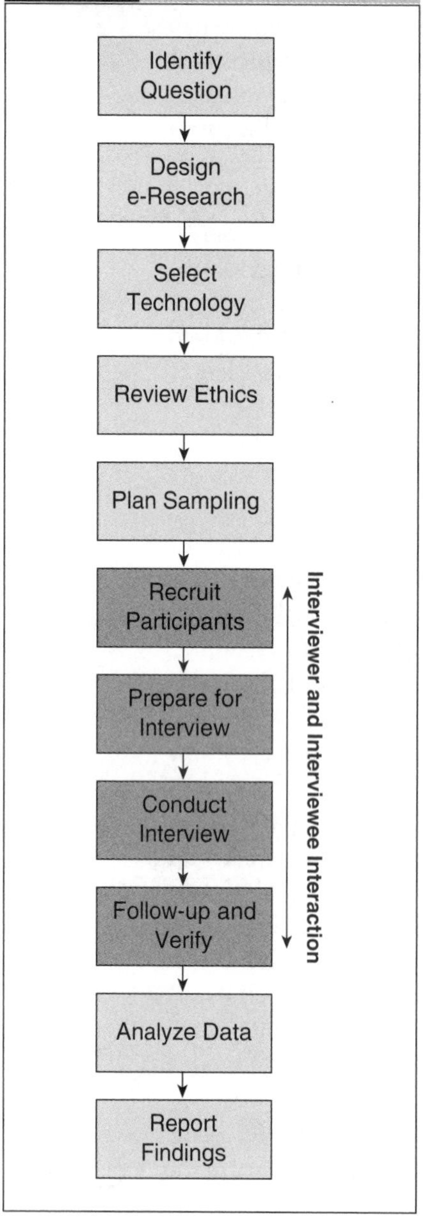

Whether through words or images, the extent and type of self-disclosure is a consideration for all interviewers. Online, understanding of the sample population may help interviewers decide what will contribute to, or detract from, the social presence and trusting communication necessary for productive interviews.

Mason (2002) recommends that interviewers practice skills, taking steps such as recording and listening to pilot or rehearsal interviews. As noted in Chapter 6, a part of preparation may involve rehearsing with fellow researchers (or fellow students), friends, or colleagues who will provide candid feedback. Such practice is even more essential for the online researcher, who must be confident and fluent in the selected technology tools before conducting interviews with research participants. The online interviewer also may ask for feedback on impressions conveyed by written and visual communications. Another suggestion is to ask a colleague or more experienced interviewer to observe a practice interview or interview recording and offer suggestions.

In large studies multiple interviewers may be involved in data collection. But typically the interviewer also is the researcher, the person who designed the study and will analyze the results. As

Figure 7.2   Building Connections in All Interactions

- Identify Question
- Design e-Research
- Select Technology
- Review Ethics
- Plan Sampling
- Recruit Participants
- Prepare for Interview
- Conduct Interview
- Follow-up and Verify
- Analyze Data
- Report Findings

Interviewer and Interviewee Interaction

such, the interviewer has many opportunities to interact with research participants. Each step, from initial contact, negotiation of consent to participate, through interview and follow-up, offers the interviewer opportunities to build the research relationship and listen and learn from the research participant.

Conducting a Research Interview

Some researchers lay out the entire interview prior to the session and articulate some or all questions and sequence in advance. Others create a plan or guide to refer to and use the list of topics to word questions during the interview. A conversational style is used by those who prefer to allow the interview to flow in its own unique way. As discussed in Chapter 3, schools of thought and practice exist for each approach, and, as discussed in Chapter 6, some level of preparation is associated with each. On the practical side, all interviewers share a common need: to begin, carry out, and end the interview. Even when researchers conduct interviews with a flexible sequence, they will want to consider the overall flow (Arthur & Nazroo, 2003; Rubin & Rubin, 2005).

For simplicity's sake, four interview stages are defined here as *Opening, Questioning and Guiding, Closing,* and *Following Up.* While steps taken within these stages may vary depending on the purpose, structure, or approach of the interview, principles discussed here apply in most cases. Each interviewer can adapt them to fit the style and communication technology used in the study.

Ethics Tip: Make sure interview steps and approaches are consistent with the protocols laid out in preinterview discussions and verified in the consent agreement signed by the research participants.

OPENING THE INTERVIEW

The introduction allows the interviewer to build on preinterview communication and set the style and pace. Three main tasks should be accomplished: reintroducing the study and its purpose, establishing protocols, and developing rapport. The interviewer reminds the participant of the research previously discussed during recruitment and preparation stage and acknowledged in the consent agreement. Significance of the experience and perspectives of the participant to the study are recognized, and appreciation for potential contribution to new understandings and knowledge is conveyed. Protocols, expectations, and ground rules for both parties are discussed. These may include confidentiality, recording, or note-taking during the interview, timing, or breaks.

Rapport means "an understanding, one established on a basis of respect and trust between an interviewer and respondent" (Gray, 2004, p. 22). It also means "establishing a safe and comfortable environment for sharing the interviewee's personal experiences and attitudes as they actually occurred" (DiCicco-Bloom & Crabtree, 2006, p. 316).

Interviewers may try to establish rapport before the interview, beginning warm and open communication to start relationship-building with the initial contact. Beginning the interview with some informal conversation or a simple "How are you?" check-in with the research participant can help set the stage for the interview. Inviting the participant to ask for clarification on any issues related to interview participation before beginning formal questioning can help to clear away unresolved matters that could distract the participant. A formula does not exist that reliably contributes to rapport and a perception of safety. Personal qualities, social identities, characteristics, and/or chemistry make one person seem trustworthy and another not.

QUESTIONING AND GUIDING

The interviewer may ask research participants direct or indirect questions, suggest themes for discussion, or otherwise guide the conversation. Research questions and the purpose of the study typically inform the questions including both content and types of questions or conversation themes. Usually interviews include several approaches to allow researchers to collect data of the depth and breadth needed to answer the research questions. Ritchie and Lewis (2003) describe questioning as a process of "mapping." To open a new topic, "ground mapping questions" help the researcher identify relevant issues and generate multiple dimensions of the subject of inquiry. To focus the participant more narrowly on particular topics or concepts raised in response to ground-mapping questions, "dimension-mapping questions" are posed. "Perspective mapping" questions are used to encourage interviewees to look at issues from different perspectives, to gain more richness and context. Probes for the purpose of "content mining" explore detail and allow the interviewer to "obtain a full description of phenomena, understanding what underpins the participant's attitude or behavior" (Ritchie & Lewis, 2003, p. 150). Patton (2002) looks at the process a little differently. He distinguishes between five kinds of questions, including background and demographic questions as well as the following:

- Opinion and values questions: What is your opinion of _____?
- Feeling questions: How do you feel about _____?
- Knowledge questions: What do you know about _____?
- Sensory questions: What do you experience when you are in the _____ situation?

Patton suggests detail-oriented follow-up questions (p. 372):

When did that happen?

Who else was involved?

Where were you during that time?

What was your involvement in that situation?

How did that come about?

Where did that happen?

Rubin and Rubin (2005) describe using "open the locks," the "tree and branch," or "river and channel" styles. An "open the locks" interview aims to create a broad picture, usually as the basis for additional interviews. One or two broad, open-ended questions are asked with the intention of unlocking a flood of response. They suggest that the tree and branch style is best for exploring multiple themes with a focus on breadth. The researcher divides research problem (trunk) into parts, each covered by a main question (branch). When exploring one theme in depth the researcher uses a river and channel approach. The researcher has a topic and follows it wherever it goes.

Numerous types, approaches, and styles of interview questioning exist; explaining all of them is beyond the scope of this book. The principles common to most include the use of main, follow-up, and probing questions. As explained in Chapter 6, researchers working at the most structured end of the continuum may state all in advance of the interview.

Semistructured interview researchers may state ground-mapping questions to use with all interviews (perhaps varying wording or sequence) and develop some follow-up dimension-mapping and/or perspective-widening questions to use depending on answers and interview flow. In some cases they may share the ground-mapping questions with interviewees prior to the interview to allow time for reflection ahead of time.

Researchers using less-structured interview styles may create a guide, outline, or list of ground-mapping, dimension-mapping, and/or perspective-widening topics and create key phrases or descriptors. Such researchers may familiarize themselves with types of probes but articulate probing questions during the interview based on responses. In an unstructured interview, the researcher could discuss a ground-mapping, dimension-mapping, and/or perspective-widening framework in the context of the study and identify themes for discussion.

CLOSING THE INTERVIEW

Closure of the interview provides a transition from the interactive event of the interview back to everyday life. Depending on the nature and subject

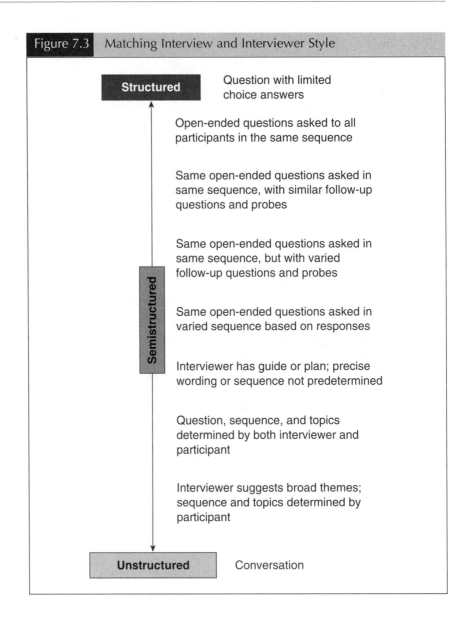

Figure 7.3   Matching Interview and Interviewer Style

Structured — Question with limited choice answers

Open-ended questions asked to all participants in the same sequence

Same open-ended questions asked in same sequence, with similar follow-up questions and probes

Same open-ended questions asked in same sequence, but with varied follow-up questions and probes

Semistructured

Same open-ended questions asked in varied sequence based on responses

Interviewer has guide or plan; precise wording or sequence not predetermined

Question, sequence, and topics determined by both interviewer and participant

Interviewer suggests broad themes; sequence and topics determined by participant

Unstructured — Conversation

of the interview, an emotional "cool down" may be needed. Ritchie and Lewis (2003) suggest that shortly before the end of the agreed-upon time frame, the researcher should signal the approaching close of the interview. One way is by introducing questions with phrases such as, "For the final question. . . ." Another is by closing with a summative or reflective question such as, "Is there anything we have not discussed that you would like to share before we end?" Gray (2004) says, "It is worth noting that interviewees often make some of their most interesting and valuable points once they think that the interview is over" (p. 226).

The closing phase of the interview is a time when any remaining expectations for interviewees can be discussed, including postinterview follow-up.

POSTINTERVIEW FOLLOW-UP

As you segue from closing the interview into data analysis, the postinterview follow-up is essential and should be seen as an opportunity for potentially valuable interaction with the research participant. In Chapter 6, qualitative methods generally encourage in-depth interaction with research participants at each stage of the process: preparing to collect data, collecting data, and analyzing data (see Appendix and the book's website).

After the interview, while it is fresh on the mind, reflect on what you heard and carry out a preliminary data review. Make notes on key ideas; where relevant, refine questions for subsequent interviews.

Once transcription is complete, verify data with participants and ask for clarification on missing, incomplete, or confusing statements. This step offers participants one more chance to add illuminating details and closes the circle, completing the interview contract they accepted in the consent agreement. This step strengthens the study through data triangulation, the use of a variety of data sources in a study (Patton, 2002).

Conducting a Research Interview Using Synchronous Technologies

Four main types of synchronous communication tools are explored in this book for online interviews: text-based, videoconferencing or video calls, multichannel, and immersive virtual environments. These types offer various degrees of media richness, meaning they vary in the availability of instant feedback and the use of multiple cues (such as facial expressions, voice inflections, and gestures). However, "richer" does not necessarily mean it is better. (Media Richness Theory is discussed in Chapter 1.) More important than richness per se is alignment with research design, with participants' usage preferences, access, and availability.

Many variations are possible within—and across—each of these online communication types, and new tools are continuously being developed. (See book's website for updates.) Some platforms allow for combinations of text, audio, and visual forms, enabling researchers to collect in diverse ways.

The four interview stages defined here as *Opening, Questioning and Guiding, Closing,* and *Following Up* characterize research interviews regardless of setting. The way they occur—and the role of the interviewer in carrying them out—will vary depending on what ICT is used. Researchers may choose to use different synchronous and asynchronous technologies for each respective stage: preparation (see Chapter 6), Opening, Questioning and Guiding, and Closing.

TEXT-BASED INTERVIEW

Text-based synchronous interviews use text messaging or chat. Several strategies introduced in Chapter 6 can help researchers conduct a text-based interview. By developing questions and key phrases in advance, the interviewer can cut and paste into the window rather than take the time to write out each item. Prompt response is essential; if needed, paste in a placeholder such as "I'd like follow-up" or "give me a second to think about what you've just shared" to signal the interviewee that you are writing a question or comment.

Suggestions for each stage are outlined in Table 7.1.

Table 7.1	Suggestions for Text-Based Interviews
Stages	**Suggestions for Text-Based Interviews**
Preparing	See preparation steps in Chapter 6. Make sure participant can use any tools needed, such as file sharing. Confirm agreed upon uses of emoticons or abbreviations.
Opening	Review research purpose and process, and answer any questions. Confirm time frame, anticipated length for interview. Offer photo through file-sharing or a link to a research project website with picture and bio. Establish protocols for the interview. These may include agreement on signals to indicate need for more time to answer or time for a break. Clarify/define any communication shortcuts you (or the participant) want to use.
Questioning and Guiding	Break longer questions into shorter subquestions to keep back-and-forth of dialogue moving. Use active listening with brief paraphrased comments to keep interview flowing. Type encouraging notes when the participant is writing long responses to show you are paying attention. Use the written equivalent of the nod, "uh huh," or emoticons to signal that you are listening and paying attention. Offer reassurance with short comments as appropriate. Respond promptly. Be prepared with follow-up or probes to avoid gaps in conversation. Write out core ideas or key phrases so you can cut and paste into message window more quickly.

Stages	Suggestions for Text-Based Interviews
Closing	Signal last question so interviewee knows you are ready to close the interview.
	Make sure interviewee has finished with responses.
	Reiterate any post-interview follow-up steps as well as expectations for research participant.

Videoconference Interview

Videoconferencing combines real-time sound and images of conversation partners. This kind of exchange would be considered "richer" than a text interview based on Media Richness Theory, because social cues and visual exchange are possible. Videoconferencing can give meetings and interactions a "human feeling," because participants have the ability to see people on the other side and hear them talk, which helps to develop personal relationships and a sense of immediacy (Olaniran, 2009). Some nonverbal immediacy behaviors such as physical gestures, body posture, facial expressions, and vocal expressiveness can be conveyed. (See Chapter 6 for more about videoconference interview preparation.)

Studies of videoconferencing in other contexts offer insights for those who want to adopt these technologies for scholarly purposes. The 2007 *Good Practice Guidelines for Participatory Multi-Site Videoconferencing* published by the Canadian National Research Council Institute for Information Technology draws on research experience with videoconferencing in education and community development work in remote and rural First Nations in Canada (Molyneaux et al., 2007; O'Donnell et al., 2008). The Canadian National Research Council identified four variables to consider in the study of effective videoconferencing. All of these variables apply in an online research interview, albeit in a slightly different context than the studies' authors (2007, 2008) may have envisioned:

- *Social relations:* Researchers and participants must be able to relate to one another, develop trust, and create a sense of social presence.

- *Content:* The purpose for the interview and types of questions to be discussed should be appropriate for the medium.

- *Interaction between the users and the technology:* Access and ease of use should promote, not distract from, interactions between researcher and participant.

- *Technical infrastructure:* The type of videoconference and the attributes of the technical infrastructure and the capacity of the system to incorporate new features and elements may influence the quality of the interview communication conducted in video-conference. "Clear audio and visual signals can increase participation by increasing the quality of the auditory and visual cues (Molyneaux et al., 2007, p. 4).

Interrelationships between users, content and purpose, and the technology are discussed in business videoconference examples. In an effort to cut costs in a global talent market, larger companies are using videoconferencing for recruitment purposes. Employment interviews share some characteristics with research interviews. Chapman and Rowe's (2002) study of videoconferencing in employer interviews found correlations between the level of structure in the interview and the choice of communication media:

> The use of videoconference technology for conducting employment interviews appears to have either no effect or a positive effect on the recruiting function of the employment interview for interviewers conducting highly structured interviews. (p. 195)

Applicants reported that structured interviews "eased the anxiety" of the exchanges where videoconferencing was used. "The question-answer format of the structured interview is well suited to the limitations of videoconference technologies that can interfere more with the normal flow of an unstructured conversation" (Chapman & Rowe, 2002, p. 194). However, the study showed that less structured interactions had a negative effect on the recruiting function of their interview. The findings were opposite for face-to-face interviews, where applicants preferred the more informal, less structured interview style (Chapman & Rowe, 2002).

In addition to framing the interaction with some level of structure, eye contact is mentioned as a dynamic of communication that merits attention when planning a videoconference interview. Eye contact is a natural part of face-to-face communication and considered by many people to be essential in building trusting relationships. Grayson and Monk describe mutual gaze as a "synchronization signal or 'hand shake'" with important functions in regulating conversation (Grayson & Monk, 2003, p. 222). The impression of failure to maintain eye contact is considered in many cultures to be a sign of deception and may lead to feelings of mistrust (Bekkering & Shim, 2006; Wegge, 2006). This is not merely a matter of the technology per se; user choices also influence perceptions; when one participant looks down at the screen and not at the camera, it appears to the other that he or she is looking away and breaking contact. This can easily happen when a researcher is trying to read a list of questions or take notes. Figures 7.4 to 7.6 illustrate variations in a desktop video call.

Grayson and Monk (2003) describe the dilemma:

> Were they to look at the camera it would appear to the partner that they are being looked at in the eyes, but then the user can no longer judge whether their partner is looking at them (as they are looking at the camera, not the image), preventing mutual gaze from serving its purpose as a synchronization signal. (pp. 221–222)

Yuzar (2007) uses the term *virtual eye contact* to describe interactions that come as close as possible to direct visual contact. He suggests that meaningful eye contact is possible in desktop videoconferencing when close-up camera views are used (Yuzar, 2007). Bekkering and Shim (2006) also discussed camera angles and positioning to maximize the value of visual exchange in videoconferencing. Chen's study of eye contact in videoconferencing suggests that simple improvements enhance participants' perceptions of eye contact:

> Because our sensitivity in the downward direction is lower than in other directions, the camera should be placed above the display to support eye contact . . . a conservative solution is to make the visual angle between the camera and the eyes rendered on the display less than 5°. (Chen, 2002, p. 55)

Grayson and Monk (2003) observe that experienced users of conventional desktop video conferencing

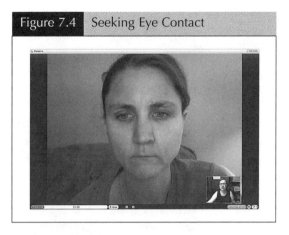

Figure 7.4   Seeking Eye Contact

Figure 7.5   Building Rapport With "Virtual Eye Contact"

Figure 7.6   Building Rapport With "Virtual Eye Contact" Plus Text Chat

equipment soon get used to the slightly off version of mutual gaze. They point out that because videoconferencing also allows for conversation, participants who speak in a way that treats the video image of the other person as if they were really there offer enough information for them both to "recalibrate their expectations and to learn a new signal for mutual gaze"(p. 224). Desktop videoconferencing or video calls can mesh with other technologies. Some platforms include text chat, allowing researchers to clarify interview questions or offer encouraging comments while the participant is talking.

Consumers are driving the development of these increasingly user-friendly technologies—in particular, grandparents and deployed military members' families. If experience in the medium improves interaction between the users and the technology, then as more people become accustomed to using Web chats, video calls, and other desktop tools, researchers may find more interview participants willing to meet through a videoconference. Integration with other interactive ICTs, as explored in the next section on multichannel groupware, can be expected as more devices include both audio and video capability. At the same time, as sophisticated videoconference systems become a common fixture in office and institutional environments, they may become more accessible for use by researchers.

Table 7.2	Suggestions for Videoconference Interviews
Stages	**Suggestions for Videoconference Interviews**
Preparing	See preparation steps in Chapter 6.
	Desktop:
	Adjust the webcam to allow for close-up view.
	Carefully review questions or interview guide so you can minimize need to look down at notes. Take the time, before looking down to read notes, to make the best "virtual eye contact" possible.
	Discuss options and parameters for participant's Web camera. Is it acceptable for the participant to turn the camera off and use audio only?
	Start recording.
	Facility:
	In a videoconference facility: position microphone; mute until start time.
	Focus, position cameras, or work with technician to do so.
Opening	Review research purpose, process, and structure, and answer any questions.
	Begin with broad questions to establish comfort with interview process and medium.

Stages	Suggestions for Videoconference Interviews
Questioning and Guiding	Stick with agreed upon structure and time frame. Try to keep eye contact with minimum attention to taking or reading notes. Use follow-ups and probes to keep dialogue moving.
Closing	Signal last question so interviewee knows you are ready to close the interview. Make sure interviewee has finished with responses. Ask how the participant felt about the interview and about the medium. Reiterate any postinterview follow-up steps as well as further expectations for research participant.

MULTICHANNEL ONLINE MEETING SPACES

Online researchers can take advantage of the diverse communication channels in these meeting spaces to conduct substantive online interviews. Online meeting or conferencing platforms integrate text chat, audio, and videoconferencing functions with various combinations of tools that may include shared applications and shared whiteboard. Use of text and videoconference applications have been discussed earlier in this chapter and the visual research potential for the shared whiteboard is addressed in Chapter 8. Three other components found in most online meeting platforms are considered here: the central workspace, shared applications, and the Web tour.

As noted in Chapter 6, for a structured or semistructured interview, questions or key discussion topics can be prepared in advance and presented on PowerPoint slides or other documents loaded into the meeting space. This allows the interviewer to focus on the conversation, without the need to cut and paste from another document or type during the interview. Interview questions or themes can be presented in the workspace, one by one, by advancing through the slides or pages. Because the medium is flexible, it is possible to move back and forth through the preset questions if a different sequence is called for.

For less structured interviews, themes for discussion can be written or drawn on the shared whiteboard during the interview. The interviewer can speak and write the question, or pose a question related to a diagram, image, or media clip presented on the shared whiteboard. See Chapter 8 for more about the visual studies that can be conducted with these tools.

Participants have numerous options for communicating responses. They can say them, write them, draw them, and/or show examples. If an interviewee seems at a loss for words, the interviewer can encourage the participant to express the response in another way.

Given the multiple communications options in one place, the interviewer can use varied, complementary approaches at each stage of the interview.

Table 7.3	Suggestions for Meeting Space Interviews
Stages	**Multichannel Online Meeting Spaces**
Preparing	See preparation steps in Chapter 6.
	Test microphone and audio; set turn-taking protocol if the system is set up for one speaker at a time.
	If using a webcam:
	Adjust the webcam to allow for close-up view. Take the time, before necessarily looking down to read notes, to make the best "virtual eye contact" possible.
	Discuss options and parameters for participant's web camera. Is it acceptable for the participant to turn the camera off and use audio only? Introduce other features participants can use to present their answers.
	Demonstrate and allow participant to practice using tools for writing, drawing, and so on.
	Start recording.
Opening	Confirm time frame, anticipated length for interview.
	Review research purpose, process, and structure, and answer any questions.
	If webcams are available, use them to share introduction and set the tone for the interview. Discuss how or whether to use the webcam throughout the interview—or not.
Questioning and Guiding	Use shared whiteboard to convey questions—whether prepared in advance or during interview. Say each question and ask whether clarification is needed.
	Vary communication approaches, making use of visual and shared application features as relevant.
	Use follow-ups and probes to keep dialogue moving.

Stages	Multichannel Online Meeting Spaces
Closing	Signal last question so interviewee knows you are ready to close the interview.
	Make sure interviewee has finished with responses.
	Reiterate any postinterview follow-up steps as well as expectations for research participant.

IMMERSIVE VIRTUAL ENVIRONMENT

The preceding interview strategies involve people who communicate from the vantage point of their "real-world" identities. Interviews in immersive virtual environments are conducted by communicating through avatars in 3-D environments. An *immersive virtual environment* is defined as "one that perceptually surrounds the user, increasing his or her sense of presence or actually being within it" (Bailenson et al., 2008). The interviewer must "immigrate" into the virtual world and create an online persona that will represent the interviewer to the research participant. (See Chapter 6 for more on the creation of an avatar.)

This visual representation of the individual in virtual space creates new dimensions of communication. "Forms of interaction need no longer be restricted to text as both proxemical and kinesical features in everyday communication can be replicated in avatar form. Social interaction becomes more complex, with the combination of the textual utterance and the corresponding avatar gesture" (Williams, 2007, p. 9). With the addition of a microphone and speakers, voice can be added to this already complex set of interactions.

The presence of avatars and a 3-D environment are undeniably major factors for interviewers to consider; however, the means of communication is still primarily through text. As such, some of the guidelines on text interviews apply.

At this point, scholarly research about the immersive experience and avatars' behaviors in Second Life, gaming, and other environments is beginning to emerge. So far, most of this research uses observation or laboratory simulations with limited examples of interview research. Corporations, however, are holding job fairs and conducting interviews in Second Life. When prospective employees interact in Second Life, they demonstrate technical, personal, communication, and social skills they could use to handle a real situation. As noted earlier, talent-focused companies with the resources to use innovative recruitment and interview approaches may provide useful examples for researchers. Clearly, researchers designing interview studies in immersive environments have the opportunity to conduct foundational research. The potential exists to elicit new understandings of the human presence behind the graphical presence through interviews in immersive environments.

Table 7.4	Suggestions for Interviews in Immersive Environments
Stages	**Suggestions for Interviews in Immersive Environments**
Preparing	See preparation steps in Chapter 6. If using text, see text interview suggestions. If using, test microphone and audio. Make sure note cards or other features are in place. Make sure participant has all information needed, including meeting place.
Opening	Review research purpose and process, and answer any questions. Confirm time frame, anticipated length for interview. Depending on the nature of the study, offer a link to a research project website with researcher's picture and bio or more background on the study. Establish protocols for the interview. These may include agreement on signals to indicate need for more time to answer or time for a break. Clarify/define any communication shortcuts or tools such as note cards you (or the participant) want to use. Establish whether the interview will take place in one setting or whether it will involve moving from one place to another.
Questioning and Guiding	Break longer questions into shorter sub-questions to keep back-and-forth of dialogue moving. Your avatar can display nonverbal cues to show listening, including gestures and expressions. Brief paraphrased comments can be said or posted, to keep interview flowing. Offer reassurance with short comments as appropriate. Respond promptly. Be prepared with follow-up or probes to avoid gaps in conversation. Write out core ideas or key phrases so you can cut and paste into message window more quickly.
Closing	Signal last question so interviewee knows you are ready to close the interview. Make sure interviewee has finished with responses. Reiterate any postinterview follow-up steps as well as expectations for research participant. Determine best follow-up contact approach.

Closing Thoughts

People are people, online or off. Interviews are successful when the researcher is able to convey warmth, sincerity, and curiosity in the role of interviewer. The online interviewer needs more people skills, not less, than does the face-to-face interviewer. The relationship and trust-building begins with the initial contact and recruiting, and steps involved to prepare for the interview. As noted in Chapter 6, researchers should find someone willing to practice process—the technology tools—and content—the questions—before conducting an actual interview. By the time the interviewer and interviewee meet online for the interview, both individuals should be ready to proceed.

In addition to developing rapport, the online interviewer must demonstrate interest and attention throughout the interview. In interviews where only one person can speak at a time, or where the exchange is text-based, short comments or use of emoticons can assure the speaker that someone is indeed listening.

Easy access to text or desktop tools makes it possible to arrange for more short interviews instead of one or two long ones. Researchers and participants can agree to log in for one or two questions over lunch hour each day, for example. This can be a strategic advantage, allowing researchers to collect data on events as they unfold, or observations of present experiences.

When considering the features and potential for an online communications technology, it is natural to compare it with face-to-face communication. When making decisions about selection of tools for online interviews, it may be more productive to look at online interaction as a means of communication unto itself, in a unique online environment that has its own culture. Adopting the mannerisms, norms, and attitudes of the online culture will enable the researcher to create the warm and welcoming social presence needed to make research participants feel confident and comfortable in the online interview.

Researchers' Notebook: Stories of Online Inquiry

CONDUCTING INTERVIEWS IN A MULTICHANNEL MEETING SPACE

I conducted interviews for two related studies on collaborative e-learning, online on the Elluminate platform, using videoconferencing, VoIP two-way audio, text chat, and shared whiteboard.

The interviews ranged from fifty minutes to one hour and twenty minutes. Each interview followed the same sequence and procedure. An overview of research interview process was provided, reiterating points made in preinterview discussion. Using the webcam helped establish rapport and make sure interviewees understood the steps of the interview. The research purpose and research questions were briefly explained.

As noted in previous Notebooks, these interviews with instructors and learners were focused on understanding their experiences in relation to the Taxonomy of Online Collaboration I was developing. A semistructured interview approach involved questions that corresponded to levels of the taxonomy. Questions were written on PowerPoint slides. (See Chapter 8 for more about the visual research methods used in this interview.)

This approach allowed for collection of comparable information across all participants, in relation to the stated research questions and themes of inquiry. However, because the questions were open-ended, the interviews also solicited instructors' stories, thoughts, and feelings about planning and teaching collaboratively. Participants were encouraged to talk as long as they wanted and discuss the topics as fully as they wished. This approach negated some of the inflexibility associated with standardized, structured interviews. The features of the Elluminate platform enabled the research participants to respond using verbal, text, and/or visual responses. (The visual data collection will be discussed in Chapter 8's Researchers' Notebook.)

A follow-up process allowed participants to verify and enhance data collected in the interview. The online interviews were saved, which allowed participants to review and suggest any needed modifications. Follow-up by e-mail was used to solicit additional comments or sample materials. This ensured that participants had conveyed the full extent of their experience in the context of the interview focus and scope.

CONDUCTING INTERVIEWS BY VIDEOCONFERENCE

Dr. Monique Sedgwick conducted research interviews with nursing students in rural Canadian hospitals. Each participant used the hospital's Telehealth videoconferencing system. This system, designed for medical consultation, is set up by an office worker to run without presence of a technician. This allowed participants to interact with Dr. Sedgwick without need for attention to equipment—and without concerns about privacy.

Dr. Sedgwick found that the basic approach used in other settings required little alteration in the videoconference setting.

> All of the interviews in this study regardless of the medium we used to conduct them were booked for a 2-hour period. We began each interview with some small talk, which then led us to collect demographic information. We answered any questions the participants might have concerning the study and/or videoconferencing technology, which was then followed by the grand tour question. Although some in-person interviews lasted only 1.5 hours, the majority lasted the full 2 hours. All of the videoconferenced interviews also lasted 2 hours, which gave the participants ample time to share their experiences with us. (M. Sedgwick, personal communication, May 21, 2009)

The approach to questioning was consistent in all the interview settings used for the study.

> Each interview in this study, regardless of whether it was in person, or conducted by telephone or videoconferencing, began with a grand-tour question: "Describe what the rural hospital experience is like for you." Questions eliciting ethnographic explanations, such as "What was it like being a student in a rural hospital?" were then asked. Finally, to help discover the meanings of words that the participants used to describe their culture, questions structured to find similarities and differences in how they see the words were asked. For example, participants were asked to describe a typical shift and an atypical shift. (Sedgwick & Spiers, 2009, p. 6)

The process of active listening on the part of the researcher and the back-and-forth exchange between interviewer and interviewee were comparable across all interviews. Camera angles allowed for a waist-up view and clear visibility of participants' facial expressions. Monique felt the ways of arranging cameras did not convey a mismatch of eye contact as noted by other videoconference interviewers (M. Sedgwick, personal communication, May 21, 2009).

Although Dr. Sedgwick saw few real disadvantages for using videoconferencing in interview research, she expressed a concern for "participants who have sensitive information and difficult experiences to share" (Sedgwick & Spiers, 2009, p. 7). In such cases "the researcher's lack of the physical presence might have a negative influence on the degree of sharing" (p. 7). In such circumstances the researcher may "offer the participant tissues, rest periods, and the occasional physical touch of the hand or shoulder" (p. 7). She observed that "although compassion can be expressed through tone of voice and nonverbal facial expression through videoconferencing, none of the behaviors that rely on tactile sensation could be expressed through this medium" (p. 7).

With the potential exclusion of very sensitive subject matter in mind, Dr. Sedgwick hopes to conduct further research using videoconference interviews because they offer her a way to study perspectives of participants in very remote areas who would otherwise be difficult or impossible to interview.

Key Concepts

Four main types of online interviews are text-based, videoconferencing, online meeting spaces, and immersive virtual environments for communications. These tools can be combined in some online environments, or different tools can be used for the interview and for preparation and/or follow-up communications. Each has advantages and disadvantages, depending on the research purpose, context, and characteristics of the sample population.

Discussions and Assignments

1. As noted in Chapter 1, we live in an "interview society." This means we have readily available examples of interviews. Although an interview for news or entertainment has a different purpose than a scholarly interview, interviewers still must open, conduct, and close the interview. Search the Internet for a recorded one-to-one interview that lasts at least five minutes. Review the recording several times to identify how the interviewer conducted each step of the interview, transitioned between steps, and responded to any unexpected responses from the interviewee.

2. What worked or didn't? Why? What would you recommend?

3. If the interviewer were using this interview to collect data, what would be done differently?

4. Select one of the four synchronous modes described in this book. If the interview was conducted using that technology, what different styles or strategies would you recommend?

5. Review the planning timeline and checklist for an online interview using the ICTs you developed in the Chapter 6 assignment.

6. Based on what you learned in Chapter 7, are any changes needed? Why or why not?

7. What steps will be appropriate for implementing this plan?

8. What types of responses or events—including technical issues—could derail your interview? Make a contingency plan for addressing them.

On the Book's Website

Check the website for updated information about conducting interviews with various synchronous technologies.

Terms

Mediated immediacy: Communicative cues in mediated channels that can shape perceptions of psychological closeness between interactants. Immediacy cues can be seen as a language of affiliation (O'Sullivan et al., 2004, p. 471).

Visual Research and the Synchronous Online Interview

8

Questions, after all, raise some profound issues about what kind of knowledge is possible and desirable, and how it is to be achieved. For example, do all questions have to be made in words?

—Michael Pryke, 2003

The world told *is a different world to the world* shown.

—Gunther Kress, 2003

After studying Chapter 8, you will be able to do the following:

- Define and explain the meaning of visual literacy;

- Offer an overview of visual research methods; and

- Distinguish different types of online visual research using the Typology of Online Visual Interview Methods.

Communication between researcher and participant in interviews, as discussed in Chapter 7, occurs primarily through words—written or spoken. This chapter discusses the use of visual communication as a complement to verbal and textual exchanges during online interviews.

Seeing the Interview: Visual Questions, Visual Answers

Visual research has long been essential to inquiries into culture or artifacts in fields such as sociology, ethnography, and anthropology. Contemporary communications media increasingly emphasize images over text. This change in emphasis makes visual methods of interest to researchers from a wider range of disciplines that plan to communicate with participants in research interviews. Ethnographer Pink (2007) observes that "each individual produces meanings by relating the image to his or her existing personal experience, knowledge and wider cultural discourses" (p. 82). Such meanings might not be communicated to researchers who use only verbal communications.

Interview researchers may choose to complement a mostly verbal process of questioning with some visual approaches or complement a mostly visual approach with verbal interview exchanges. Researchers may use images that allow a viewer to visualize what is otherwise not intrinsically visual. Data organized into graphs or charts, or relationships between concepts or numbers in a diagram or visual map, are examples. Researchers also can use images that extend vision across space and time through photographs or videos. As always, alignment with the research purpose and methodology drives the data collection decision.

Visual research methodologies, according to Banks (2007), have traditionally encompassed two main strands. Researchers have long used visual images to capture observations in the field or to graphically describe field data. Photography (still or moving images) or graphics (drawings or diagrams) are used to document research phenomena.

The second classic approach to visual research revolves around collecting and studying images created by research participants or others in the participants' culture. This approach is used when researchers want to understand the significance or function of artistic or creative expressions.

This approach is used when researchers want to understand the significance or function of artistic or creative expressions. Two additional visual research methods have emerged. The first is the study of the "collaborative image," where social researcher and the subjects of study work together to add to preexisting images or create new images (Banks, 2007, p. 7).

The second is the use of visuals to elicit responses and stimulate discussion about research participants' experiences generally. Visual elicitation stimuli are artifacts employed during interviews where the subject matter defies the use of a strictly verbal approach (Crilly, Blackwell, & Clarkson, 2006, p. 341). Goldstein points out that fruitful dialogue can take place based on the viewer's response to the content, perception of intent, and context of the image (Goldstein, 2007). Stanczak (2007) describes an interview process:

In conjunction with or as an alternative to conversational questions, particpants are asked open-ended questions about a photograph. Prompting a participant with "tell me about this photograph," for example, shifts the locus of meaning away from empirically objective representations of objects or interactions. Instead, images gain significance through the way that participants engage and interpret them. (pp. 10–11)

The image becomes a common frame of reference to both parties. By sharing photographs or video, researchers and participants can visit other time periods or spaces it would be difficult for them to enter physically (Näykki & Järvelä, 2008). When the subject matter is of a sensitive nature, interviewee and interviewer can both turn to the visual image "as a kind of neutral third party" (Banks, 2007, p. 65).

Pink (2007) suggests that rather than simply "eliciting" or drawing out responses to the image or media, the researcher and participant can

discuss images in ways that create a "bridge" between their different experiences of reality. Photographs [graphics, or media] can become reference points through which [researchers and participants] represent aspects of their realities to each other. (p. 84)

Using the image as a "bridge" will help avoid the danger Crilly and colleagues (2006) point to: presenting interviewees with a single graphic or photographic image could constrain their thinking. Interviewees may be inclined to suggest only modifications to the diagram or image rather than offering new conceptualizations. In other words, simply presenting an image to elicit responses can constrain the more creative and collaborative part of the process.

Visual research methods, whether used online or off, can enrich the otherwise word-intensive process of data collection through in-depth interviews.

Multimodal Communication in a Multilingual World

ICT advances have made it possible to communicate in more ways, more immediately, more cheaply, using more kinds of tools and devices. In related or parallel developments, an increasingly global economy and global culture has emerged. In this multilingual world communication is not limited to words; it also occurs through still and moving images, icons, and emoticons. Gergle and colleagues observe that "using visual information to infer what another person knows facilitates efficient communication and reduces the ambiguity otherwise associated with particular linguistic expressions" (Gergle, Kraut, & Fussell, 2004, p. 492). Kress

(2003) suggests that this shift from words to pictures is interrelated with a shift from print to digital:

> There is, on one hand, the broad move from the centuries-long dominance of writing to the new dominance of the image and, on the other hand, the move from the dominance of the medium of the book to the dominance of the medium of the screen. (p. 1)

Kress points out that even when the screen contains text it is inherently visual as a result of the layout of the online page, and use of colors, fonts, and other elements. Kress (2003) calls this type of communication *multimodality.*

> In multimodal ensembles, of writing and image, or of writing, speech, image, music and so on, the possibilities of supplementing messages with meaning multiply, and incorporate the demands and potentials of imagination of all the modes involved. (p. 170)

Kress argues that understanding these multimodel messages requires new literacies. The term **visual literacy,** coined by John Debes in 1968, can be defined as the ability to decode and interpret (make meaning from) visual messages and also to be able to encode and compose meaningful visual communications (Debes, 1968). It includes the ability to visualize internally, communicate visually, and read and interpret images (Bamford, 2003). In addition, visual literacy "encompasses the ability to be an informed critic of visual information, able to ethically judge accuracy, validity, and worth" (Metros, 2008, p. 103). Burkdall points out that higher education is recognizing this shift as evidenced by the 2009 Conference on College Composition and Communication, where workshops focused on how faculty can assess multimodal assignments rather than traditional essays, and a 2008 Modern Language Association annual convention with an opening panel on multimedia (Burkdall, 2009). Words and images are easily meshed electronically; thus visual literacy in an online world intersects with ICT or information literacy, defined as follows:

> Using digital technology, communications tools, and/or networks to access, manage, integrate, evaluate and create information in order to function in a knowledge society. (ETS, 2006, p. 2)

Developing 21st-century literacies (information, digital, and visual) among students and faculty is one of the top five priorities identified by the higher education technology organization, EDUCAUSE, in its 2009 Top Teaching and Learning Challenges (Little & Page, 2009). The 21st-century literate individual can critically evaluate diverse types of information, including visual and textual, and integrate elements in new ways to create and communicate complex messages using technology tools.

Visual Literacy and Spatial Intelligence

Howard Gardner's (1983) theory of multiple intelligences also aligns with Kress's thinking about multimodal communication and with related ideas about new literacies. Gardner suggests that intelligence comes in many flavors—including linguistic, interpersonal, and spatial. While people with linguistic intelligence think in words and people with interpersonal intelligence gain understanding by discussing concepts with others, people with spatial intelligence "see" and understand meaning through interaction with images and patterns.

> Central to spatial intelligence are the capacities to perceive the visual world accurately, to perform transformations and modifications upon one's initial perceptions, and to be able to re-create aspects of one's visual experience, even in the absence of relevant physical stimuli. (Gardner, 1983, p. 183)

Using Gardner's and Kress's terminologies, it is possible to describe an integrated "intelligence" comprised of linguistic, interpersonal, and spatial abilities used by people who relate to one another using multimodal communications. They have the necessary levels of literacy needed to access, consume, create, communicate, and evaluate messages that integrate written and spoken words, images, and sounds.

How are these matters relevant to interviewers? Researchers need to be flexible and able to hear—and see—a full range of responses. Online researchers have unique opportunities to use a full range of multimodal communications to engage participants by connecting to their diverse intelligence styles and literacies. All of these strands are possible in online research and are described here in a conceptual framework called a Typology of Online Visual Interview Methods.

Typology of Online Visual Interview Methods

The established practices of researchers creating or gathering a visual record of their work and of using images to facilitate in-person communications were noted earlier in this chapter. New communication technologies enable researchers who conduct online interviews to extend those methods over the Internet to achieve similar results. Four main types of visually oriented interactions are available to researchers and participants online. They can do the following:

- *Transmit* visual images. Image or media files, links to images posted on a server or website, or images captured in the moment are sent to the other party during the interview.

- *View* visual representation of phenomena together: Researchers can view photos, graphics, artifacts, or media during the interview. Digital cameras, Web cameras, and compact video cameras allow for new uses of media, since previously researchers were constrained because a player or projector was needed to view tapes or film.

- *Navigate* in a visual virtual environment. Observe and experience websites, software applications, or 3-D virtual environments.

- *Generate* visual images. Access shared tools that allow researchers and/or participants to create drawings, diagrams or visual maps, snapshots, or videos.

Visual research methods can make use of these four types of enabling technologies to accomplish various tasks in the interview. Methods introduced earlier are adapted for online research and categorized here as visual elicitation, visual communication, and visual collaboration.

One way to think about visuals in research is by their potential use as either stimulus or response. When researchers ask questions or introduce themes, they hope to stimulate a fruitful response. Interviews generally use a verbal stimulus to produce a verbal response. Images can complement words as stimulus or response. A verbal stimulus can bring forth a visual response. Researchers and participants may use *visual communication* techniques to convey the stimulus or represent the response. Visual communication describes the use of images to communicate abstract concepts, relationships between concepts or data, or examples of research phenomena.

Visual elicitation refers specifically to the process of using a visual stimulus to draw out a verbal or a visual response. The scenery or events in an immersive virtual environment navigated by researcher and participant, the images or media viewed together, or the graphic generated during the interview may stimulate response.

Visual collaboration refers to a collaborative approach to either stimulate new thinking or create responses in relation to visual representations of the research phenomena. Researchers and participants can create, edit, or embellish images together during the interview. "A collaborative method assumes that the researcher and participant are consciously working together to produce visual images and specific types of knowledge through technological procedures and discussions" (Pink, 2007, p. 53).

These principles align with the interview structure continuum discussed throughout this book. Researchers can variously use visual elicitation, communication, and/or collaboration in structured, semistructured, or unstructured interviews (see Figure 8.1).

> **Research Tip:** In general, novice researchers should choose a style with at least some structure and preparation, since managing the visual interview requires focus and also it may be hard to devise meaningful questions on the fly.

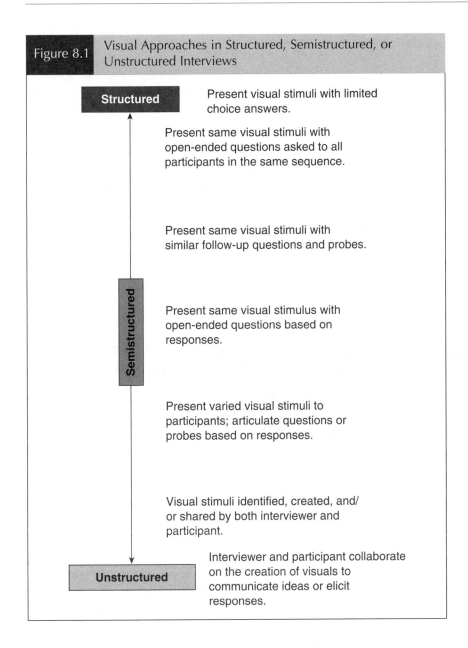

Figure 8.1 Visual Approaches in Structured, Semistructured, or Unstructured Interviews

Structured
Present visual stimuli with limited choice answers.

Present same visual stimuli with open-ended questions asked to all participants in the same sequence.

Present same visual stimuli with similar follow-up questions and probes.

Semistructured
Present same visual stimulus with open-ended questions based on responses.

Present varied visual stimuli to participants; articulate questions or probes based on responses.

Visual stimuli identified, created, and/or shared by both interviewer and participant.

Unstructured
Interviewer and participant collaborate on the creation of visuals to communicate ideas or elicit responses.

These types of visually oriented interactions can be used in various combinations in text-based, multichannel, videoconferencing, or immersive virtual environments.

Visual Methods in Synchronous Online Interviews

Visual research methods for communication, elicitation, and collaboration can variously augment verbal communication in the four types of

📖
🛐   Research Tip: Steps for preparation
     discussed in Chapter 7 should be
observed.

synchronous interviews (see Figure 8.2). Visual communication can complement verbal communication to stimulate answers or show responses to the research phenomena.

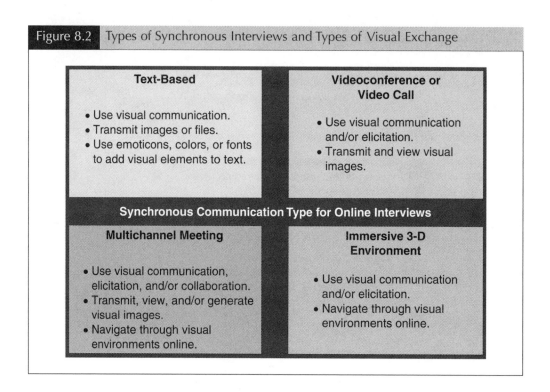

Figure 8.2 | Types of Synchronous Interviews and Types of Visual Exchange

Text-Based

- Use visual communication.
- Transmit images or files.
- Use emoticons, colors, or fonts to add visual elements to text.

Videoconference or Video Call

- Use visual communication and/or elicitation.
- Transmit and view visual images.

Synchronous Communication Type for Online Interviews

Multichannel Meeting

- Use visual communication, elicitation, and/or collaboration.
- Transmit, view, and/or generate visual images.
- Navigate through visual environments online.

Immersive 3-D Environment

- Use visual communication and/or elicitation.
- Navigate through visual environments online.

Text-Based Interviews

Interviews via text generally apply fewer visual research techniques than are possible with other technologies. They can communicate visually through textual elements such as emoticons or colored text with different fonts (see Figure 8.3).

Researchers and participants can transmit images using file sharing before, during, or after the interview. Computer or mobile device text or chat spaces have file-sharing capabilities that can be used to transmit images. Some mobile devices have cameras, making it possible for participants to take, send, and view pictures, or even video clips, during the interview. Alternatively, participants can keep a photo or video diary over a period of time by using the camera feature to record events, and transmit

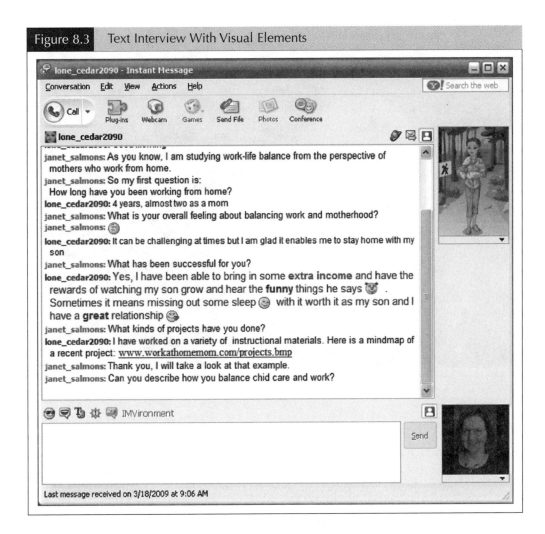

Figure 8.3   Text Interview With Visual Elements

the file(s) to the researcher. These images—while not visible within the text chat—can be used to elicit responses and stimulate discussion about their significance (see Figure 8.4).

Videoconference or Video Call

Interviews via videoconferencing can make use of two interactive visual research dimensions. Live images of interviewer and interviewee are transmitted, in addition to audio, and in some cases live text chat. Artifacts or items of interest can be shown on camera for researcher or participant to view. These images may serve communication or elicitation purposes.

Figure 8.4   Sharing an Image to Elicit a Response in a Desktop Video Call Interview

Multichannel Meeting Spaces: Interviews in meeting spaces can be used with any visual research and ICT type. Researchers and participants can transmit images, view visuals together, navigate virtual environments, and generate images individually or collaboratively. They can weave together Visual Communication, Elicitation, and Collaboration to complement and enhance the verbal exchange of the interview.

Ahead of the interview, images can be loaded and organized for sequential viewing in tandem with interview questions. Images also can be transmitted during the interview.

Photographs, diagrams, or media can be viewed together and discussed. Video clips created by the researcher or participant, or publicly available media that show examples of the research phenomenon in action can also be viewed together and discussed. Using Web tour features the researcher and participant can navigate to other websites, shared software applications, or even 3-D environments.

Using the shared whiteboard, researchers and participants can generate charts or illustrations. Collaborative diagramming can be used to show ideas or represent experiences in nonlinear ways. Uploaded images such as photographs or graphics can be individually or collaboratively manipulated by using the drawing tools to label elements or arrange

Figure 8.5   Creating a Diagram to Illustrate Points in the Interview Response

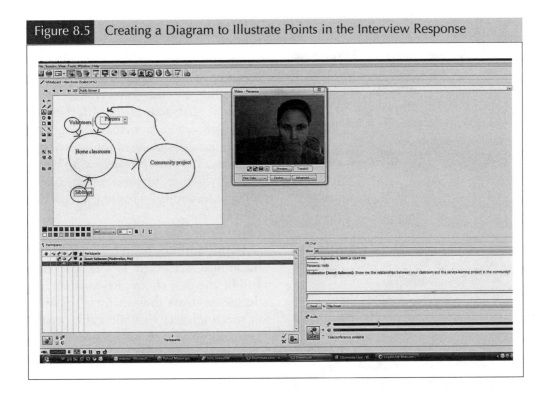

them on the whiteboard to show relationships between people, places, objects, and/or concepts.

Immersive Virtual Environments

Interviews in immersive environments such as Second Life can use varied interactive approaches to transmit, view, and navigate visual stimuli in real time.

The researcher and participant communicate through audio, text chat, or written note cards. They can transmit virtual objects or artifacts into the virtual inventory of the other. Through avatars they can communicate visually by using gestures or physical expressions. They can navigate through the virtual environment, which can offer a variety of visual stimuli. These may result in intended, or unintended, influences on the interview.

Research Tip: Choice of communication media also influences style to some extent. You need to think about what medium your sample will have and be comfortable with: audio, text, both?

Research Tip: If the interview will use text for verbal exchange, see preparation and considerations for text-based interviews described in Chapter 7.

Research Tip: If the interview will use audio, consider the setting. If eavesdropping is possible, consider using external audio (telephone or Skype call). Also, consider using a digital recording device to capture audio.

Ethics Tip: The ethical dilemma—alluded to in the discussion of Fair Information Processing in earlier chapters—is in the degree of observation that you may want to complement the interview. Typically researchers take stock of attire, surroundings, and so on if they conduct the interview *in situ*. Or, you may want to observe and discuss phenomena with participants. How do you handle observational activities—in different kinds of immersive 3-D settings? What aspects of observation should be discussed with participants and spelled out in the consent agreement?

Ethics Tip: Fair Information Processing principles point out that personal data should be collected in a context of free speech, for one specific purpose. Additional information available in a participant's online profile may be outside the data agreed upon in the consent agreement.

As noted earlier in the book, every researcher needs a safe, neutral location conducive to the interview. A preferred location will be comfortable for and accessible to the interviewee, with minimal distractions or interference. When choosing a virtual setting, the researcher faces many of the same issues as does the interviewer, who must decide whether to meet in an agency office, community location, or participant's home.

In some cases a neutral location, without stimuli of relevance to the meanings exchanged in the interview, will be the best choice. Researchers may decide to create their own virtual office or meeting space that allows for private, permission-only access by selected participants. A private space can deter eavesdropping or accidental interruptions. Many academic institutions, libraries, and nonprofit organizations have virtual spaces in Second Life available for educational use. Such settings have fewer distractions. These settings do not communicate the personal expressions of the interviewer or participant or reveal potentially private information about the avatar (see Figures 8.6 and 8.7).

For other interviews, the environment may offer visual representation of phenomena and thus elicit response in the interview. Together researchers and participants can navigate the virtual environment to observe, participate in, simulate, or experience some aspect of the subject of inquiry.

In some cases the participant's environment, which visually communicates choices in design, mood, purpose, and/or creativity, can be an appropriate setting. If observations of such settings are part of the research data, the consent agreement should reflect that intention.

Figure 8.6   Meeting in a Neutral Location for an Interview in Second Life

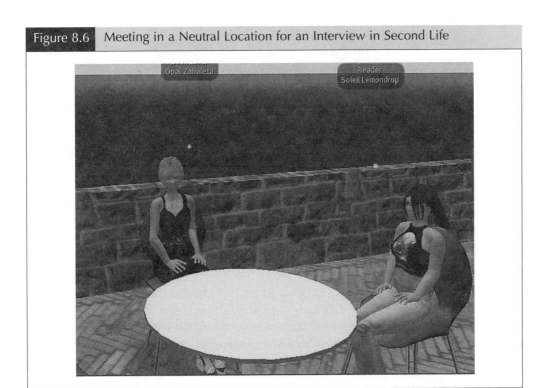

Figure 8.7   Talking About Observations of Second Life in a Tour Guided by a Research Participant

USING VISUAL METHODS
TO ENRICH ONLINE INTERVIEW DATA

Visual research methods for communication, elicitation, and collaboration using technologies allow researchers to transmit or view images or media, navigate online environments, or generate images together. Online visual methods offer researchers and participants the chance to visit and discuss virtual environments as well as enabling them to explore the participant's world. Digital and Web cameras enlarge the possibilities for communication, elicitation based on photography or video, because images can easily be taken and shared. Readily available drawing and graphics software makes it possible to easily create charts, graphs, maps, or diagrams that convey complex information and relationships between concepts.

- These approaches can add richness to the interview exchange and appeal to individuals with the kinds of spatial-visual intelligences Gardner identified (Gardner, 1983). The integration of any or all of these approaches should be congruent with the stated purpose of the study.

Issues in Online Visual Research

PERCEPTUAL ISSUES

Images are not value-free. Whether generated by people associated with the study or not, they were created from someone's subjective perspective, and that perspective enters the research discourse. Goldstein (2007) discusses issues as they pertain to photography:

> When looking at a photograph, it is useful to first consider all of the technical choices made by the photographer. All of these results in the content of the image: what's in the frame (or, more accurately, what's before us, since the frame itself may be an important part of the image). However, the more interesting question is often why the photographer made these choices. Were they conscious or unconscious? What did he or she intend that we notice, and why? Do we see something that was perhaps unintended? If we decide that certain intent is present, does it work effectively, or could other choices have been more effective? What makes these questions interesting is that they often have more than one answer, or no answer at all. (p. 75)

Comparable choices are made for graphics, including what to include or omit, how to present, what colors to use, and where to draw visual attention. One reason visuals are valuable in interviews is the fact that they do not present or evoke one "right" answer. Stanczak (2007) holds that

> reflexive epistemologies of visual research hold that the meaning of the images resides most significantly in the ways that participants interpret those images, rather than as some inherent property of the images themselves. (pp. 10–11)

The researcher—and, to some extent, the participant—needs to demonstrate visual literacy skills to decode and interpret visual images. It is important to evaluate, acknowledge, and discuss perspectives, choices, and potential biases represented in images associated with the study.

ETHICAL ISSUES

Issues of public versus private settings and related need for informed consent should be handled with the same care as any data collection (see Chapter 4). Covert research is unacceptable; "covert research implies that the researcher is videoing and photographing the behavior of [research participants] in a secretive rather than collaborative way, for example, using a hidden camera" (Pink, 2007, p. 53). Images should be treated as private data, with appropriate permissions articulated within the consent agreement (Banks, 2007). Permission to publish or disseminate images also must be part of informed consent. Ownership of images created for or during the interview should be spelled out. If images belonging to research participants are used in the interview (for example, family photographs), permissions to use them should be discussed and stated in informed consent or in a separate agreement. If images are *not* the intellectual property of the researcher or participant, copyright regulations must be observed.

Ethics Tip: Observe consent agreement and make sure participant is aware of video or still photography.

Ethics Tip: Always observe copyright laws and respect others' intellectual property.

Closing Thoughts

Much of the early literature about online interviews described exchanges using the early bare-bones text communications. The evolution of ICTs, with the advent of myriad Internet-connected handheld devices with cameras, as well as computers with built-in Web cameras and varied drawing and diagramming software, has changed online communications.

These changes provide researchers with many options for visual research previously limited to well-funded studies with budgets for film or video cameras, technicians, and graphic artists. At the same time, the changes toward more visual communication styles—and greater orientation to the screen versus the page—mean research participants may be more comfortable expressing themselves with pictures. Drawing relevant practices from visual ethnography, sociology, and/or anthropology, contemporary researchers can design studies that build new understandings from verbal, text, and visual data collected in online interviews.

Researchers' Notebook: Stories of Online Inquiry

VISUAL INTERVIEWS IN A MEETING SPACE

Interviews for my study on e-learning took place using the meeting space on the Elluminate platform, with dialogue through VoIP two-way audio, text chat, and shared whiteboard. These interviews involved transmitting images, viewing images together, and participants' generating images. The interviews used visual communication, elicitation, and collaboration.

The study proposed a Taxonomy of Collaborative e-Learning and refined it based on interviews with research participants (Salmons, 2006, 2008). Since the taxonomy is a model with a series of visual diagrams, the shared whiteboard in the electronic meeting room was a central focus of the interview. The features of the Elluminate platform enabled the research participants to respond using verbal, text, and/or visual responses.

Interview questions related to the phenomenological concepts of noema, that which is experienced, and noesis, the act of experiencing (Husserl, 1994). This study explored the examples of e-learning activities that promote collaboration as noema, and the instructors' experience of preparing, facilitating, and evaluating this kind of learning activity as noesis. The in-depth interviews conducted for this study generated two forms of data: verbal and visual. Verbal data related to inquiry about purpose, preparation, and evaluation of collaborative e-learning while visual data related to how research participants' experiences fit with the prototype Taxonomy of Online Collaboration.

The interview opened with transmission of my image to welcome the interviewee, and visual presentation to reinforce verbal description of the interview process.

Images of each of the six stages of the taxonomy were introduced. Then, research participants used the taxonomy to categorize and map stages of e-learning activities they had planned and taught. This entailed

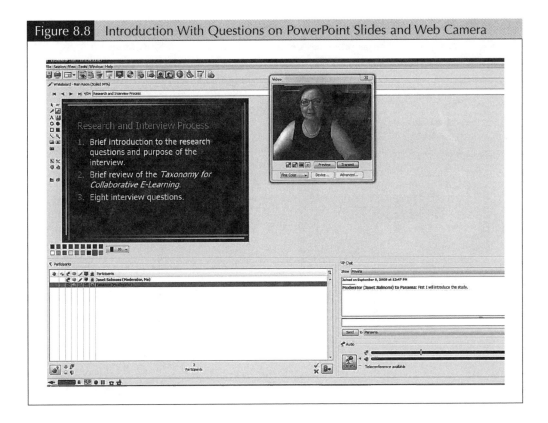

Figure 8.8   Introduction With Questions on PowerPoint Slides and Web Camera

generating visual depictions of relationships between concepts and steps described in the taxonomy.

Participants also were given the opportunity to suggest or illustrate adaptations to the five levels of collaboration described by the prototype Taxonomy of Online Collaboration, or to generate images depicting new levels or approaches.

In the interviews or the follow-up dialogue, none of the participants chose to add new levels or to revise existing levels in the taxonomy (see Figure 8.9). However, they did add to the model. Five research participants described projects or series of related assignments where individual assignments were intrinsically connected to the collaborative project. For example, some participants asked learners to keep a journal to record experiences or impressions of the project or asked them to keep track of participation. In these situations this icon is used: The single arrow and star icon is now used in the model to describe individual processes and outcomes that take place in the context of the collaborative project.

The visual data generated in the interviews included images from the drawings done by research participants. These images were transcribed

| Figure 8.9 | Participants Drew on the Symbols for Each Level of the Taxonomy to Show the Sequence of Activities in Their Own Collaborative Projects |

into Microsoft Visio and presented as graphic depictions of reported collaborative e-learning activities. A key was developed to illustrate the elements of each example (see Figure 8.10).

| Figure 8.10 | A Key to the Composite Diagrams |

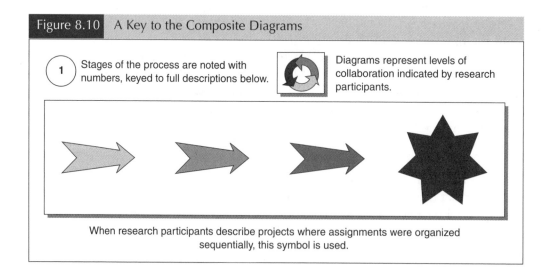

These descriptions and graphic representations were submitted to the research participants for further refinement and approval as part of the interview follow-up. Changes were made as needed to create accurate descriptive accounts of reported collaborative e-learning activities. The online interviews were saved, which allowed participants to review and suggest any needed modifications. Follow-up by e-mail was used to solicit additional comments or sample materials. This ensured that participants had conveyed the full extent of their experience in the context of the interview focus and scope.

Figure 8.11 A Sample Diagram of a Collaborative e-Learning Activity, Illustrated With the Taxonomy of Online Collaboration Iconography

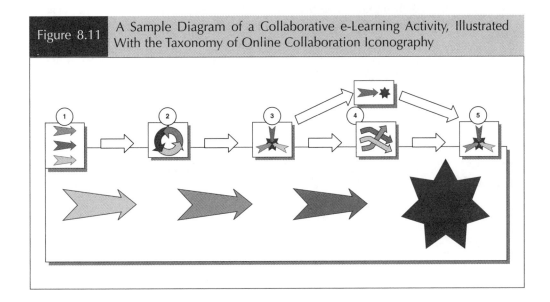

Given the nature and purpose of this study, the visual exchange was essential. The visual data allowed me to refine the taxonomy, initially described as the Taxonomy of Collaborative e-Learning, and to develop a new set of materials. After the study, the model was renamed the Taxonomy of Online Collaboration to reflect the broader applicability to other settings where people collaborate (Salmons, 2010).

Research Tip: See the visual knowledge map of the entire study in Chapter 3. Find a template for creating your own knowledge map on the book's website.

COMMUNICATING THE RESEARCH DESIGN VISUALLY

Dr. Lynn Wilson's doctoral research used mixed methods in a Q-study (Wilson, 2006). This complex multistage study generated a large amount of data. She used diagrams to visually communicate the design of the overall study and to describe key relationships in the data. Lynn's work offers an example of visual methods used after the interview, to share, verify, and present research findings to various stakeholders in the process and audiences interested in the results.

This fishbone diagram (see Figure 8.12) of the Q-study on ocean policy illustrates an augmented Q-method statistical study; it is augmented by rigorous qualitative work not only in creating the Q-study through an analysis of interviews, participant observations and literature to identify underlying collective perspectives, but throughout the entire analytical process. The V diagramming and surrounding narrative analysis grounds the Q statistical study. While there is direct feedback from the Q-study spawning additional interviews, other continuous input is inherent in the research design and cannot be separated. (L. Wilson, personal communication, June 3, 2009)

| Figure 8.12 | Visual Representation of Dr. Wilson's Research Design |

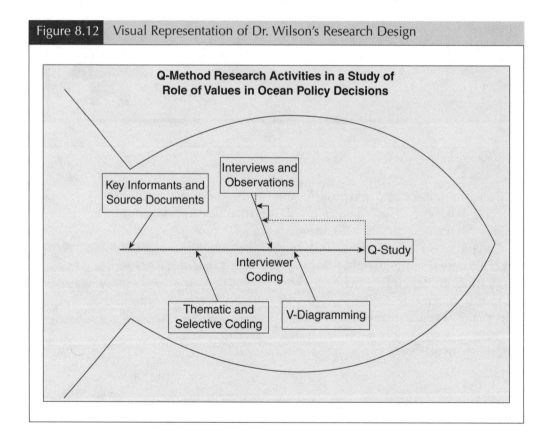

Dr. Wilson used the diagram to communicate with and elicit responses from different audiences about different aspects of the research.

> One was on methodology—about how to integrate methods (qualitative and quantitative) with Q and address some of the criticisms of Q by checking results of the factor analysis with qualitative methods as well as using qualitative methods to construct the dialogue upon which the Q-study was based. Another instance was using it to show how my *thinking* progressed in analyzing the U.S. Commission on Ocean Policy process and products. In this case, the diagram was illustrative of how I achieved that analysis, rather than how the study itself was conducted. (L. Wilson, personal communication, June 3, 2009)

Key Concepts

- Narratives and pictures go together and, likewise, the online interviewer can tell a more comprehensive story by more fully understanding the interviewee's experiences and perspectives by using images.

- Text-based, videoconferencing, online meeting space, or immersive environment technologies offer different ways to accomplish visual research purposes, including Visual Ideation, Visual Elicitation, Visual Communication, or Visual Collaboration.

Discussions and Assignments

Review an article or report of a study based on verbal interview data. Develop an alternative data collection plan using online visual interview methods. Use at least two visual research method types (Visual Ideation, Visual Elicitation, Visual Communication, or Visual Collaboration) and two synchronous approaches (View, Transmit, Navigate, Generate). Provide a rationale for your choices.

1. Create a planning checklist for visual interview preparation. Exchange with peer learners to compare, contrast, and refine your checklists.

2. Think of a time when someone successfully used visual approaches to communicate with you. Describe the experience and identify why the message got through to you by a visual means.

3. What does "visual literacy" mean to you?

4. Do you think in words or pictures? Which form of Howard Gardner's intelligences is strongest for you—and how does it impact your inclinations and abilities as a researcher?

5. How "visually literate" are you? What can you do to become more visually literate?

6. Conduct a practice online interview using visual research methods with a peer.

   • Using the same interview questions, experiment with different combinations: verbal stimulus/verbal response; verbal stimulus/ visual response; visual stimulus/verbal response; and visual stimulus/visual response.

   • Compare and contrast the ways you communicated and the kinds of results you obtained.

   • Based on your experience, what kinds of questions elicit the richest responses?

On the Book's Website

• Links to articles and resources about visual research methods, and technologies that enable researchers to use them online

Terms

Visual literacy: The ability to recognize, draw meaning from, and convey ideas through visible symbols, pictures, or images.

Online Communications and Online Interviews

9

Trends and Influences

The future often appears strange just before it becomes ordinary . . . trying to grapple with what comes next is a deep problem. Doing so is partly a matter of science fiction, which consists, after all, of the stories we tell about the future.

—Bryan Alexander, 2009

After studying Chapter 9, you will be able to do the following:

- Identify and discuss emerging trends and implications for online interview research; and

- Analyze and generate recommendations for further discussion and development of online interview research methodology.

Online Communications and Online Interviews

ANYWHERE, ANYTIME COMMUNICATION

It is hard to predict what information and communications technology, tool, or gadget will next enthrall experienced users and attract new ones. It seems likely that coming generations of ICTs will be faster, with more options for integrating visual media, audio, and text. As devices become smaller, they will go with their owners into more parts of daily personal, social, community, as well as professional life. More of the important events of life will be experienced in the presence of or recorded on, if not mediated through, some form of communications technology.

In addition to changes in ICT tools and communication types, the use of these tools and ways people think about them are changing. Given the focus here on the use of technology for research purposes, two phenomena that merit consideration are as follows: **online collaboration** and **disintermediation**.

Online Collaboration

The ease of online communication allows people to **collaborate** in new ways. Examples of online collaboration are evident across the World Wide Web. Companies, educational institutions, governmental, and social sector agencies are collaborating electronically to complete projects and solve complex problems. In these examples collaboration occurs within an established framework or organizational structure. Another trend is what is being called **mass collaboration** (Tapscott & Williams, 2008).

Mass collaboration occurs when people who do not know each other write, think, or work on projects together. People write collaboratively and edit each other's comments on wikis; they design, implement, test, and improve on open-source software. They form social networks of new and old friends who keep in touch in online communities. These networks fulfill niches for people of varied ages and interests. According to two recent reports from the Pew Internet and American Life Project, while younger users may be more active in mobile communications, Generation X, the Baby Boomers, and older generations tend to dominate Internet use in other areas (Jones & Fox, 2009). "The share of adult internet users who have a profile on an online social network site has more than quadrupled in the past four years—from 8% in 2005 to 35% at the end of 2008" (Lenhart, 2009). These vocal multigenerational users join together to make a loud collective voice on everything from politics to product reviews and development (Shirky, 2008).

Li and Bernoff created a "social technographics" model to describe people-people technology activities (Li & Bernoff, 2008). Their "Technographics Ladder" illustrates six progressive levels of activity from "Spectators" who read or view others' posted materials to "Critics" who post comments ratings or reviews and "Creators" who publish and post materials that inspire others' contributions (p. 43).

Similarly, those creating models for ICT literacy point to a progression that aligns critical thinking with the skills to use them in a technological environment. The seven identified levels start with the basic ability to define needs, use appropriate tools to access relevant information to more sophisticated levels of ability to make judgments about the quality, relevance, usefulness, or efficiency of information, as well as to create, generate, and communicate new information (ETS, 2003, 2006).

By participating in mass collaboration, individuals move up the Technographics Ladder and increase their respective levels of ICT literacy. They are not "Spectators" or consumers of information; they are active contributors who interact with people known and unknown, adding, editing, and sharing ideas. In the process they gain skills and attitudes beneficial to online research. It is reasonable to expect that people who are comfortable collaborating with others "co-constructing" wikis or open-source software might also be comfortable co-constructing knowledge with researchers. Individuals who share photographs and video clips with Internet friends may be more willing to do so with researchers. As Figure 9.1 illustrates, in general, more structured interviews require fairly basic

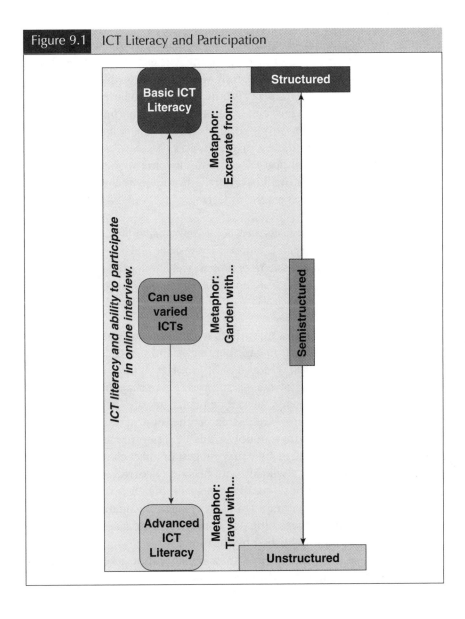

Figure 9.1   ICT Literacy and Participation

online skills. Advanced skills will allow more substantive responses and more generation of data within the context of less structured interviews.

Trust is essential in any online collaboration, whether it is in a workplace team or a mass collaboration wiki. Kouzes and Posner (2007) observe, "At the heart of collaboration is trust. . . . To build and sustain social connections, you have to be able to trust others and others have to trust you" (pp. 224–225). Trust also is essential in the online interview, particularly in the less structured types where a more collaborative approach to "gardening" or "traveling" is desired. People who are experienced with online collaboration may find it easier to develop trusting connections with interviewers.

Disintermediation

A companion trend to mass collaboration is **disintermediation.** This term refers to the removal of the middlemen, the gatekeepers. Individuals can communicate immediately and directly with experts, people in authority, or producers of the services or products they purchase or consume. E-mail, blog postings, review, and comment sections on publications and company websites offer ways—often very public ways—to convey thoughts, opinions, experiences, or preferences.

Although disintermediation is occurring in some way in almost every major industry, a poignant illustration is found in the world of print media. Shirky (2008) observes the following:

> The media landscape is transformed, because personal communication and publishing, previously separate functions, now shade into one another. One result is to break the older pattern of professional filtering of the good from the mediocre before publication; now such filtering is increasingly social, and happens after the fact. (p. 81)

Where before editors and publishers served as gatekeepers, today anyone with an online connection can share news and perspectives. Whether they are accurate, truthful, relevant, or appropriate will be determined by the readers and addressed by mass responses. There is an implicit sense of caveat emptor—let the buyer, viewer, or reader beware. Readers or viewers must utilize their own awareness about the topic at hand to filter the extensive volume of information now available. They may simply shut out unacceptable information, or they may suggest or enact changes as needed to correct it. Postings on a wiki site can be simply corrected by other site visitors, while incorrect posts to a blog may simply elicit readers' suggestions—or ire. If the individual's work is considered valuable and reaches its audience, the solo writer's blog or site may compete directly for readers with websites of long-established publications.

One way disintermediation and mass collaboration intersect is in the use of crowdsourcing. Crowdsourcing is a strategy for groups to solve problems by stating them clearly and succinctly, distributing that request for help to the world at large (Alexander, 2009). In this environment terms like *professional* and *amateur* are no longer polar opposites.

The phenomenon of disintermediation has two potential implications for online research. On one hand, disintermediation may contribute to a culture where individuals are accustomed to communicating with strangers in very frank, personal, and self-revealing ways. If individuals associate a free and trusting sensibility to their online interactions, such expectations may transfer to the online interviewer. In this milieu of direct communication, potential interviewees may be more willing to participate in research.

From another perspective disintermediation places even more responsibility on the researcher to be accountable to high ethical standards and produce credible new knowledge. In a world where casual observations can be so easily distributed, the discipline of empirical research is even more important.

ICT TRENDS AND IMPLICATIONS FOR RESEARCHERS

These trends and the increasingly pervasive aspect of ICT are important to online researchers for several reasons:

First, social researchers are interested in studying human behavior and social interactions. If more behaviors and interactions occur online, then it is to be expected that researchers will be interested in studying them. Online researchers have focused on online behaviors; with new tools and broader adoption, researchers can use online interviews to explore behaviors that occur online or offline. The processes used to communicate electronically about any area of life experience, and the significance of such experiences offer fertile ground for empirical study through online interview research.

Second, sampling possibilities enlarge as more people from diverse demographic groups become accustomed to using ICTs in everyday life. When the total pool of potential participants is larger and more ICT literate, researchers have more sampling options. Researchers can be more specific and particular about selection criteria. Or, they can choose to conduct larger mixed methods studies with varied sampling techniques.

Third, the increasing variety of communication types means there are more ways to collect different types of audio, visual, and text-based data. As more people develop personal communication styles through online cultural life and mass collaboration, interview researchers will have more options in terms of type of interview and ways to conduct it.

Does popularization of online communication and collaboration develop the same skills and attitudes needed for participation in online interview research? This is a question that merits further investigation.

The relationships and assumptions suggested here offer a variety of fertile areas for empirical study.

Closing Thoughts and Recommendations for Further Research

Trends in ICT adoption and their potential for online interview research were explored in this chapter and throughout the book. Yet these discussions may raise more questions than they answer! Clearly, research about online research is needed. In addition, more work is needed to develop standards and criteria for excellence and integrity in online interview research. Two priorities are research ethics and online interview methodology.

Chapter 4 examined some of the ethical dilemmas online researchers face and proposed some guidelines. One area where greater clarity is needed is in the distinction between public and private settings.

This distinction is directly related to the determination of informed consent requirements. The public-private distinction also has implications for sampling and participant recruitment, as discussed in Chapter 5. Better understanding of the distinctions and consensus in the research field are needed to ensure that respect for privacy is respected.

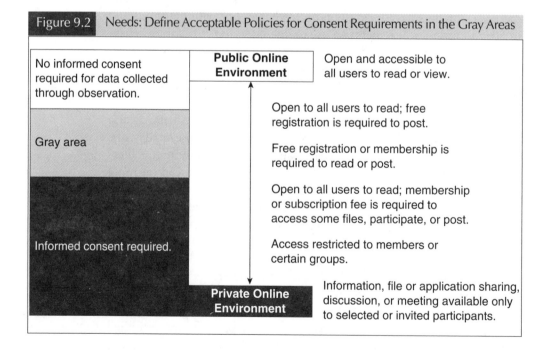

Figure 9.2   Needs: Define Acceptable Policies for Consent Requirements in the Gray Areas

Methodological and methods issues have been explored throughout this book, and numerous areas deserve more consideration.

Each stage of the interview process—and each stage of interaction with research participants—deserves more study. Which approaches for interview preparation enable researchers to develop relationships needed to conduct the type of interview that best serves the purpose of the study? What approaches motivate participants to stick with the interview—and resist the urge to click the window closed when some discomfort arises? What are the benefits of multiple short interviews over a more conventional approach with one longer interview? What level(s) of structure work best with which ICT? How can data best be collected when interviews are conducted in virtual—or highly visual—environments? These are a few of the many questions the research community will need to answer to fulfill the potential of online interview research as a valuable approach for studying human behavior in the digital age.

Terms

Collaborate: The word *collaborate* has its origins in the Latin word *collaborare,* "to work together" (OED, 2005). The working definition used here is as follows: collaboration is an interactive process that engages two or more participants who work together to achieve outcomes they could not accomplish independently (Salmons, 2008).

Disintermediation: Disintermediation is the process of cutting out the middleman so individuals communicate directly with producers and sellers of products and services.

Electronic collaboration: This occurs when the "interactive process" is conducted using ICT.

Mass collaboration: Mass collaboration occurs when people who do not know each other write, think, or work on projects together (Tapscott & Williams, 2008). Wikis exemplify mass collaboration.

Appendix

Qualitative Data Analysis

There is no particular moment when data analysis begins.

—Robert Stake, 1995

There are no clearly agreed rules or procedures for analyzing qualitative data.

—Liz Spencer, Jane Ritchie, and
William O'Connor, 2003

Once data have been collected from online interviews, they can be handled and analyzed much the same way as data collected through live, face-to-face interviews. That said, there is no one-size-fits-all approach for qualitative data analysis within a fully qualitative or mixed methods study. Researchers may use inductive analysis to discover patterns, themes, or categories in the data or a deductive analysis to analyze data according to an existing theory or framework or a hybrid approach (Fereday & Muir-Cochrane, 2006; Patton, 2002). Researchers can choose or combine elements from a number of analysis strategies. With the advent of numerous software packages for qualitative analysis, researchers also must decide which steps of the process to do by hand and which to carry out with the help of technology. This exploration of qualitative data analysis will introduce researchers to some of the many available options and resources. Additional links and updates are posted on the book's website.

A Short Survey of the Literature:
Qualitative Data Analysis by Methodology

"How do I go about finding out what the interviews tell me about what I want to know?" (Kvale & Brinkman, 2009, p. 192). Interview researchers constructing life histories are looking for different things in the data than interview researchers constructing new theories. As noted in Chapter 3, interview approaches can be organized by degree of structure. At the analysis stage this means some researchers begin analysis with some classifications that naturally emerge when consistent sets of questions are asked to all participants. Other researchers who conducted unstructured interviews have a wide-ranging collection of data they will need to classify. The following books offer guidance for data analysis specific to various qualitative methodologies.

Kvale and Brinkman and Rubin and Rubin write specifically about interview research—and their respective books discuss analysis of data collected through interviews (Kvale, 2007; Kvale & Brinkman, 2009; Rubin & Rubin, 2005). Rubin and Rubin's approach builds on the semistructured **"responsive interview"** described throughout the book. The stages they lay out are described in Chapter 7. Kvale and Brinkman approach analysis a little differently. They look at modes of analysis focusing on meaning, language, and/or theory. In the broad category "language analysis," they cover linguistic analysis, conversation analysis, narrative analysis, discourse analysis, and deconstruction. In *Doing Interviews,* Kvale offers an overview in one chapter while the more comprehensive *InterViews* provides a chapter on each mode.

In *Qualitative Inquiry and Research Design: Choosing Among Five Approaches,* Creswell explores narrative research, phenomenology, grounded theory, ethnography, and case study (Creswell, 2007). This volume surveys all stages of the research process for the five selected traditions. After introducing a general organizing framework, he addresses distinctive data analysis characteristics for each one. Creswell's clear explanations will be most valuable for the researcher who is trying to decide which methodology (or combination) to use. In practice, researchers will want more specific steps and examples. While Creswell deals with researchers' decisions from design to report, *Analyzing Qualitative Data: Systematic Approaches* (Bernard & Ryan, 2009) provides a multimethodology exploration of the data analysis stage for discourse analysis, narrative analysis, grounded theory, content analysis, and schema analysis.

Postmodern Interviewing and *Inside Interviewing: New Lenses, New Concerns* (Gubrium & Holstein, 2003b; Holstein & Gubrium, 2003c) are edited collections. In *Postmodern Interviewing,* some of the contributions discuss analysis in the context of their chapters. *Inside Interviewing: New Lenses, New Concerns* offers more specific strategies, with one section of the book devoted to "Analytic Options" (Holstein & Gubrium, 2003c, pp. 311–414). The five chapters in this section discuss analysis in narrative, oral history, ethnographic, and grounded theory studies. These are critical examinations, not practical how-to steps for carrying out data analysis.

The expectations for grounded theory analysis are very specific—to generate new theoretical principles. Grounded theory researchers build on the understanding of individuals' experiences derived through phenomenological methods to generate theoretical principles (Creswell, 2007; Strauss, 1987). They look at categories discovered in the data and construct explanatory theoretical frameworks, which provide abstract, conceptual understandings of the studied phenomena. For practical steps, one contributor to *Inside Interviewing*, Kathy Charmaz, also wrote a more in-depth book titled *Constructing Grounded Theory: A Practical Guide Through Qualitative Analysis* (Charmaz, 2006). She emphasizes "flexible guidelines, not methodological rules, recipes and requirements" (p. 9). Situational analysis is a style of grounded theory. Situational analysis looks at the social *situation* while grounded theory looks at social *process*. Situational analysts diagram elements in the research *situation* to capture the complexities and show relationships in the data. In *Situational Analysis: Grounded Theory After the Postmodern Turn*, Adele Clarke (Clarke, 2005) uses examples, illustrations, and clear explanations to promote situational and positional maps as "analytic exercises . . . provoking the researcher to analyze more deeply" (p. 83). The situational analysis approach may be useful beyond grounded theory contexts for researchers investigating policies, opinions, or other social science arenas where research participants express distinctive positions on the topic of inquiry.

Researchers who use interviews to build case studies can learn appropriate ways to analyze data from *Case Study Research* by Robert Yin (Yin, 2009) or *The Art of Case Study Research* by Robert Stake (Stake, 1995). The updated, more detailed text by Yin offers four different strategies for organizing the case study and five techniques for data analysis. Stake's book offers one example for analyzing data and generating naturalistic generalizations.

When researchers collect visual data, they add another set of analytic steps and concerns. Pink's second edition of *Doing Visual Ethnography* is a useful book for online researchers. She offers chapters on video as well as photographic materials, and Part 3 of the book is devoted to "Visual Images and Technologies" (Pink, 2007). Banks' *Using Visual Data in Qualitative Research* (Banks, 2007) includes a chapter on "Presenting Visual Research" but does not specifically address analysis of visual data. Neither Pink nor Banks addresses visuals such as charts, diagrams, or illustrations. In *Qualitative Researching* Mason (2002) offers a more comprehensive look in a chapter titled "Using Visual Methods." Although more work is needed, Mason's section on "Turning Documents and the Visual into Data" is a start.

Each qualitative methodology may offer some specific foci for researchers. However, every research methods writer or theorist seeks resolutions to the interview researcher's common dilemma: moving from a large collection of data to some useful, well-supported answers to the research questions.

STAGES OF THE ANALYTIC PROCESS: COMPARISON

Approaches to analysis of qualitative interview data are presented here to demonstrate the general flow recommended by respected analysts. They may each use different language, but they describe a comparable process.

Rubin and Rubin and Kvale and Brinkman write specifically about analysis of interview data; Ritchie and Lewis et al. speak more broadly to analysis of any qualitative data but include detailed discussions of interview research (Kvale, 2007; Kvale & Brinkman, 2009; Northcutt & McCoy, 2004; Ritchie, Lewis, & Elam, 2003). All three describe data analysis as a process that begins with research design and is ongoing throughout the research. While the researcher moves through distinct phases, analysis is iterative and deeply reflective, not linear. Some critical steps described in these three books are summarized in Table A.1.

Increasingly, researchers are using software for some of these data analysis steps. Data management and storage, text retrieval, and coding are possible with various computer-assisted qualitative data analysis software (CAQDAS) programs. One researcher observed the following:

> I found that switching from paper-based to electronic, software-based research allowed more freedom to play with ideas, because researchers can link and compare patterns within and across documents and the results can be saved, printed, or undone at will. When beginning a project, researchers create new documents or import text, numerical data, and graphics files from compatible software programs. [The software] organizes raw data (interviews, observations, etc.) and links them with memos where researchers might make codes and analytical notes, and then edit and rework ideas as the project progresses. For those involved in multiple projects, it is helpful to keep track of activities from one session to the next. Video images can also be linked to text documents. (Walsh, 2003, p. 253)

 CAQDAS options for data analysis, with links to demonstrations and reviews, can be found on the book's website.

Table A.1	Comparative Approaches to Data Analysis		
	Rubin and Rubin (Rubin & Rubin, 2005)	**Kvale and Brinkman** (Kvale, 2007; Kvale & Brinkman, 2009)	**Ritchie et al.** (Ritchie et al., 2003)
During and immediately after interviews	Reflection and note-taking are carried out throughout the interview research.	Interviewees may "discover new relationships" . . . interviewer condenses, interprets, and sends meaning back for further reply (Kvale, 2007, p. 102).	The "Framework" approach centers on an iterative "analytic hierarchy" (p. 212). The first step is familiarization with the data and ongoing review of research proposal, questions, and so on.
	Recognition occurs when the researcher finds concepts, themes, events, or topical markers in the data.	Analysis can focus on meaning, language, or theoretical concepts in the data.	*Data Management* refers to the process of sorting and synthesizing data to identify initial themes and create an index.
	Synthesis occurs when the researcher systematically clarifies meanings of concepts and themes.		
	Researchers *code* to label and designate themes and concepts.		*Descriptive Accounts* refers to the process of defining elements and dimensions, refining categories, and classifying data.
	Researchers *sort* by grouping data units with the same code or label.	*Re-interview* to allow subject the opportunity to comment on interviewer's interpretation.	
	At the stage of *final synthesis* researchers combine concepts to suggest conclusions or recommend policies.	Continue description and interpretation.	*Explanatory Accounts* refers to the process of developing explanations and applications to wider theory or practice.

Glossary of Terms

Abductive: A form of reasoning that, along with inductive and deductive reasoning, shows a way to come to a conclusion. Abductive reasoning is used when the researcher has an insight or makes a guess or an assumption that a connection exists in an incomplete or seemingly unrelated set of observations. Philosopher Charles Sanders Peirce (1839–1914) is credited with the origination of this concept and for applying it to pragmatic thinking.

Active interview: In an active interview, both parties to the interview are *active*, putting less focus on the interviewer as the one responsible for the interview process and focus. Meaning is actively assembled in the interview encounter (Holstein & Gubrium, 2004; Kvale, 2007).

Alienation: "[T]he appropriation of the products of somebody's action for purposes never intended or foreseen by the actor herself, drawing these products into a system of relations over which the producer has no knowledge or control" (Bakardjieva & Feenberg, 2001, p. 206).

Asynchronous communication: Communications that involve a delay between message and response, meaning it is not necessary to be online at the same time.

The Belmont Report: The basis for protection of human subjects regulations in the United States.

Beneficence: To do no harm and to reduce risks involved in research, a fundamental principle of research ethics.

Broadband: High-speed connection that permits transmission of images, audio and video, and large files.

Co-constructed narratives: Researchers and interviewees share jointly created stories. Narratives are called *mediated* when the researcher monitors the exchange or *unmediated* when a researcher and interviewee, or two researchers, exchange and study their own stories (Ellis & Berger, 2003).

Collaborate: The word *collaborate* has its origins in the Latin word *collaborare,* "to work together" (OED, 2005). The working definition used here is as follows: collaboration is an interactive process that engages two or more participants who work together to achieve outcomes they could not accomplish independently (Salmons, 2008).

Computer Mediated Communication (CMC): This term refers to human communication that occurs when messages are conveyed by computers.

Consequentialism: Ethical framework concerned with moral rightness of acts.

Constructivism: The premise of constructivism is that we construct reality based on our perceptions of the world. Subjects construct their own meanings in different ways, even in relation to the same phenomenon (Gray, 2004). The term *interpretivism* is often used synonymously with constructivism. The premise of interpretivism is that we "interpret" our experiences in the social world.

Convergence: A multimedia environment and/or network where signals regardless of type (i.e., voice, quality audio, video, data, and so on) are merged and can be accessed through the same devices (Knemeyer, 2004; Seybold, 2008, p. 11).

Creative interview: Jack Douglas' book *Creative Interviewing* introduced a life-story approach to interviews. These unstructured interviews occur on location in situational everyday worlds of people in society (Douglas, 1984; Fontana & Frey, 2003).

Criterion sampling: Selecting all participants on the basis of criteria selected to align with the research purpose.

Data analysis: Approach for deriving meaning, findings, or results.

Deductive reasoning: Reasoning used for research in which a specific explanation is deduced from a general premise and is then tested (Schutt, 2006).

Deontological ethics: Deontological ethics, building on the philosophies of Immanuel Kant (1785), views morality as the responsibility to fulfill duties and to follow principles.

Digital divide: Term describing unequal access to ICTs across social, economic, and demographic groups.

Disintermediation: Disintermediation is the process of cutting out the middleman so individuals communicate directly with producers and sellers of products and services.

Electronic collaboration: This occurs when the "interactive process" is conducted using ICT.

Epistemology: A branch of philosophy that considers the criteria for determining what constitutes and does not constitute valid knowledge. In research, *epistemology* refers to the study of the nature of knowledge or the study of how knowledge is justified (Gray, 2004).

Epoche: "Setting aside prejudgments and opening the research interview with unbiased, receptive presence" (Moustakas, 1994, p. 85).

Existing sample frame: Existing lists or collections of information about groups of people such as membership rolls or administrative records.

Experimental research: A research methodology based upon cause-and-effect relationships between independent and dependent variables by means of the manipulation of independent variables (Creswell, 2008).

Follow-up questions: Follow-up questions build on interviewee responses to get a clearer or deeper understanding of the interviewee's response.

Forum: A form of asynchronous discussion where original comments and responses are organized by topic. Threaded discussion occurs when one user posts a message that is visible to other users, who respond in their own time. Also known as *threaded discussion.*

Human subject: A living individual about whom an investigator (whether professional or student) conducting research obtains the following:

- Data through intervention or interaction with the individual, or
- Identifiable private information (HHS, 2005).

ICT literacy: Using digital technology, communications tools, and/or networks to access, manage, integrate, evaluate, and create information in order to function in a knowledge society (ETS, 2002).

Immediacy: Communicative behaviors that reduce the physical or psychological distance between individuals and foster affiliation (Mehrabian, 1971).

In-depth interview: An in-depth interview is a qualitative research technique involving a researcher who guides or questions a participant to elicit information, perspectives, insights, feelings or behaviors, experiences, or phenomena that cannot be observed. The in-depth interview is conducted to collect data that allow the researcher to generate new understandings and new knowledge about the subject of investigation.

Inductive reasoning: Reasoning used for research in which general conclusions are drawn from specific data (Schutt, 2006).

Information and Communications Technologies (ICTs): Umbrella term describing communication devices or applications including the following: cellular phones, computer and network hardware and software, satellite systems, as well as the various services and applications associated with them.

Institutional Review Board (IRB), Research Ethics Board: Body responsible for verifying that the research design protects human subjects.

Interactivity: The degree of mutuality and reciprocation present in a communication setting (Kalman et al., 2006).

IRB approval: The determination of the IRB that the research has been reviewed and may be conducted at an institution within the constraints set forth by the IRB and by other institutional and federal requirements (HHS, 2005).

Main interview questions: Main interview questions are articulated to elicit overall experiences and understandings.

Mass collaboration: Mass collaboration occurs when people who do not know each other write, think, or work on projects together (Tapscott & Williams, 2008). Wikis exemplify mass collaboration.

Mediated immediacy: Communicative cues in mediated channels that can shape perceptions of psychological closeness between interactants; immediacy cues can be seen as a language of affiliation (O'Sullivan et al., 2004, p. 471).

Methodologies: The study of, and justification for, methods used to conduct research. The term describes approaches to systematic inquiry developed within a particular paradigm with associated epistemological assumptions (Gray, 2004). Methodologies emerge from academic disciplines in the social and physical sciences and while considerable cross-disciplinary exchange occurs, choices generally place the study into a disciplinary context.

Methods: The practical steps used to conduct the study (Anfara & Mertz, 2006; Carter & Little, 2007).

Minimal risk: The probability and magnitude of harm or discomfort anticipated in the research are not greater in and of themselves than those ordinarily encountered in daily life or during the performance of routine physical or psychological examinations or tests (HHS, 2005).

Mixed methods: A research design that combines more than one method of qualitative and quantitative data collection and analysis (Creswell & Clark, 2007).

Mobile access: Ability to connect to the Internet anywhere using computers, cell phones, handheld computers, and personal digital assistants.

Nonverbal communication: Aspects of communication that convey messages without words. Types of nonverbal communication include the following:

- Chronemics communication is the use of pacing and timing of speech and length of silence before response in conversation.
- Paralinguistic or paralanguage communication describes variations in volume, pitch, or quality of voice.
- Kinesic communication includes eye contact and gaze, facial expressions, body movements, gestures, or postures.
- Proxemic communication is the use of interpersonal space to communicate attitudes (Gordon, 1980; Guerrero et al., 1999; Kalman et al., 2006).

Online interviews: For the purpose of this book "online interviews" refer to interviews conducted with CMC. Scholarly interviews are conducted in accordance with ethical research guidelines; verifiable research participants provide informed consent before participating in any interview.

Phenomenological research: Research method used to investigate the meaning, structure, and essence of human experience (Patton, 2002).

Positivism: A belief, shared by most scientists, that there is a reality that exists apart from our perceptions of it, that can be understood through observation, and that follows general laws (Schutt, 2006). The positivist tradition's view of social reality as "knowable" relies on a concept of validity in terms of measurement (Hesse-Biber & Leavy, 2006).

Postmodern interview: "Postmodern" refers to a set of "orienting sensibilities" rather than a particular kind of interviewing (Holstein & Gubrium, 2003b). These sensibilities include new ways to look at theory as "stories linked to the perspectives and interests of their storytellers" (Fontana, 2003; Holstein & Gubrium, 2003b, p. 5).

Postpositivism: A set of "orienting sensibilities" rather than a particular kind of interviewing (Holstein & Gubrium, 2003b). These sensibilities include new ways to look at theory as "stories linked to the perspectives and interests of their storytellers" (Fontana, 2003; Holstein & Gubrium, 2003b, p. 5).

Pragmatism: A worldview that draws on both objective and subjective knowledge (Creswell & Clark, 2007).

Probability sampling: A sampling method that relies on a random selection method so that the probability of selection of population elements is known (Schutt, 2006).

Probes: Probes encourage the interviewee to provide detail to flesh out and expand on the answer.

- A continuation probe encourages the interviewee to keep going with the current response.
- Elaboration probes ask for more explanation on a particular point.
- Attention probes ("Okay, I understand," and so on) let the interviewee know you are listening.
- Clarification probes ask for better definition or explanation if the researcher is confused or could not follow the thread of the story.
- Steering probes intend to get the story back on topic (Rubin & Rubin, 2005).

Purposive or purposeful sampling: A nonprobability sampling method in which participants or cases are selected for a purpose, usually as related to ability to answer central questions of the study.

Q-method: A structured approach to studying subjectivity. It is self-referential, and it is communicable by the participants (Amin, 2000). More than 2,000 theoretical and applied Q studies have been published in a variety of disciplines including medicine, psychology, and policy (Valenta & Wiggerand, 1997). Invented in 1935 by British physicist-psychologist William Stephenson, Q methodology is frequently associated with quantitative analysis because of its use of factor analysis (Stephenson, 1935). Q also can be used as a qualitative technique because it concentrates on the perceptions, attitudes, and values from the perspective of the person who is participating in the study and relies heavily on qualitative methods in developing the Q concourse. In correlating persons instead of tests, Q-method provides a holistic perspective of a participant's subjectivity in relationship to the research question.

Qualitative research: Methods of inquiry directed at providing an "in-depth and interpreted understanding of the social world of research participants by learning about their social and material circumstances, their experiences, perspectives and histories" (Ritchie & Lewis, 2003, p. 3).

Quantitative research: Methods of inquiry that analyze numeric representations of the world; the systematic and mathematical techniques used to collect and analyze data (Gray, 2004). Survey and questionnaire data are often analyzed in quantitative units (Yoshikawa et al., 2008).

Quasi-experimental research: A research approach that uses elements of the experimental design, such as use of a control group, but without the ability to randomly select the sample (Gray, 2004).

Research design: A comprehensive strategic plan for the study that "provides the glue that holds the research project together. A design is used to structure the research, to show how all of the major parts of the research project . . . work together to try to address the central research questions" (Trochim, 2006, Chapter 5).

Responsive interview: Rubin and Rubin use the term *responsive interview* to describe their approach that is characterized by a flexible design. They acknowledge the human feelings and common interests that allow interpersonal relationships to form between interviewer and interviewee. Responsive interviews aim for depth of understanding through ongoing self-reflection (Rubin & Rubin, 2005).

Sample: The subjects or participants selected for the study.

Sample frame: Lists or collections of information about groups of people, either already existing or constructed by the researcher for the purpose of selecting the sample.

Sampling: Procedure for selecting cases or participants to study.

Saturation or redundancy: The point at which selection is ended; when new interviews seem to yield little additional information (Schutt, 2006).

Second Life: A massive multiplayer universe (MMU) set in a 3-D virtual world created by San Francisco–based software maker Linden Labs (Wigmore & Howard, 2009).

Skype: An IP telephony service provider that offers free calling between computers and low-cost calling to regular telephones that aren't connected to the Internet. Included in the free service is a softphone.

Structured or survey interview: Interviewers ask fixed-choice questions and record responses based on a coding scheme. All interviews ask the same questions in the same order, and interviewers are trained to maintain a consistent, neutral approach to questioning and responding to all participants (Fontana & Frey, 2003; Schaeffer & Maynard, 2003; Schutt, 2006).

Survey: An investigation into one or more variables in a population that may involve collection of qualitative and/or quantitative data (Gray, 2004). Data may be analyzed with qualitative or quantitative methods.

Synchronous communication: Communications that involve a delay between message and response, meaning it is not necessary to be online at the same time.

Technology leapfrogging: The implementation of a new and up-to-date technology in an area where the previous version of the technology has not been deployed, bypassing technological stages that others (other countries) have gone through (Davison et al., 2006; Ehrhardt et al., 2008).

Theory: An explanation of a phenomenon that is internally consistent, is supportive of other theories, and gives new insights into the phenomenon. Some qualitative researchers frame the study in theoretical terms while others aim to discover and "ground" theoretical principles in the data. In quantitative research, theory "is an inter-related set of constructs (or variables) formed into propositions, or hypotheses, that specify the relationship among variables" (Creswell, 2003, p. 120).

Utilitarian approach: Ethical view that actions should provide the most good or do the least harm.

Variable: A characteristic that is measurable (Gray, 2004).

Virtual worlds: Synchronous, persistent network of people, represented by avatars, facilitated by computers (Bell, 2008).

Virtue ethics: Ethical actions ought to be consistent with certain ideal virtues that provide for the full development of our humanity (Velasquez et al., 2008).

Visual literacy: The ability to recognize, draw meaning from, and convey ideas through visible symbols, pictures, or images.

Voice over Internet protocol (VoIP): A generic term used to describe the techniques used to carry voice traffic over the Internet (infoDev, 2008).

Webinar: A workshop or lecture delivered over the Web. Webinars may be a one-way webcast, or there may be interaction between participants and presenters. VoIP audio, shared whiteboard, and shared applications may be used.

Whiteboard: The equivalent of a blackboard, but on a computer screen. A whiteboard allows one or more users to draw on the screen while others on the network watch, and can be used for instruction the same way a blackboard is used in a classroom (*Computer User High Tech Dictionary*, 2008).

Wiki: A web application designed to allow multiple authors to add, remove, and edit content (infoDev, 2008).

Wireless: Generic term for mobile communication services that do not use fixed-line networks for direct access to the subscriber (infoDev, 2008).

References

Ahern, N. R. (2005). Using the Internet to conduct research. *Nurse Researcher,* *13*(2), 55–68.

Alexander, B. (2009). Apprehending the future: Emerging technologies, from science fiction to campus reality. *EDUCAUSE Review, 44*(3), 12–29.

Amin, Z. (2000). Q methodology: A journey into the subjectivity of the human mind. *Singapore Medical Journal, 41*(8), 410–414.

Anfara, V. A., & Mertz, N. T. (Eds.). (2006). *Theoretical frameworks in qualitative research.* Thousand Oaks, CA: Sage Publications.

Arthur, S., & Nazroo, J. (2003). Designing fieldwork strategies and materials. In J. Ritchie & J. Lewis (Eds.), *Qualitative research practice: A guide for social science students and researchers* (pp. 109–137). London: Sage Publications.

Atkinson, P., & Silverman, D. (1997). Kundera's immortality: The interview society and the invention of the self. *Qualitative Inquiry, 3*(September), 304–325.

Baggini, J., & Fosl, P. S. (2007). *The ethics toolkit: A compendium of ethical concepts and methods.* Malden, MA: Blackwell Publishing.

Bailenson, J. N., Yee, N., Blascovich, J., Beall, A. C., Lundblad, N., & Jin, M. (2008). The use of immersive virtual reality in the learning sciences: Digital transformations of teachers, students, and social context. *Journal of the Learning Sciences, 17*, 102–141.

Bakardjieva, M. (2005). *Internet society: The Internet in everyday life.* London: Sage Publications.

Bakardjieva, M., & Feenberg, A. (2001). Respecting the virtual subject, or how to navigate the private/public continuum. In C. Werry & M. Mowbray (Eds.), *Online communities: Commerce, community action, and the virtual university* (pp. 195–213). Upper Saddle River, NJ: HP Prentice Hall.

Bamford, A. (2003). *The visual literacy white paper.* Uxbridge: Adobe Systems Pty Ltd., Australia.

Bampton, R., & Cowton, C. J. (2002). The e-Interview. *Forum: Qualitative Social Research, 3*(2).

Banks, M. (2007). *Using visual data in qualitative research.* London: Sage Publications.

Baños, R. M., Botella, C., Rubió, I., Quero, S., García-Palacios, A., & Alcañiz, M. (2008). Presence and emotions in virtual environments: The influence of stereoscopy. *CyberPsychology & Behavior, 11*(1), 1–8.

Baym, N. K. (2009). What constitutes quality in qualitative Internet research? In A. N. Markham & N. K. Baym (Eds.), *Internet inquiry: Conversations about method* (pp. 173–190). Thousand Oaks, CA: Sage Publications.

Bekkering, E., & Shim, J. P. (2006). Trust in videoconferencing. *Communications of the ACM, 49*(7), 103–107.

Bell, M. (2008). *Definition and taxonomy of virtual worlds.* Paper presented at the New Digital Media (Audiovisual, Games and Music): Economic, Social and Political Impacts, Sao Paulo, Brazil.

Bernard, H. R., & Ryan, G. (2009). *Analyzing qualitative data.* Thousand Oaks, CA: Sage Publications.

Berry, D. M. (2004). Internet research: Privacy, ethics and alienation: An open source approach. *The Journal of Internet Research, 14*(4), 323–332.

Biswas, R., Maniam, J., Lee, E. W. H., Umakanth, S., Das, P. G., Dahiya, S., et al. (2009). Electronic collaboration toward social health outcomes. In J. E. Salmons & L. Wilson (Eds.), *Handbook of research on electronic collaboration and organizational synergy* (Vol. 2, pp. 710–724). Hershey, PA: Information Science Reference.

Blackwell, N. C. A. F., & Clarkson, P. J. (2006). Graphic elicitation: Using research diagrams as interview stimuli. *Qualitative Research, 6*(3), 341–366.

Bloomberg, L. D., & Volpe, M. (2008). *Completing your qualitative dissertation: A roadmap from beginning to end.* Thousand Oaks, CA: Sage Publications.

Bowker, N. I., & Tuffin, K. (2007). Understanding positive subjectivities made possible online for disabled people. *New Zealand Journal of Psychology, 36*(2), 63–71.

Brown, S. R. (1980). *Political subjectivity: Applications of Q methodology in political science.* New Haven, CT: Yale University Press.

Brown, S. R. (1993). A primer on Q methodology. *Operant Subjectivity, 16,* 91–138.

Brown, S. R., & Melamed, L. E. (1990). *Experimental design and analysis.* Thousand Oaks, CA: Sage Publications.

Browne, K. (2005). Snowball sampling: Using social networks to research nonheterosexual women. *International Journal of Social Research Methodology, 8*(1), 47–60.

Burkdall, T. (2009). The persistence of writing. *EDUCAUSE Review, 44*(3), 58–59.

Cabiria, J. (2008a). Benefits of virtual world engagement: Implications for marginalized gay and lesbian people. *Media Psychology Review* (Vol. Summer).

Cabiria, J. (2008b). *A Second Life: Online virtual worlds as therapeutic tools for gay and lesbian people.* Santa Barbara, CA: Fielding Graduate University.

Cabiria, J. (2008c). Virtual world and real world permeability: Transference of positive benefits for marginalized gay and lesbian populations. *Journal of Virtual Worlds Research, 1.*

Calhoun, E. F. (1993). Action research: Three approaches. *Educational Leadership, 51*(2), 62–66.

Carter, S. M., & Little, M. (2007). Justifying knowledge, justifying method, taking action: Epistemologies, methodologies, and methods in qualitative research. *Qualitative Health Research, 17*(10), 1316–1328.

Carusi, A. (2008). Data as representation: Beyond anonymity in e-research ethics. *International Journal of Internet Research Ethics, 1*(1), 37–65.

Cascio, J. (2009). *Politics: Participatory panopticon, ten-year forecast.* Palo Alto, CA: Institute of the Future.

Chapman, D. S., & Rowe, P. M. (2002). The influence of videoconference technology and interview structure on the recruiting function of the employment interview: A field experiment. *International Journal of Selection and Assessment, 10*(3), 185–197.

Charmaz, K. (2003). Qualitative interviewing and grounded theory analysis. In J. A. Holstein & J. F. Gubrium (Eds.), *Inside interviewing: New lenses, new concerns* (pp. 311–330). Thousand Oaks, CA: Sage Publications.

Charmaz, K. (2006). *Constructing grounded theory: A practical guide through qualitative analysis.* Thousand Oaks, CA: Sage Publications.

Chen, M. (2002). *Leveraging the asymmetric sensitivity of eye contact for videoconference.* Paper presented at the Special Interest Group on Computer-Human Interaction Conference on Human Factors in Computing Systems, Minneapolis, MN.

Chen, P., & Hinton, S. M. (1999). Realtime interviewing using the World Wide Web. *Sociological Research Online, 4.*

Chin-Sheng, W., & Wen-Bin, C. (2006). Why are adolescents addicted to online gaming? An interview study in Taiwan. *CyberPsychology & Behavior, 9*(6), 762–766.

Chou, C. (2001). Internet heavy use and addiction among Taiwanese college students: An online interview study. *CyberPsychology & Behavior, 4*(5), 573–585.

Clandinin, D. J., & Connelly, F. M. (2000). *Narrative inquiry: Experience and story in qualitative research.* Thousand Oaks, CA: Sage Publications.

Clarke, A. (2005). *Situational analysis: Grounded theory after the postmodern turn.* Thousand Oaks, CA: Sage Publications.

Computer user high tech dictionary. (2008). Retrieved September 8, 2008, from http://www.computeruser.com

Connor, H. O. (2006). *Exploring online research methods in a virtual training environment.* Leicester, UK: University of Leicester.

Connor, H. O., & Madge, C. (2001). Cyber-mothers: Online synchronous interviewing using conferencing software. *Sociological Research Online, 5*(4).

Corbin, A. S. J. (1998). *Basics of qualitative research: Grounded theory procedures and techniques* (2nd ed.). Newbury Park, CA: Sage Publications.

Covey, S. R. (2004). *The 7 habits of highly effective people: Powerful lessons in personal change.* New York: Free Press.

Coyne, I. T. (1997). Sampling in qualitative research. Purposeful and theoretical sampling; merging or clear boundaries? *Journal of Advanced Nursing, 26*, 623–630.

Creswell, J. W. (1998). *Qualitative inquiry and research design: Choosing among five traditions* (1st ed.). Thousand Oaks, CA: Sage Publications.

Creswell, J. W. (2003). *Research design: Qualitative, quantitative and mixed methods approaches* (2nd ed.). Thousand Oaks, CA: Sage Publications.

Creswell, J. W. (2007). *Qualitative inquiry and research design: Choosing among five approaches* (2nd ed.). Thousand Oaks, CA: Sage Publications.

Creswell, J. W. (2008). *Research design: Qualitative, quantitative and mixed methods approaches* (3rd ed.). Thousand Oaks, CA: Sage Publications.

Creswell, J. W., & Clark, V. L. P. (2007a). *Designing and conducting mixed methods research* (2nd ed.). Thousand Oaks, CA: Sage Publications.

Creswell, J. W., & Clark, V. L. P. (2007b). *The mixed methods reader* (2nd ed.). Thousand Oaks, CA: Sage Publications.

Crilly, N., Blackwell, A. F., & Clarkson, P. J. (2006). Graphic elicitation: Using research diagrams as interview stimuli. *Qualitative Research, 6*(3), 341–366.

Crotty, M. (1998). *The foundation of social research: Meaning and perspectives in the research process.* London: Sage Publications.

Daft, R. L., & Lengel, R. H. (1986). Organizational information requirements, media richness and structural design. *Management Science, 32*(5), 554–571.

Davis, M. (1999). *Ethics in the university.* Florence, Italy: Routledge.

Davis, M., Bolding, G., Hart, G., Sherr, L., & Elford, J. (2004). Reflecting on the experience of interviewing online: Perspectives from the Internet and HIV study in London. *AIDS Care, 16*(8), 944–952.

Davison, R., Vogel, D., Harris, R., & Jones, N. (2006). Technology leapfrogging in developing countries. *Electronic Journal on Information Systems in Developing Countries, 1*(5), 1–10.

Debes, J. (1968). Some foundations of visual literacy. *Audio-Visual Instruction, 13,* 961–964.

Denzin, N. K. (1989). *Interpretive biography* (Vol. 17). Newbury Park, CA: Sage Publications.

Denzin, N. K. (2001). The reflexive interview and a performative social science. *Qualitative Research, 1*(23), 23–25.

DeVault, M., & L. McCoy. (2002). Institutional ethnography: Using interviews to investigate ruling relations. In J. F. Gubrium & J. A. Holstein (Eds.), *Handbook of interviewing: Context and method.* Thousand Oaks, CA: Sage.

Dewey, J. (1916). *Democracy and education.* New York: Macmillan Company.

DiCicco-Bloom, B., & Crabtree, B. F. (2006). The qualitative research interview. *Medical Education, 40,* 314–321.

Dodge, M. (2005). The role of maps in virtual research methods. In C. Hine (Ed.), *Virtual methods: Issues in social research on the Internet* (pp. 113–128). Oxford, UK: Berg.

Douglas, J. D. (1984). *Creative interviewing.* Thousand Oaks, CA: Sage Publications.

Dourish, P. (2004). What we talk about when we talk about context. *Journal of the ACM, 8*(1), 19–30.

e-CFR. (2008). *Protection of human subjects.* In U. S. Department of Health and Human Services (Ed.) (Vol. 21 CFR Part 50).

Ehrhardt, D., Gale, S., McKinlay, A., & Sethi, P. (2008). Module 7: New technologies and impact on regulation. In *ICT regulation toolkit* (Vol. 2008). Washington, DC: Information for Development Program.

Ellis, C., & Berger, L. (2003). Their story/my story/our story. In J. F. Gubrium & J. A. Holstein (Eds.), *Postmodern interviewing* (pp. 157–186). Thousand Oaks, CA: Sage Publications.

Elm, M. S. (2008). How do various notions of privacy influence decisions in qualitative Internet research? In A. N. Markham & N. K. Baym (Eds.), *Internet inquiry: Conversations about method* (pp. 69–87). Thousand Oaks, CA: Sage Publications.

Emerson, R. W. (1838). *Literary ethics.* Hanover, NH: Dartmouth College.

Erickson, T., & Herring, S. C. (2005). *Persistent conversation: A dialog between research and design.* Paper presented at the International Conference on System Sciences, Manoa, Hawaii.

Ess, C. (2002). *Ethical decision making and Internet Research: Recommendations from the AOIR ethics working committee.* Retrieved December 10, 2003, from http://www.aoir.org/reports/ethics.pdf

ETS. (2003). *Succeeding in the 21c: What higher education must do to address the gap in information and communications technology.* Retrieved September 10, 2004, from http://www.ets.org/ictliteracy/ICTwhitepaperfinal.pdf

ETS. (2006). *ICT literacy assessment preliminary findings.* Retrieved February 25, 2007, from http://www.ets.org/Media/Products/ICT_Literacy/pdf/2006_Preliminary_Findings.pdf

Eysenbach, G., & Till, J. (2001). Ethical issues in qualitative research on Internet communities. *British Medical Journal, 323*(7321), 1103–1105.

Fereday, J., & Muir-Cochrane, E. (2006). Demonstrating rigor using thematic analysis: A hybrid approach of inductive and deductive coding and theme development. *International Journal of Qualitative Methods, 5*(1), 80–92.

Fielding, N. (2007). *New technologies, new applications: Using access grid nodes in field research and training.* Swindon, UK: Economic & Social Research Council.

Fontana, A. (2003). Postmodern trends in interviewing. In J. F. Gubrium & J. A. Holstein (Eds.), *Postmodern interviewing* (pp. 51–66). Thousand Oaks, CA: Sage Publications.

Fontana, A., & Frey, J. H. (2003). The interview: From structured questions to negotiated text. In N. K. Denzin & Y. S. (Eds.), *Collecting and interpreting qualitative materials* (pp. 61–106). Thousand Oaks, CA: Sage Publications.

Fox, S., & Fallows, D. (2003). *Internet health resources.* Retrieved October 25, 2005, from http://www.pewinternet.org/pdfs/PIP_Instantmessage_Report.pdf

Frankel, M. S., & Siang, S. (1999). *Ethical and legal aspects of human subjects research on the Internet.* Washington, DC: American Association for the Advancement of Science.

Franklin, B. (1757). *The autobiography of Benjamin Franklin* (2004 ed.). New York: Simon & Schuster.

Gardner, H. (1983). *Frames of mind: The theory of multiple intelligences.* New York: Basic Books.

Garg, A. (2008). Sampling hurdles: "Borderline illegitimate" to legitimate data. *International Journal of Qualitative Methods, 7*(4), 59–67.

Garrison, D. R., Anderson, T., & Archer, W. (2004). Critical thinking and computer conferencing: A model and tool to assess cognitive presence. *American Journal of Distance Education, 15*(1).

Gehling, R., Turner, D., & Rutherford, B. (2007). Defining the proposed factors for small business online banking: Interviewing the IT professionals. *Financial Services Marketing, 12*(3), 189–196.

Geiser, T. (2002). Conducting online focus groups: A methodological discussion. In L. Burton & D. Goldsmith (Eds.), *The medium is the message: Using online focus groups to study online learning* (Vol. 2003, pp. 1–14). New Britain: Connecticut Distance Learning Consortium.

Gergle, D., Kraut, R. E., & Fussell, S. R. (2004). Language efficiency and visual technology minimizing collaborative effort with visual information. *Journal of Language and Social Psychology, 23*(4), 491–517.

Goldstein, B. M. (2007). All photos lie: Images as data. In G. C. Stanczak (Ed.), *Visual research methods: Image, society, and representation* (pp. 61–81). Thousand Oaks, CA: Sage Publications.

Gordon, R. L. (1980). *Interviewing: Strategy, techniques and tactics.* Homewood, IL: Dorsey.

Gray, D. (2004). *Doing research in the real world.* London: Sage Publications.

Gray, D. (2009). *Doing research in the real world* (2nd ed.). London: Sage Publications.

Grayson, D. M., & Monk, A. F. (2003). Are you looking at me? Eye contact and desktop video conferencing. *Transactions on Computer-Human Interaction, 10*(3).

Groenwald, T. (2004). A phenomenological research design illustrated. *International Journal of Qualitative Methods, 3*(1). Retrieved August 1, 2009, from http://www.ualberta.ca/~iiqm/backissues/3_1/pdf/groenewald.pdf

Gubrium, E., & Koro-Ljungberg, M. (2005). Contending with border making in the social constructionist interview. *Qualitative Inquiry, 5*(11), 689–715.

Gubrium, J., & Holstein, J. (2003a). From the individual interview to the interview society. In J. F. Gubrium & J. A. Holstein (Eds.), *Postmodern interviewing* (pp. 21–50). Thousand Oaks, CA: Sage Publications.

Gubrium, J., & Holstein, J. (Eds.). (2003b). *Postmodern interviewing.* Thousand Oaks, CA: Sage Publications.

Guerrero, L. K., DeVito, J. A., & Hecht, M. L. (Eds.). (1999). *The nonverbal communication reader: Classic and contemporary readings.* Prospect Hills, IL: Waveland Press.

Hargrove, R. (2001). *E-leader: Reinventing leadership in a connected economy* (1st ed.). Cambridge, MA: Perseus Publishing.

Heeter, C. (2003). Reflections on real presence by a virtual person. *Presence: Teleoperators & Virtual Environments, 12*(4), 335–345.

Herring, S. C. (2003). Computer-mediated discourse. In D. Schiffrin, D. Tannen, & Heidi E. Hamilton (Eds.), *The handbook of discourse analysis* (pp. 612–634). New York: Wiley-Blackwell.

Hesse-Biber, S. N., & Leavy, P. (2006). *The practice of qualitative research.* Thousand Oaks, CA: Sage Publications.

HHS. (2005). *Code of Federal Regulations: Protection of human subjects* (Vol. Part 46).

Higginbottom, G. (2004). Sampling issues in qualitative research. *Nurse Researcher, 12*(1), 7–19.

Hine, C. (2005). Internet research and the sociology of cyber-scientific knowledge. *The Information Society, 21,* 239–248.

Holstein, J. A., & Gubrium, J. F. (2003a). Active interviewing. In J. F. Gubrium & J. A. Holstein (Eds.), *Postmodern interviewing* (pp. 67–80). Thousand Oaks, CA: Sage Publications.

Holstein, J. A., & Gubrium, J. F. (2003b). Postmodern sensibilities. In J. F. Gubrium & J. A. Holstein (Eds.), *Postmodern interviewing* (pp. 3–20). Thousand Oaks, CA: Sage Publications.

Holstein, J. A., & Gubrium, J. F. (Eds.). (2003c). *Inside interviewing: New lenses, new concerns.* Thousand Oaks, CA: Sage Publications.

Holstein, J. A., & Gubrium, J. F. (2004). The active interview. In D. Silverman (Ed.), *Qualitative research: Theory, method and practice* (pp. 140–161). Thousand Oaks, CA: Sage Publications.

Hull, C. L. (1943). *Principles of behavior.* New York: Appleton-Century-Crofts.

Hunt, N., & McHale, S. (2007). A practical guide to the email interview. *Qualitative Health Research, 17*(10), 1415–1421.

Husserl, E. (1931). *Ideas: General introduction to pure phenomenology.* London: George Allen and Unwin, Ltd.

Husserl, E. (1994). Logical investigations. In C. Moustakas (Ed.), *Phenomenological research methods* (p. 45). Thousand Oaks, CA: Sage Publications.

infoDev. (2008). Glossary. In *ICT regulation toolkit* (Vol. 2008). Washington, DC: Author.

Jacobsen, M. M. (1999). *Orality, literacy, cyberdiscursivity: Transformations of literacy in computer-mediated communication.* Unpublished doctoral dissertation, Texas A&M University.

James, N., & Busher, H. (2006). Credibility, authenticity and voice: Dilemmas in online interviewing. *Qualitative Research, 6*(3), 403–420.

Johnson, R. B., & Onwuegbuzie, A. J. (2004). Mixed methods research: A research paradigm whose time has come. *Educational Researcher, 33*(7), 14–26.

Joinson, A. (2001). Self-disclosure in computer-mediated communication: The role of self-awareness and visual anonymity. *European Journal of Social Psychology, 31*, 177–192.

Jones, S., & Fox, S. (2009). *Generations online in 2009*. Washington, DC: Pew Research Center.

Kahai, S. S., & Cooper, R. B. (2003). Exploring the core concepts of Media Richness Theory: The impact of cue multiplicity and feedback immediacy on decision quality. *Journal of Management Information Systems, 20*(3), 263–299.

Kalman, Y. M., Ravid, G., Raban, D. R., & Rafaeli, S. (2006). Pauses and response latencies: A chronemic analysis of asynchronous CMC. *Journal of Computer-Mediated Communication, 12*(1), 1–23.

Kaplan, H. B. (1975). The self-esteem motive. In H. B. Kaplan (Ed.), *Self-attitudes and deviant behavior* (pp. 10–31). Pacific Palisades, CA: Goodyear.

Kehrwald, B. (2008). Understanding social presence in text-based online learning environments. *Distance Education, 29*(1), 89–106.

Kitchen, R. (1998). Towards geographies of cyberspace. *Progress in Human Geography, 22*(3), 385–406.

Kitto, R. J., & Barnett, J. (2007). Analysis of thin online interview data: Toward a sequential hierarchical language-based approach. *American Journal of Evaluation, 28*(3), 356–368.

Knapik, M. (2006). The qualitative research interview: Participants' responsive participation in knowledge making. *International Journal of Qualitative Methods, 5*(3), 1–13.

Knemeyer, D. (2004). Digital convergence: Insight into the future of Web design. *Digital Web Magazine*.

Koerber, A., & McMichael, L. (2008). Qualitative sampling methods: A primer for technical communicators. *Journal of Business and Technical Communication, 22*(4), 454–473.

Kouzes, J. M., & Posner, B. Z. (2007). *The leadership challenge* (4th ed.). San Francisco: Jossey Bass.

Kress, G. (2003). *Literacy in the new media age*. London: Routledge.

Kvale, S. (2006). Dominance through interviews and dialogues. *Qualitative Inquiry, 12*(3), 480–500.

Kvale, S. (2007). *Doing interviews*. Thousand Oaks, CA: Sage Publications.

Kvale, S., & Brinkman, S. (2009). *InterViews: Learning the craft of qualitative research interviewing* (2nd ed.). Thousand Oaks, CA: Sage Publications.

Lebo, H. (2004). *Center for the Digital Future identifies the 10 major trends emerging in the Internet? First decade of public use*. Retrieved October 27, 2005, from http://www.digitalcenter.org/downloads/DigitalFutureReport-Year4-2004 .pdf

Lee, N., & Lings, I. (2008). *Doing business research: A guide to theory and practice*. London: Sage Publications.

Lenhart, A. (2009). *Adults and social network websites*. Retrieved January 25, 2009, from http://www.pewinternet.org/Reports/2009/Adults-and-Social-Network-Websites.aspx

Lester, S. (1999). *An introduction to phenomenological research.* Retrieved August 1, 2009, from http://www.sld.demon.co.uk/resmethy.pdf

Lévi-Strauss, C. (1983). *The raw and the cooked: Mythologiques, Volume 1.* Chicago: University of Chicago Press.

Li, C., & Bernoff, J. (2008). *Groundswell: Winning in a world transformed by social technologies.* Boston: Harvard Business School Press.

Licoppea, C., & Smoredab, Z. (2005). Are social networks technologically embedded? How networks are changing today with changes in communication technology. *Social Networks, 27*(4), 317–335.

Lincoln, Y. S., & Guba, E. G. (1985). *Naturalistic inquiry.* Thousand Oaks, CA: Sage Publications.

Little, J. K., & Page, C. (2009). *The EDUCAUSE top teaching and learning challenges 2009.* Retrieved May 29, 2009, from http://www.educause.edu/eli/Challenges/127397

Lombard, M., & Ditton, T. (1997). At the heart of it all: The concept of presence. *Journal of Computer-Mediated Communication, 3*(2).

Loue, S. (2000). *Textbook of research ethics: Theory and practice.* Hingham, MA: Kluwer Academic Publishers.

Madden, M. (2005). *Do-it-yourself information online.* Retrieved October 25, 2005, from http://www.pewinternet.org/PPF/r/157/report_display.asp

Mann, C., & Stewart, F. (2000). *Internet communication and qualitative research: A handbook for researching online.* London: Sage Publications.

Mann, C., & Stewart, F. (2003). Internet interviewing. In J. F. Gubrium & J. A. Holstein (Eds.), *Postmodern interviewing* (pp. 81–105). Thousand Oaks, CA: Sage Publications.

Markham, A. N. (2005). Disciplining the future: A critical organizational analysis of Internet studies. *The Information Society, 21*, 257–267.

Mason, J. (2002). *Qualitative researching* (2nd ed.). Thousand Oaks, CA: Sage Publications.

Mehrabian, A. (1971). *Silent messages.* Belmont, WA: Wadsworth.

Messinger, P. R., Ge, X., Stroulia, E., Lyons, K., & Smirnov, K. (2008). On the relationship between my avatar and myself. *Journal of Virtual Worlds Research, 1*(2).

Metros, S. E. (2008). The educator's role in preparing visually literate learners. *Theory Into Practice, 47*, 107–109.

Miles, M., & Huberman, A. M. (1994). *Qualitative data analysis: An expanded sourcebook* (2nd ed.). Thousand Oaks, CA: Sage Publications.

Miller, J., & Glassner, B. (2004). The "inside" and the "outside": Finding realities in interviews. In D. Silverman (Ed.), *Qualitative research: Theory, method and practice* (pp. 125–139). Thousand Oaks, CA: Sage Publications.

Molyneaux, H., O'Donnell, S., Liu, S., Hagerman, V., Gibson, K. B. M., et al. (2007). *Good practice guidelines for participatory multi-site videoconferencing.* Fredericton: National Research Council Canada Institute for Information Technology.

Morgan, D. L. (2007). Combining qualitative and quantitative methods. Paradigms lost and pragmatism regained: Methodological implications. *Journal of Mixed Methods Research, 1*(1), 48–76.

Moustakas, C. (1994). *Phenomenological research methods.* Thousand Oaks, CA: Sage Publications.

Näykki, P., & Järvelä, S. (2008). How pictorial knowledge representations mediate collaborative knowledge construction in groups. *Journal of Research on Technology in Education, 40*(3), 359–387.

Neuman, W. L. (1994). *Social research methods: Qualitative and quantitative approaches.* Needham Heights, MA: Allyn and Bacon.

Norris, D., Mason, J., & Lefrere, P. (2004). Experiencing knowledge. *Innovate: Journal of Online Education, 1*(1).

Northcutt, N., & McCoy, D. (2004). *Interactive qualitative analysis: A systems method for qualitative research.* Thousand Oaks, CA: Sage Publications.

O'Connor, H. (2006). Online interviews, *Exploring online research methods: Online interviews.* Leicester, UK: The University of Leicester.

O'Donnell, S., Perley, S., & Simms, D. (2008). *Challenges for video communications in remote and rural communities.* Paper presented at the IEEE International Symposium on Technology and Society, New Brunswick, Canada.

O'Hara, P. (2005). *Strategic Initiative for Developing Capacity in Ethical Review (SIDCER).* Paper presented at the International Conference on Ethical Issues in Behavioural and Social Sciences Research, Montreal, Canada.

O'Sullivan, P. B., Hunt, S. K., & Lippert, L. R. (2004). Mediated immediacy: A language of affiliation in a technological age. *Journal of Language and Social Psychology, 23*(4), 464–490.

OED. (2005). *Oxford English Dictionary.* Retrieved May 29, 2005, from http://www.askoxford.com

Olaniran, B. A. (2009). Organizational communication: Assessment of videoconferencing as a medium for meetings in the workplace. *International Journal of Technology and Human Interaction, 5*(2), 63–84.

Ong, W. (1990). *Writing and reading texts are speech events: Language as hermeneutic.* MO: Saint Louis University.

Opdenakker, R. (2006). Advantages and disadvantages of four interview techniques in qualitative research. *Forum: Qualitative Social Research, 4*(11).

Palmquist, M. (2008). *Writing guides: Case studies.* Retrieved July 18, 2008, from http://writing.colostate.edu/guides/research/casestudy/index.cfm

Patton, M. Q. (2002). *Qualitative research and evaluation methods* (3rd ed.). Thousand Oaks, CA: Sage Publications.

Pedroni, J. A., & Pimple, K. D. (2001). *A brief introduction to informed consent in research with human subjects.* Bloomington: Poynter Center for the Study of Ethics and American Institutions.

Penslar, R. L., & Porter, J. P. (2009). *IRB Guidebook chapter III: Basic IRB review.* Retrieved August 3, 2009, from http://www.hhs.gov/ohrp/irb/irb_chapter3.htm

Pink, S. (2007). *Doing visual ethnography* (2nd ed.). London: Sage Publications.

Porter, J. P. (1993). *Institutional review board guidebook.* Washington, DC: U.S. Department of Health and Human Services Office for Human Research Protections.

Pryke, M. (2003). *Using social theory: Thinking through research.* London: Sage Publications.

Ragin, C. C. (1994). *Constructing social research.* Thousand Oaks, CA: Pine Forge Press.

Rainie, L. (2005). *The state of blogging*. Retrieved October 25, 2005, from http://www.pewinternet.org/pdfs/PIP_blogging_data.pdf

Rainie, L., & Horrigan, J. (2005). *A decade of adoption: How the Internet has woven itself into American life*. Retrieved October 25, 2005, from http://www.pewinternet.org/pdfs/PIP_blogging_data.pdf

Reid, A., Petocz, P., & Gordon, S. (2008). Research interviews in cyberspace. *Journal for Qualitative Research, 8*(1), 47–61.

Reppel, A., Gruber, T., Szmigin, I., & Voss, R. (2008). Conducting qualitative research online: An exploratory study into the preferred attributes of an iconic digital music player. *European Advances in Consumer Research, 8*, 519–525.

Ritchie, J., & Lewis, J. (Eds.). (2003). *Qualitative research practice: A guide for social science students and researchers*. London: Sage Publications.

Ritchie, J., Lewis, J., & Elam, G. (2003). Designing and selecting samples. In J. Ritchie & J. Lewis (Eds.), *Qualitative research practice: A guide for social science students and researchers* (pp. 77–108). London: Sage Publications.

Roper, J. M., & Shapira, J. (2000). *Ethnography in nursing research*. Thousand Oaks, CA: Sage Publications.

Rosenblatt, P. C. (2003). Interviewing at the border of fact and fiction. In J. F. Gubrium & J. A. Holstein (Eds.), *Postmodern interviewing* (pp. 225–242). Thousand Oaks, CA: Sage Publications.

Ross, D. N. (2001). Electronic communications: Do cultural dimensions matter? *American Business Review*, 75–81.

Rubin, H. J., & Rubin, I. S. (2005). *Qualitative interviewing: The art of hearing data* (2nd ed.). Thousand Oaks, CA: Sage Publications.

Sade-Beck, L. (2004). Internet ethnography: Online and offline. *International Journal of Qualitative Methods, 3*(2), Article 4.

Salmons, J. E. (2006). *Taxonomy of collaborative e-learning*. Cincinnati, OH: Union Institute and University.

Salmons, J. E. (2008). Taxonomy of collaborative e-learning. In L. A. Tomei (Ed.), *Encyclopedia of information technology curriculum integration* (pp. 839–942). Hershey, PA: Information Science Reference.

Salmons, J. E. (2009). *Taxonomy of online collaboration: Theory and application in e-learning*. Hershey, PA: Information Science Reference.

Salmons, J. E. (2010). *Taxonomy of online collaboration: Theory and practice in e-learning*. Hershey, PA: IGI Global.

Salmons, J. E., & Wilson, L. A. (Eds.). (2009). *Handbook of research on electronic collaboration and organizational synergy*. Hershey, PA: Information Science Reference.

Schaeffer, N. C., & Maynard, D. W. (2003). Standardization and interaction in the survey interview. In J. F. Gubrium & J. A. Holstein (Eds.), *Postmodern interviewing* (pp. 51–66). Thousand Oaks, CA: Sage Publications.

Schmolck, P. (1999). *WebQ*. Retrieved June 4, 2009, from http://www.lrz-muenchen.de/~schmolck/qmethod/webq/

Schutt, R. K. (2006). *Investigating the social world: The process and practice of research* (5th ed.). Thousand Oaks, CA: Pine Forge Press.

Sedgwick, M., & Spiers, J. (2009). The use of videoconferencing as a medium for the qualitative interview. *International Journal of Qualitative Methods, 8*(1), 1–11.

Seybold, A. M. (2008). The convergence of wireless, mobility, and the Internet and its relevance to enterprises. *Information Knowledge Systems Management, 7,* 11–23.

Seymour, W. S. (2001). In the flesh or online? Exploring qualitative research methodologies. *Qualitative Research, 1*(2), 147–168.

Shin, N. (2002). Beyond interaction: The relational construct of "transactional presence." *Open Learning, 17*(2).

Shinebourne, P. (2009). Using Q method in qualitative research. *International Journal of Qualitative Methods, 8*(1), 93–97.

Shirky, C. (2008). *Here comes everybody: The power of organizing without organizations.* New York: Penguin Press.

Shiu, E., & Lenhart, A. (2004). *How Americans use instant messaging.* Retrieved October 25, 2005, from http://www.pewinternet.org/pdfs/PIP_Instantmessage_Report.pdf

Silverman, D., & Marvasti, A. (2008). *Doing qualitative research: A comprehensive guide.* Thousand Oaks, CA: Sage Publications.

Sixsmith, J., & Murray, C. D. (2001). Ethical issues in the documentary data analysis of Internet posts and archives. *Qualitative Health Research, 11*(3), 423–432.

SKMM. (2008). *Malaysian communications and multimedia commission.* Retrieved September 4, 2008, from http://www.skmm.gov.my/mcmc/index.asp

Smith, R. C. (2003). Analytic strategies for oral history interviews. In J. F. Gubrium & J. A. Holstein (Eds.), *Postmodern interviewing* (pp. 203–224). Thousand Oaks, CA: Sage Publications.

Soanes, C., & Stevenson, A. (Eds.). (2004). *Concise Oxford English dictionary* (Vol. 2005, 11th ed.). Oxford, UK: Oxford University Press.

Spencer, L., Ritchie, J., & O'Connor, W. (2003). Analysis: Practices, principles and processes. In J. Ritchie & J. Lewis (Eds.), *Qualitative research practice: A guide for social science students and researchers* (pp. 199–218). London: Sage Publications.

Stake, R. E. (1995). *The art of case study research.* Thousand Oaks, CA: Sage Publications.

Stanczak, G. C. (2007). *Visual research methods: Image, society, and representation* Thousand Oaks, CA: Sage Publications.

Starks, H., & Trinidad, S. B. (2007). Choose your method: A comparison of phenomenology, discourse analysis, and grounded theory. *Qualitative Health Research, 17*(10), 1372–1380.

Stephenson, W. (1935). Correlating persons instead of tests. *Character and Personality, 4,* 17–24.

Stern, S. R. (2009). How notions of privacy influence research choices: A response to Malin Sveningsson. In A. N. Markham & N. K. Baym (Eds.), *Internet inquiry: Conversations about method* (pp. 94–98). Thousand Oaks, CA: Sage Publications.

Strauss, A. L. (1987). *Qualitative analysis for social scientists.* Cambridge: Cambridge University Press.

Streeton, R., Cooke, M., & Campbeii, J. (2004). Researching the researchers: Using a snowballing technique. *Nurse Researcher, 12*(1), 35–45.

Sue, V., & Ritter, L. (2007). *Conducting online surveys.* Thousand Oaks, CA: Sage Publications.

Suler, J. (2003). Presence in cyberspace [Electronic Version]. *Psychology of cyber-space.* Retrieved August 5, 2008, from http://www-usr.rider.edu/~suler/psycyber/psycyber.html

Swann, W. B. Jr. (1987). Identity negotiation: Where two roads meet. *Journal of Personality and Social Psychology, 53,* 1038–1051.

Swann, W. B. Jr., Pelham, B. W., & Krull, D. S. (1989). Agreeable fancy or dis-agreeable truth? Reconciling self-enhancement and self-verification. *Journal of Personality and Social Psychology, 57*(5), 782–791.

Tapscott, D., & Williams, A. D. (2008). *Wikinomics: How mass collaboration changes everything.* New York: Portfolio Hardcover.

Thorpe, S. (2008a). *Storytelling in Second Life.* Auckland, New Zealand: Zenergy Global.

Thorpe, S. (Ed.). (2008b). *The use of story in building online group relationships.* Hershey, PA: IGI Global.

Trochim, W. (2006). *Research methods knowledge base.* Retrieved August 6, 2009, from http://trochim.human.cornell.edu/kb/index.htm

Valenta, A. L., & Wiggerand, U. (1997). Q methodology: Definition and applica-tion in health care informatics. *Journal for the American Medical Informatics Association, 6*(6), 501–510.

Velasquez, M., Moberg, D., Meyer, M. J., Shanks, T., McLean, M. R., DeCosse, D., et al. (2008). *A framework for thinking ethically.* Retrieved August 31, 2008, from http://www.scu.edu/ethics/practicing/decision/framework.html

Walsh, M. (2003). Teaching qualitative analysis using QSR NVivo. *The Qualitative Report, 8*(2).

Walther, J. (1999). *Research ethics in Internet-enabled research: Human subjects issues and methodological myopia.* Retrieved December 10, 2003, from http://www.nyu.edu/projects/nissenbaum/ethics_wal_full.html

Walther, J. B., Loh, T., & Granka, L. (2005). Let me count the ways: The inter-change of verbal and nonverbal cues in computer-mediated and face-to-face affinity. *Journal of Language and Social Psychology, 24*(1), 36–65.

Webb, B., & Webb, S. (1932). *Methods of social study.* London: Longmans, Green.

Wegerif, R. (1998). The social dimension of asynchronous learning networks. *Journal of the Asynchronous Learning Networks, 2*(1).

Wegge, J. (2006). Communication via videoconference: Emotional and cognitive consequences of affective personality dispositions, seeing one's own picture, and disturbing events. *Human-Computer Interaction, 21,* 273–318.

Wigmore, I., & Howard, A. B. (2009). *Whatis.com. The leading IT encyclopedia and learning center.* Retrieved August 6, 2009, from http://whatis.techtarget.com

Williams, M. (2007). Avatar watching: Participant observation in graphical online environments. *Qualitative Research, 7*(1), 5–24.

Wilmot, A. (2008). *Designing sampling strategies for qualitative social research.* Newport, UK: Office for National Statistics.

Wilson, L. A. (2006). *Communications between ocean scientists and policymakers: An analysis through the U.S. ocean policy review process.* Cincinnati, OH: Union Institute & University.

Wilson, L. A. (2009). Collaboration in the service of knowledge co-creation for envi-ronmental outcomes, science and public policy. In J. E. Salmons & L. A. Wilson (Eds.), *Handbook of research on electronic collaboration and organizational syn-ergy* (pp. 599–614). Hershey, PA: Information Science Reference.

Yates, S. J. (1996). Oral and written linguistic aspects of computer conferencing. In S. Herring (Ed.), *Computer-mediated communication: Linguistic, social and cross-cultural perspectives* (pp. 29–46). Amsterdam: John Benjamins.

Yin, R. K. (2009). *Case study research: Design and methods* (4th ed.). Thousand Oaks, CA: Sage Publications.

Yoshikawa, H., Weisner, T. S., Kalil, A., & Way, N. (2008). Mixing qualitative and quantitative research in developmental science: Uses and methodological choices. *Developmental Psychology, 44*(2), 344–354.

Yuzar, T. V. (2007). Generating virtual eye contacts through online synchronous communications in virtual classroom applications. *Turkish Online Journal of Distance Education, 8*(1), 43–54.

Zalta, E. N. (2008). *Stanford encyclopedia of philosophy.* Retrieved August 31, 2008, from http://plato.stanford.edu/

Index

About the Author

Janet Salmons received a B.S. in Adult and Community Education from Cornell University; an M.A. in Social Policy Studies from Empire State College, a distance-learning institution in the SUNY system; and a Ph.D. in Interdisciplinary Studies (meshing educational, technology, and leadership studies) at the Union Institute and University. She was at Cornell for many years and a few years ago moved to Colorado, where she started her own consulting business, Vision2Lead. Currently, in addition to consulting, she develops and teaches online graduate courses and mentors doctoral dissertators as a member of the Capella University School of Business and Technology faculty. She is active in online professional development and adult education and frequently conducts webinars and conference presentations. She has published three publications with IGI Global Reference.

Supporting researchers for more than 40 years

Research methods have always been at the core of SAGE's publishing program. Founder Sara Miller McCune published SAGE's first methods book, *Public Policy Evaluation*, in 1970. Soon after, she launched the *Quantitative Applications in the Social Sciences* series—affectionately known as the "little green books."

Always at the forefront of developing and supporting new approaches in methods, SAGE published early groundbreaking texts and journals in the fields of qualitative methods and evaluation.

Today, more than 40 years and two million little green books later, SAGE continues to push the boundaries with a growing list of more than 1,200 research methods books, journals, and reference works across the social, behavioral, and health sciences. Its imprints—Pine Forge Press, home of innovative textbooks in sociology, and Corwin, publisher of PreK–12 resources for teachers and administrators—broaden SAGE's range of offerings in methods. SAGE further extended its impact in 2008 when it acquired CQ Press and its best-selling and highly respected political science research methods list.

From qualitative, quantitative, and mixed methods to evaluation, SAGE is the essential resource for academics and practitioners looking for the latest methods by leading scholars.

For more information, visit **www.sagepub.com**.